GCSE
Additional Science
Higher Workbook

This book is for anyone doing **GCSE Additional Science** at higher level.

It's full of **tricky questions**... each one designed to make you **sweat** — because that's the only way you'll get any **better**.

There are questions to see **what facts** you know. There are questions to see how well you can **apply those facts**. And there are questions to see what you know about **how science works**.

It's also got some daft bits in to try and make the whole experience at least vaguely entertaining for you.

What CGP is all about

Our sole aim here at CGP is to produce the highest quality books — carefully written, immaculately presented and dangerously close to being funny.

Then we work our socks off to get them out to you — at the cheapest possible prices.

Contents

Published by Coordination Group Publications Ltd.

Editors:
Ellen Bowness, Gemma Hallam, Sarah Hilton, Ali Palin, Kate Redmond, Ami Snelling, Claire Thompson, Julie Wakeling, Sarah Williams.

Contributors:
Michael Aicken, Tony Alldridge, Steve Buckley, Peter Cecil, Claire Charlton, Steve Coggins, Vikki Cunningham, Mike Dagless, Jane Davies, Ian H. Davis, Catherine Debley, Philippa Falshaw, Max Fishel, James Foster, Paddy Gannon, Anna-fe Guy, Giles Greenway, Dr Iona MJ Hamilton, Derek Harvey, Rebecca Harvey, Frederick Langridge, Barbara Mascetti, Lucy Muncaster, John Myers, Andy Rankin, Adrian Schmit, Sidney Stringer Community School, Claire Stebbing, Paul Warren, Chris Workman, Dee Wyatt.

ISBN: 978 1 84146 535 7

With thanks to Sharon Keeley and Glenn Rogers for the proofreading.

Groovy website: www.cgpbooks.co.uk

Printed by Elanders Hindson Ltd, Newcastle upon Tyne.
Jolly bits of clipart from CorelDRAW®

Cells

Q1 Tick the boxes to show whether the following statements are **true** or **false**.

		True	False
a)	Palisade tissue makes up part of an organ.	✓	
b)	Organisms have only one organ system.		✓
c)	Palisade cells are present in leaf tissue.	✓	
d)	Mitochondria are where most of the respiration reactions take place.	✓	
e)	Most cells are specialised for their function.		✓

Q2 Complete each statement below by choosing the correct words.

a) **Plant** / **animal** cells contain chloroplasts, but **plant** / **animal** cells do not.

b) Plant cells have a **vacuole** / **cell wall**, which is made of cellulose.

c) **Both plant and animal cells** / **Only plant cells** / **Only animal cells** contain mitochondria.

d) Chloroplasts are where **respiration** / **photosynthesis** occurs, which makes **glucose** / **water**.

Q3 Below are three features of **palisade leaf cells**. Draw lines to match each feature to its function.

Lots of chloroplasts
Tall shape
Thin shape

gives a large surface area for absorbing CO_2
means you can pack more cells in at the top of the leaf
for photosynthesis

Q4 Complete the following paragraph about **guard cells** using the words below.

night **turgid** **flaccid** **photosynthesis** **stomata**

Guard cells open and close the ....stomata.... . When the plant has lots of water the guard cells are ....turgid.... . This makes the stomata open, so gases can be exchanged for ....photosynthesis.... . When the plant is short of water the guard cells become ....flaccid...., making the stomata close. They also close at ....night.... to save water.

Q5 State what the following cell structures **contain** or are **made of** and what their **functions** are.

a) The **nucleus** contains ....genetic information....

Its function is ....to control what happens in the cell....

b) **Chloroplasts** contain ....chlorophyll....

Their function is ....to absorb light energy for photosynthesis....

c) The **cell wall** is made of ....cellulose....

Its function is ....to give the plant a rigid structure....

DNA

Q1 Write out these structures in order of size, **starting with the smallest.**

nucleus	gene	chromosome	cell

1. Gene........................ 2. Chromosome.................. 3. Nucleus.................. 4. Cell..........................

Q2 Choose from the words below to complete the passage about the **structure of DNA.**

uracil	base	adenine	helix	cytoplasm
guanine	protein	nucleotides	glycine	nucleus

DNA is found in the .... of every cell. It is a double-stranded .... made up of lots of .... Each nucleotide contains a small molecule called a .... There are four of these — ...., cytosine, ... and thymine.

Q3 Number the statements below to show the correct order of the stages in **DNA replication.**

☐ Cross links form between the bases of the nucleotides and the old DNA strands.

☐ The DNA double helix 'unzips' to form two single strands.

☐ The result is two molecules of DNA identical to the original molecule of DNA.

☐ Free-floating nucleotides join on where the bases fit.

☐ The new nucleotides are joined together.

Q4 The **bases** in DNA always pair up in the **same** way.

a) Complete the diagram below to show which **bases** will form the complementary strand of DNA.

A	C	T	G	C	A	A	T	G
......	......	......	......	......	......	......	......	......

b) Suggest how this helps DNA replication.

....

Top Tips: Watson and Crick announced that they had 'found the secret of life' in the Eagle Pub in Cambridge. Rumour has it they found inspiration for the structure of DNA by drunkenly walking down a spiral staircase — seeing double.

DNA Fingerprinting

Q1 **Genetic fingerprinting** is a way of comparing people's DNA — it's useful in forensic science. Put these stages in DNA fingerprinting into the correct order.

Compare the unique patterns of DNA.

Separate the sections of DNA.

Collect the sample for DNA testing.

Cut the DNA into small sections.

1. ....

2. ....

3. ....

4. ....

Q2 Choose from the words below to complete the passage about the **DNA fingerprinting** process.

positive negatively big chromatography small positively suspended negative separated

After the DNA has been cut into fragments, these fragments are .... out using a process a bit like .... They're .... in a gel, and an electric current is passed through the gel. DNA is .... charged, so it moves towards the .... anode. .... bits travel faster than .... bits, so they get further through the gel.

Q3 A thoroughbred horse breeder has collected DNA samples from each of her horses. Her **new foal's DNA** is **sample 1**. Study the **DNA profiles** and complete the table showing which horses are the **foal's parents**.

	Foal	Mother	Father
DNA sample	Sample 1		

Sample 1 (female) Sample 2 (female) Sample 3 (female) Sample 4 (male) Sample 5 (male)

Q4 A national **genetic database** would allow everyone's unique pattern of DNA to be saved on file.

a) Give one use of a national genetic database.

....

b) Give one drawback of a national genetic database.

....

Making Proteins

Q1 Circle the correct word(s) from each pair to complete the following sentences.

a) Proteins are made up of chains of **amino acids** / **glucose**.

b) Transamination happens in the **kidneys** / **liver**.

c) Proteins are made in the cell by organelles called **chloroplasts** / **ribosomes**.

d) Each amino acid is coded for by a sequence of **three** / **four** bases.

Q2 Number the statements below to show the correct order of the stages in **protein synthesis**.

☐ Amino acids are joined together to make a polypeptide.

☐ RNA moves out of the nucleus.

☐ RNA joins with a ribosome.

☐ A molecule of RNA is made using DNA as a template.

☐ The DNA strand unzips.

Q3 Protein synthesis involves a molecule called **RNA**.

a) Why is the information contained in DNA copied onto a strand of RNA?

....

b) Give **two** differences between DNA and RNA.

....

Q4 DNA controls the production of **proteins**.

a) What is the name for a section of DNA that codes for a particular protein? ....

b) How do **amino acids** determine the function of a protein?

....

c) What happens if we don't take in the right amounts of each amino acid in our **diet**?

....

d) Explain how DNA determines the type of cell.

....

....

e) Explain the role of the **bases** in DNA in the building of a protein.

....

....

Biological Catalysts — Enzymes

Q1 a) Write a definition of the word '**enzyme**'.

....

....

b) In the space below, draw a labelled diagram to show how an enzyme's **shape** allows it to break substances down.

Q2 a) Tick the correct boxes to show whether the sentences are **true** or **false**.

	True	False
i) Most enzymes are made of fat.	☐	☐
ii) The rate of most chemical reactions can be increased by increasing the temperature.	☐	☐
iii) Most cells are damaged at very high temperatures.	☐	☐
iv) Each type of enzyme can speed up a lot of different reactions.	☐	☐

b) Write a correct version of each false sentence in the space below.

....

....

Q3 Stuart has a sample of an enzyme and he is trying to find out what its **optimum pH** is. Stuart tests the enzyme by **timing** how long it takes to break down a substance at different pH levels. The results of Stuart's experiment are shown in the table below.

pH	time taken for reaction in seconds
2	101
4	83
6	17
8	76
10	99
12	102

a) Draw a line graph of the results of the experiment on the grid above.

b) What is the **optimum** pH for the enzyme? ....

c) Explain why the reaction is very slow at certain pH levels.

....

d) Would you expect to find this enzyme in the stomach? Explain your answer.

....

Diffusion

Q1 Complete the passage below by circling the most appropriate words.

Diffusion is the **direct / random** movement of particles from an area where they are at a **higher / lower** concentration to an area where they are at a **higher / lower** concentration. The rate of diffusion is faster when the concentration gradient is **bigger / smaller** and in **liquids / gases**. It is slower when there is a **large / small** distance over which diffusion occurs and when there is **more / less** surface for diffusion to take place across.

Q2 Decide which of the following statements are **true or false**.

		True	False
a)	Diffusion takes place in all types of substances.	☐	☐
b)	Diffusion is usually quicker in liquids than in gases.	☐	☐
c)	Diffusion happens more quickly when there is a higher concentration gradient.	☐	☐
d)	A larger surface area makes diffusion happen more quickly.	☐	☐
e)	A larger distance for particles to move across speeds up the rate of diffusion.	☐	☐

Q3 The first diagram below shows a **cup of tea** which has just had a **sugar cube** added.

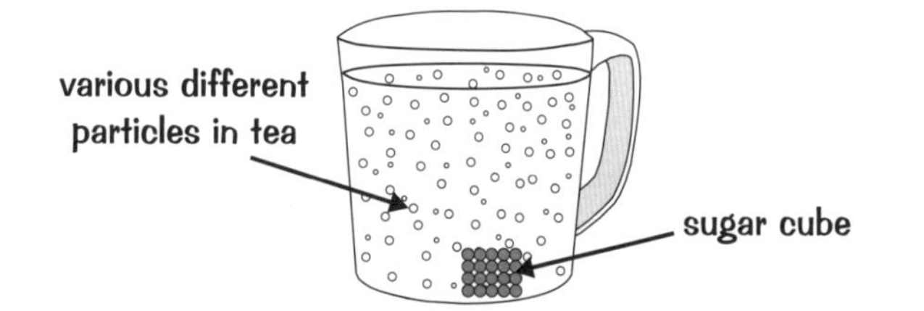

a) In the second cup above, draw the molecules of **sugar** in the tea after an hour.

b) Predict how the rate of diffusion of the sugar would change in each of the following situations:

i) sugar crystals are used rather than a sugar cube

....

ii) the tea is heated

....

iii) the sugar and tea are placed in a long thin tube

....

c) Explain the movement of the sugar particles in terms of areas of different **concentration**.

....

....

Diffusion in Cells

Q1 The passage below is about the transport of food molecules in the body. Circle the correct words.

Proteins in our food are digested to produce **amino acids / starch**. This makes the molecules **large / small** enough to enter the bloodstream by **diffusion / osmosis**. This happens because their concentration in the blood is **higher / lower** than in the gut. Later, when the blood reaches the cells in the body that are using up the food substances, the food molecules move **into / out of** the bloodstream.

Q2 Use the words below to complete the passage about transmission between nerve cells.

impulse **binds** **digestive** **diffuses** **nerve**
dove **membrane** **receptor** **synapse** **lapse** **transmitter**

The gap between one .... cell and the next is called a .... When a nerve .... arrives, it causes the release of a .... substance from the first nerve cell. This .... across the gap, and .... to a .... in the end of the next cell.

Q3 The diagram below shows an **alveolus** and a **capillary** from inside the lungs.

a) On the diagram, label the **alveolus**, a **red blood cell** and the **capillary wall**.

b) Air is being breathed **into** the lungs. On the diagram:

i) draw an arrow to show the movement of air molecules due to breathing. Label this arrow **X**.

ii) draw an arrow to show the diffusion of oxygen molecules. Label this arrow **Y**.

iii) label with the letter **Z** the red blood cell which has the lowest oxygen concentration.

c) As a person breathes **out**, is oxygen diffusing into or out of the blood? Explain your answer.

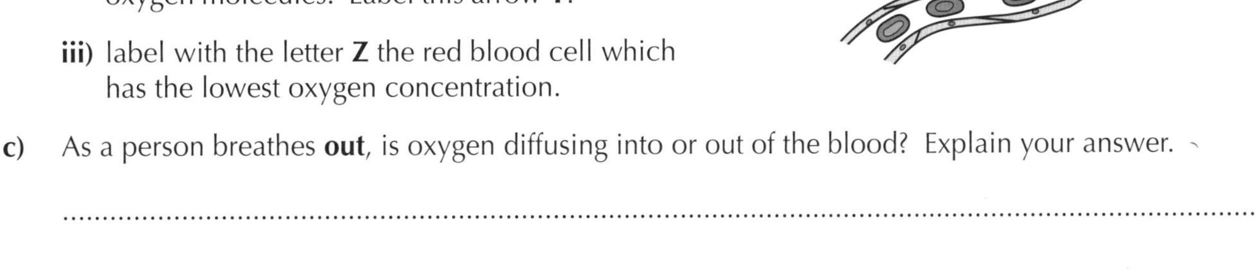

....

....

Top Tips: Things tend to spread out — that's all that diffusion is — and with cells, it's no different. Substances will move across the membrane from an area of higher concentration to an area of lower concentration.

Osmosis

Q1 This diagram shows a tank separated into two by a partially permeable membrane.

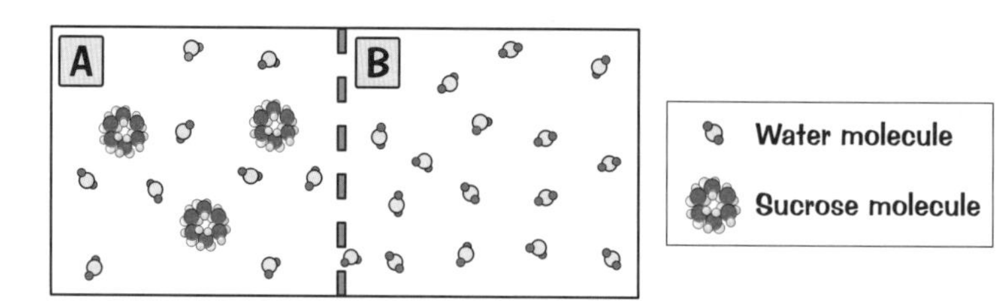

a) What is a partially permeable membrane?

....

b) On which side of the membrane is there the higher concentration of water molecules? ....

c) In which direction would you expect more water molecules to travel — from A to B or from B to A?

....

d) Predict whether the level of liquid on side B will **rise** or **fall**. Explain your answer.

The liquid level on side B will ...., because ....

....

Q2 The diagram below shows some **body cells** bathed in **tissue fluid**. A blood vessel flows close to the cells, providing water. The cells shown have a low concentration of water inside them.

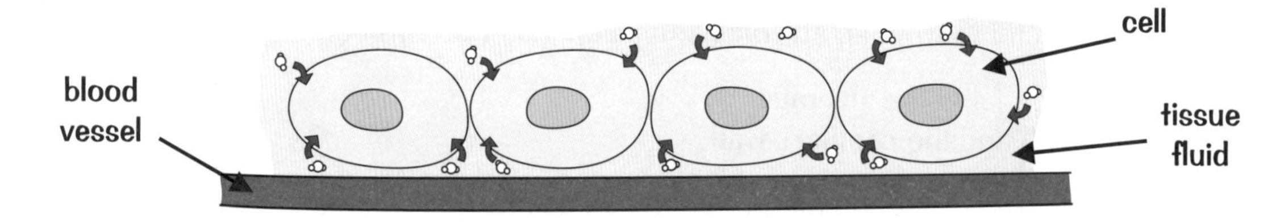

a) Is the concentration of water higher in the **tissue fluid** or inside the **cells**? ....

b) In which direction would you expect more water to travel — **into** the cells or **out of** the cells? Explain your answer.

....

....

c) Explain why osmosis appears to stop after a while.

....

....

Top Tips: Don't forget it's only small molecules that can diffuse through cell membranes, e.g. glucose, amino acids, water and oxygen. Big hulking things like proteins and starch can't fit through.

Mixed Questions — Section One

Q1 Both **plants** and **animals** are made up of cells.

a) Complete this diagram of a plant cell by filling in the labels.

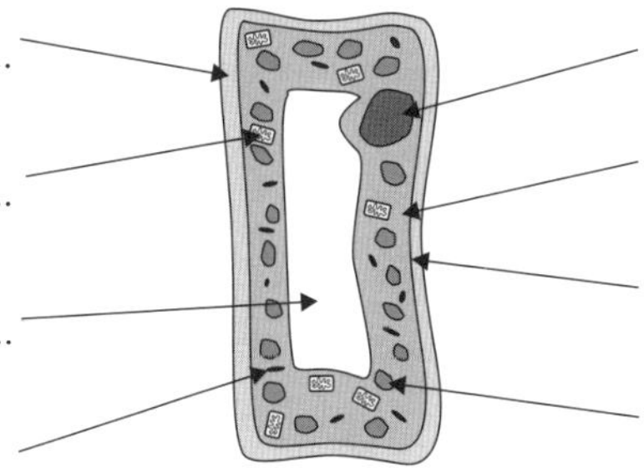

....

....

....

....

b) Name the part of the cell which:

i) produces energy from glucose, ...

ii) contains chlorophyll for photosynthesis, ...

iii) contains genetic material, ...

iv) supports the cell. ....

Q2 The **DNA code** is transferred onto **RNA**.

a) Describe how this happens. ....

....

b) Where in the cell does this process occur? ....

c) Proteins are made in which structure within cells? ....

Q3 The following **DNA samples** are being used in a **murder investigation**. The DNA samples are from the victim, three suspects and some blood which was found on the victim's shirt.

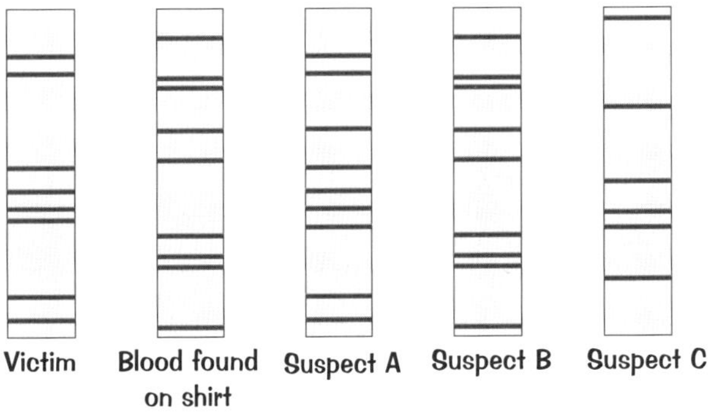

Victim | Blood found on shirt | Suspect A | Suspect B | Suspect C

a) Which two individuals are likely to be **related** to each other? Explain your choice.

....

....

b) Who is the most likely culprit based on the DNA evidence? ....

c) How do you know?

....

d) Can this suspect be accused of murder beyond all doubt?

....

....

Mixed Questions — Section One

Q4 Mollie set up the following experiment and left it for a few hours.

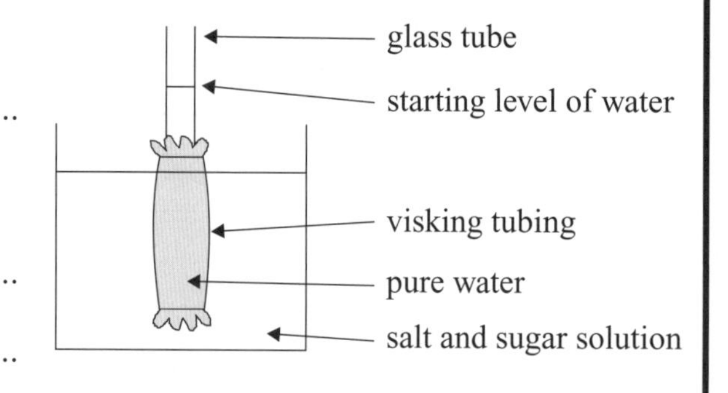

a) What will happen to the level of water in the tube?

....

b) Explain why this happens.

....

....

....

Q5 This graph shows the results from an investigation into the effect of **temperature** on the rate of an **enzyme** catalysed reaction.

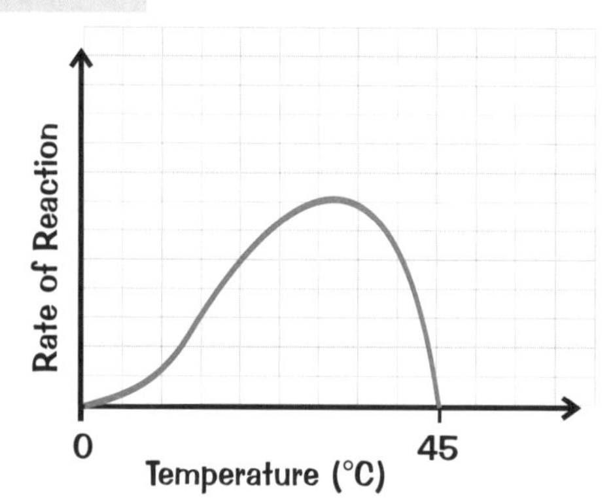

a) What is the **optimum** temperature for this enzyme?

....

b) What happens to enzymes at temperatures **above** their optimum?

....

....

Q6 Some **potato cylinders** were placed in solutions of different **salt concentrations**. At the start of the experiment each cylinder was 50 mm long. Their final lengths are recorded in the table below.

Concentration of salt (molar)	Final length of potato cylinder (mm)	Change in length of potato cylinder (mm)
0	60	
0.25	58	
0.5	56	
0.75	70	
1	50	
1.25	45	

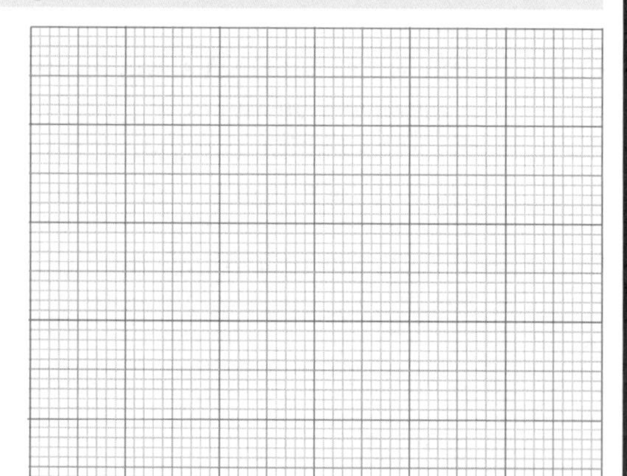

a) Plot the points for concentration of salt solution vs final length of potato cylinders on the grid.

b) Work out the change in length of each of the cylinders and complete the table above.

c) Study the pattern of the results.

i) State the salt concentration(s) that produced unexpected results. ....

ii) Suggest a method for deciding which of the results are correct.

....

Growth

Q1 Daniel wants to measure the **growth** of his new puppy.

a) Suggest two measurements he could take to record the puppy's **size**.

....

b) He also records the puppy's wet weight.

i) What is wet weight?

ii) Give a disadvantage of measuring growth by recording an organism's wet weight.

....

Q2 Describe two examples of animals that are able to grow new limbs.

1. ....

2. ....

Q3 Give two differences in **growth** between plants and animals.

1. ....

2. ....

Q4 Zapphites from the planet Zaphron have a similar growth pattern to humans. The graph shows the **head circumference** of baby zapphites between birth and 40 weeks. The shaded area shows where 90% of babies fall.

Baby's name	Age (weeks)	Head circumference (cm)
Charles	19	46.5
Edward	15	51
Engletree	34	54
George	27	49
Henry	23	49
Oliver	29	57
Richard	39	50
Xionbert	23	51.5

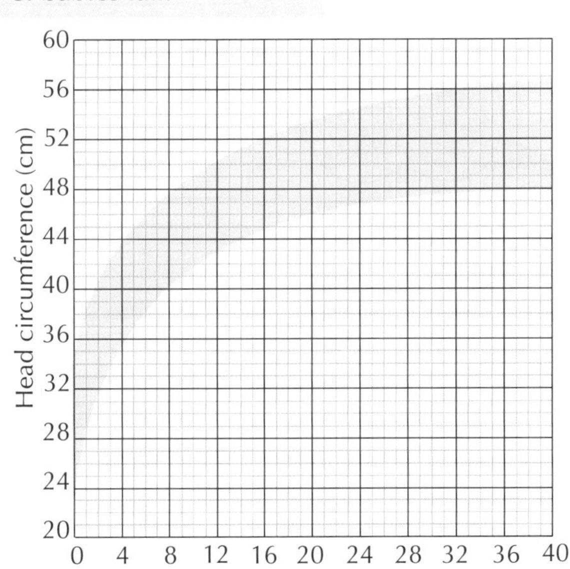

a) Plot the head circumferences of the above babies points on the graph.

b) Which baby's size may cause concern? ....

c) Why might zapphite doctors monitor a baby's head circumference? ....

....

Cell Division — Mitosis

Q1 Decide whether the following statements are **true** or **false**.

		True	False
a)	There are 46 chromosomes in most of your body cells.	☐	☐
b)	There are 20 pairs of chromosomes in a human cheek cell.	☐	☐
c)	Chromosomes are found in the cytoplasm of a cell.	☐	☐
d)	Before a cell divides by mitosis, it duplicates its DNA.	☐	☐
e)	Mitosis is where a cell splits to create two genetically identical copies.	☐	☐
f)	Mitosis produces new cells to replace those which are damaged.	☐	☐
g)	We need mitosis to grow.	☐	☐

Q2 The following diagram shows the different stages of **mitosis**.
Write a short description to explain each stage.

a) ....

b) ....

c) ....

....

d) ....

....

e) ....

Q3 Complete the following passage using the words below.

runners   strawberry   variation   asexual   reproduce   genes

Some organisms use mitosis to .... For example, ...
plants produce .... this way, which become new plants. This is known as
.... reproduction. The offspring have exactly the same
.... as the parent, which means there's no genetic ....

Cell Division — Meiosis

Q1 Tick the boxes below to show whether each statements is true of **mitosis**, **meiosis** or **both**.

		Mitosis	Meiosis
a)	Halves the number of chromosomes.	☐	☐
b)	Chromosomes line up in the centre of the cell.	☐	☐
c)	Forms cells that are genetically different.	☐	☐
d)	In humans, it only happens in the reproductive organs.	☐	☐

Q2 Draw lines to match the descriptions of the stages of **meiosis** to the right diagrams below.

a)

b)

c)

d)

e)

The pairs are pulled apart, mixing up the mother and father's chromosomes into the new cells. This creates genetic variation.

The DNA is spread out in long strands. Before the cell starts to divide it duplicates its DNA to produce an exact copy.

There are now 4 gametes, each containing half the original number of chromosomes.

For the first meiotic division the chromosomes line up in their pairs across the centre of the cell.

The chromosomes line up across the centre of the nucleus ready for the second division, and the left and right arms are pulled apart.

Q3 During sexual reproduction, two **gametes** combine to form a new individual.

a) What are gametes? ....

b) Explain why gametes have half the usual number of chromosomes.

....

....

Top Tips: It's easy to get confused between mitosis and meiosis. Meiosis is for sexual reproduction and creates sex cells. Mitosis happens everywhere else (e.g. for growth and repair).

Sexual Reproduction

Q1 Match the following adaptations of **sperm cells** to how they help the sperm get to the egg.

acrosome containing enzymes

produced in large numbers

small with long tails

lots of mitochondria

to provide energy needed to move

to digest the membrane of the egg cell

so they can swim to the egg

to increase the chance of fertilisation

Q2 **Sexual** reproduction produces **genetic variation**.

a) Explain how we get genetic variation from:

i) the fusion of gametes. ....

....

ii) meiosis. ....

....

b) Suggest why variation might be an advantage.

....

....

Q3 Human pregnancies may be **terminated**.

a) What is the legal limit for a termination? ....

b) Explain why the limit was set at this stage of the pregnancy in Britain.

....

c) Give two situations when a termination may be carried out later than this date.

1. ....

2. ....

d) Give an argument against abortion at any stage of the pregnancy.

....

e) Why do many people feel that the legal limit for abortion should be changed?

....

....

Stem Cells and Differentiation

Q1 The following terms are related to **stem cells**. Explain what each term means.

a) specialised cells ....

b) differentiation ....

c) undifferentiated cells ....

....

Q2 How are **embryonic** stem cells different from **adult** stem cells?

....

....

....

Q3 Describe a way that stem cells are already used in medicine.

....

....

....

Q4 In the future, **embryonic stem cells** might be used to replace faulty cells in sick people. Match the problems below to the potential cures which could be made with stem cells.

diabetes	**heart muscle cells**
paralysis	**insulin-producing cells**
heart disease	**brain cells**
Alzheimer's	**nerve cells**

Q5 People have **different opinions** when it comes to **stem cell research**.

a) Give one argument **in favour** of stem cell research.

....

....

b) Give one argument **against** stem cell research.

....

....

Growth in Plants: Plant Hormones

Q1 Decide whether the following statements are **true** or **false**.

		True	False
a)	Plant shoots grow away from light.	☐	☐
b)	Plant roots grow towards water.	☐	☐
c)	Plant roots grow away from gravity.	☐	☐
d)	If the tip of a shoot is removed, the shoot may stop growing.	☐	☐

Q2 Cedrick placed some seedlings on the surface of damp soil which was exposed to light from a lamp. The appearance of the seedlings are shown in the diagram.

start
bean
shoot
root

5 days later
bean
shoot
root

a) What **hormones** are responsible for these changes?

....

b) Where are these hormones produced?

....

c) Explain the results observed with the:

i) shoot. ....

....

ii) root. ....

....

Q3 Ronald owns a fruit farm which grows seedless satsumas. The fruit is picked before it is ripe and transported to a market.

fruit picked → fruit packaged → fruit transported to market → fruit displayed

a) Explain how seedless satsumas can be grown without pips.

....

b) Suggest why the satsumas are picked before they are ripe.

....

c) How will the unripened satsumas be ripened in time to reach the market?

....

....

Selective Breeding

Q1 Garfield wants to breed one type of plant for its **fruit**, and another as an **ornamental house plant**.

Suggest **two** characteristics that he should select for in each kind of plant.

Fruit plant: ....

Ornamental house plant: ....

Q2 Describe two **disadvantages** of selective breeding.

1. ....

....

2. ....

....

Q3 Describe how **selective breeding** could be used to improve the following:

a) The number of offspring in sheep. ....

....

b) The yield from dwarf wheat. ....

....

Q4 The graph shows the **milk yield** for a population of cows over three generations.

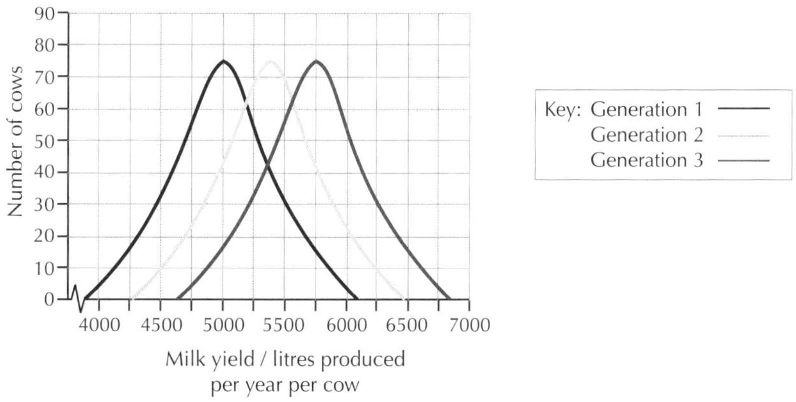

a) Do you think that selective breeding is likely to have been used in these cows? Explain your answer.

....

b) What is the increase in the average milk yield per cow from generation 1 to generation 2?

....

Top Tips: So, if you wanted to take over the world using goldfish, you would probably want to breed together the more aggressive goldfish with long memories, rather than the dappy ones that just idly swim around in a circle all day long. (You can tell which ones are aggressive — they bite.)

Genetic Engineering

Q1 **Human insulin** can be produced quickly using **genetic engineering**.

a) Put these stages involved in the production of human insulin in order by numbering them 1–4.

☐ The human insulin gene is inserted into the host DNA of a bacterium.

☐ The human insulin gene is cut from human DNA.

☐ Insulin is extracted from the medium.

☐ The bacteria are cultivated in a fermenter.

b) Suggest an **advantage** of using bacteria to produce insulin.

....

Q2 Plants can be genetically engineered.

a) Describe how genetic engineering could improve crop yield.

....

b) Describe how genetic engineering can help people get the vitamins they need.

....

....

Q3 Some people are **worried** about genetic engineering.

a) Explain why some people are concerned about genetic engineering.

....

....

b) Do you think that scientists should be carrying out genetic engineering? Explain your answer.

....

....

....

Q4 Look carefully at this headline about a new type of **GM salmon**.

Monster food? Scientists insert a growth hormone gene and create fish that grow much faster than ever before!

Some scientists have warned that the GM salmon should be tightly controlled so they don't escape into the sea. What might happen if the GM salmon were allowed to escape?

....

....

Cloning

Q1 Define the following terms.

a) Clones ....

b) Surrogate mother ....

c) Embryo ....

Q2 Joe has a herd of cows and he wants them all to have calves, but he **only** wants to breed from his champion bull and prize cow.

a) Name a method Joe could use to achieve this. ....

b) Describe the steps involved in this method in detail.

....

....

....

c) Which of the animals involved in this process will be genetically identical?

....

d) Give one disadvantage of this method.

....

....

Q3 Grace decided to increase the number of plants in her pot plant garden by taking **cuttings**.

a) Explain why all cuttings taken from a plant are clones of each other.

....

b) Give another way that we can clone plants. ....

Q4 Read the passage before deciding whether the statements that follow are **true** or **false**.

> Sperm was collected from Gerald the stallion and used to artificially inseminate Daisy the mare. An embryo was then removed from Daisy and divided into separate cells, each of which was allowed to grow into a new embryo. These new embryos were then implanted into other horses, including Rosie, Ruby and Jilly.

		True	False
a)	Each embryo is genetically identical to Daisy.	☐	☐
b)	Gerald is genetically identical to the embryos.	☐	☐
c)	All the embryos are genetically identical.	☐	☐
d)	The embryo carried by Jilly is her natural daughter.	☐	☐

Adult Cloning

Q1 Dolly the sheep was cloned from an adult cell.

Egg cell
Adult body cell
A
B
C
D

a) Write the correct letter (A, B, C or D) next to each label below to show where it belongs on the diagram.

removing and discarding a nucleus ....

implantation in a surrogate mother ....

useful nucleus extracted ....

formation of a diploid cell ....

b) What type of cell division does the fertilised egg divide by? ....

c) Give a risk associated with this type of cloning.

....

Q2 Some animals can be genetically engineered to produce **human blood clotting agents**.

a) Why would it be useful to be able to clone these animals?

....

....

b) Suggest why some people might be reluctant to use medicines produced by cloned animals.

....

Q3 Adult cloning may help to make **xenotransplantation** safe.

a) What is xenotransplantation?

....

b) Explain the role of cloning in xenotransplantation.

....

....

Q4 Summarise the **ethical** issues involved in cloning humans.

....

....

....

Genetic Diagrams

Q1 Mendel crossed different combinations of **tall** and **dwarf** pea plants.

a) Complete the genetic diagrams below showing crossings of different pea plants.
T represents the dominant allele for **tall plants** and **t** represents the recessive allele for **dwarf plants**.

Cross 1

tall dwarf
Parents: TT tt
T T t t
Offspring: Tt Tt
tall tall ....

Cross 2

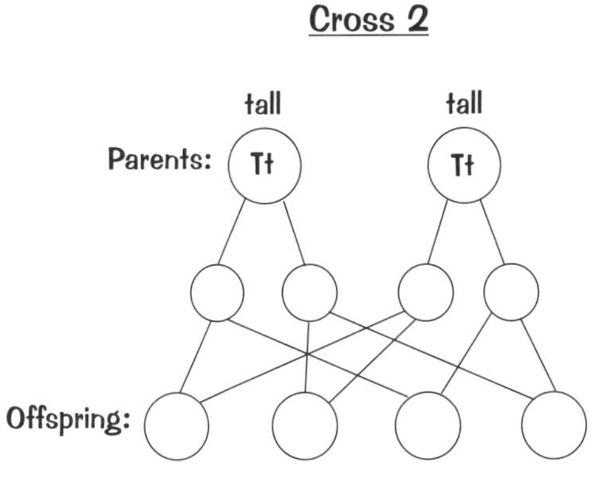

....

b) In **cross 2**, what is the probability that an offspring plant will be tall?

....

Q2 A type of fly usually has **red** eyes. However, there are a small number of white-eyed flies. Having **white** eyes is a **recessive** characteristic.

a) Complete the following sentences with either '**red eyes**' or '**white eyes**'.

i) **R** is the allele for ....

ii) **r** is the allele for ....

iii) Flies with alleles **RR** or **Rr** will have ....

iv) Flies with the alleles **rr** will have ....

b) Two flies have the alleles **Rr**. They fall in love and get it on.

i) Complete this genetic diagram to show the alleles of the possible offspring.
One's been done for you.

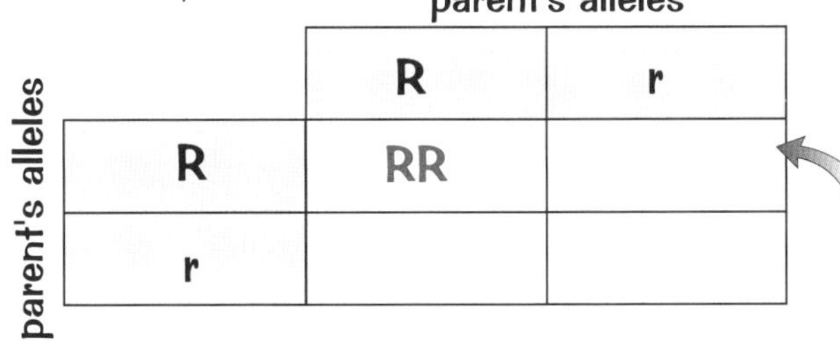

parent's alleles (across); parent's alleles (down)

	R	r
R	RR	
r		

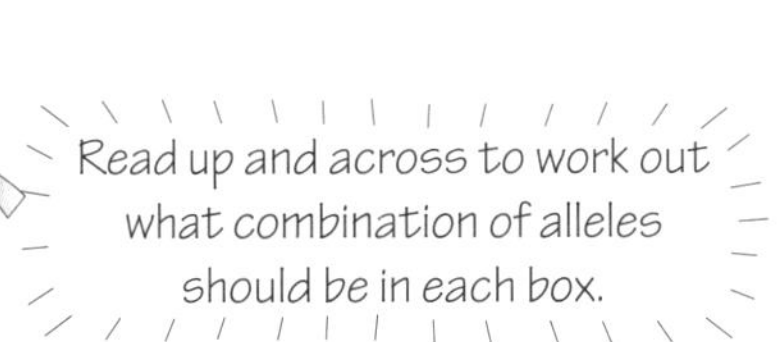

ii) What is the probability that one of the flies' offspring will have white eyes?

....

iii) The flies have 96 offspring. How many of the offspring are **likely** to have **red eyes**?

....

Top Tips: Genetic diagrams look like alphabet spaghetti at first — but they're OK really. They're useful for working out the possible combinations of alleles that offspring can get from their parents — and the probability of each combination.

Genetic Disorders

Q1 **Cystic fibrosis** is a **genetic disorder** which affects cell membranes. It is caused by a **recessive** allele, which can be passed on from parents to their children.

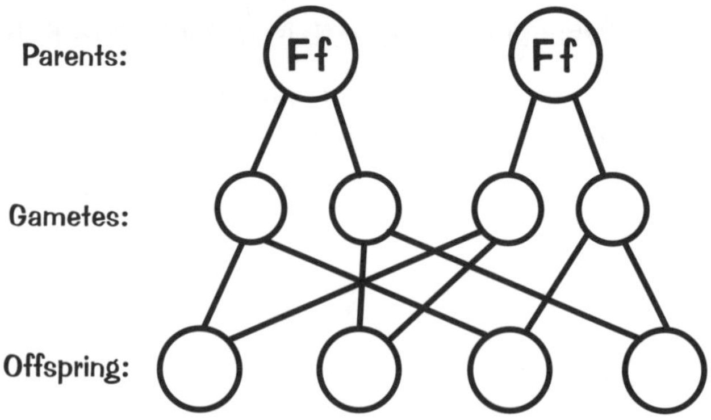

a) Complete the following genetic diagram showing the inheritance of cystic fibrosis. The recessive allele for cystic fibrosis is **f**, and the dominant allele is **F**.

Parents: Ff Ff

Gametes:

Offspring:

b) **i)** In the above genetic diagram, what is the probability of a child having cystic fibrosis?

....

ii) In the above genetic diagram, what is the probability of a child being a **carrier** of the cystic fibrosis allele but not having the disease?

....

Q2 Huntington's disease is a genetic disorder caused by a **dominant** allele. The genetic diagram shows the inheritance of Huntington's disease.

Parents: Nn nn

Gametes: N n n n

Offspring: Nn nn Nn nn

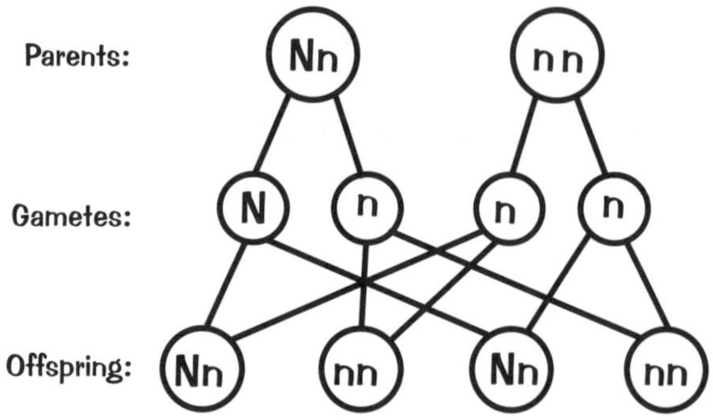

a) Two adults with the alleles Nn and nn decide to have children. What is the probability of their first child inheriting the allele for Huntington's disease?

....

b) Symptoms of Huntington's disease may not appear until a person is over 40 years old. Why does this increase the chance of the disease being passed on?

....

....

Q3 During in vitro fertilisation (IVF) a cell can be removed from an embryo and screened for genetic disorders like Huntington's disease. If a faulty allele is present, the embryo is destroyed.

a) Explain why some people think embryo screening is a **bad** thing.

....

....

b) Explain why some people think embryo screening is a **good** thing.

....

....

Mixed Questions — Section Two

Q1 a) What unique characteristic do **stem cells** have which ordinary body cells don't have?

....

b) Scientists have experimented with growing stem cells in different conditions.

i) What is the name of the process by which stem cells **divide** for growth?

....

ii) Suggest why scientists are interested in **embryonic** stem cells.

....

....

c) Although there is potential for medical breakthroughs, some people disagree with stem cell research on ethical grounds. Describe one **ethical issue** surrounding stem cell research.

....

....

Q2 Genetic disorders are inherited. Huntington's disease has been passed on through the family shown in the diagram below:

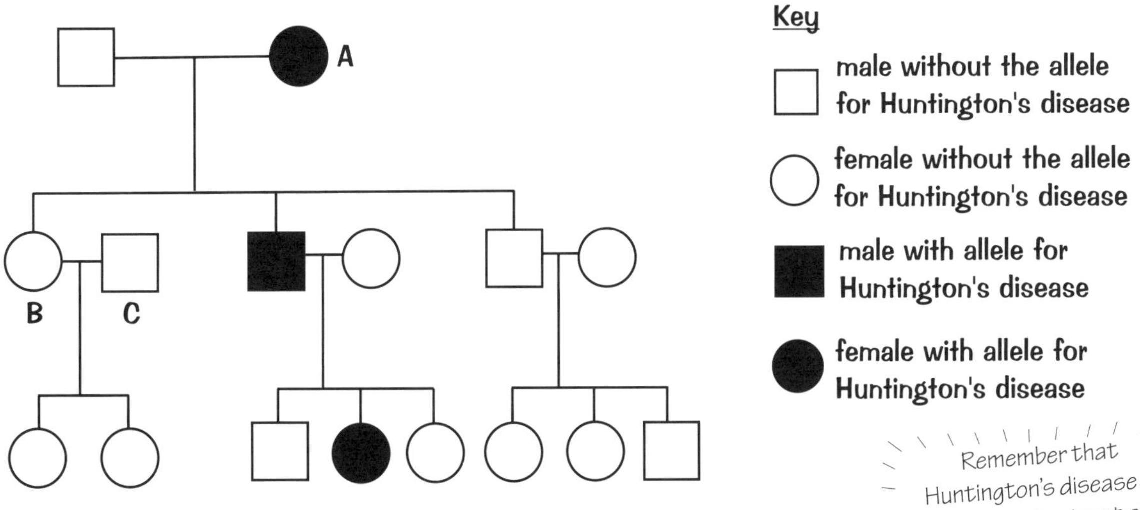

Remember that Huntington's disease is caused by a dominant allele.

a) Will person A develop Huntington's disease at some point in their life?

....

b) Is it possible that the couple B and C could have a child with the allele for Huntington's disease? Explain your answer.

....

....

Mixed Questions — Section Two

Q3 The life cycle of the honey bee is unusual. Fertilised eggs always develop into females. Males develop only from unfertilised eggs. The life cycle is summarised in the diagram below.

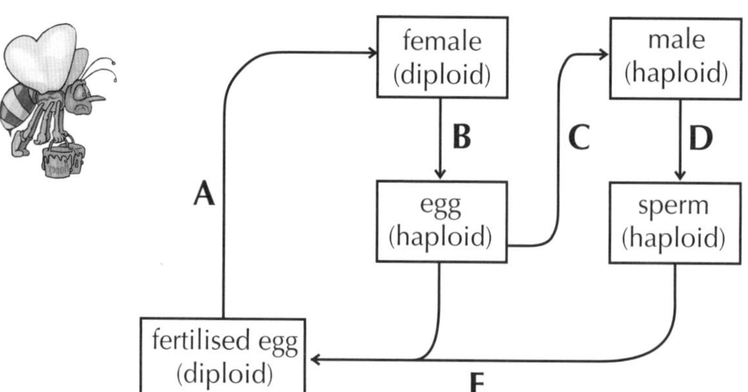

a) Identify each of the arrows A–E as **mitosis**, **meiosis** or **fertilisation**.

A: .... B: .... C: ....

D: .... E: ....

b) Explain the importance of meiosis in sexual reproduction.

....

....

Q4 The **Jungle Fowl** is the wild ancestor of all farm-bred chickens. **Farm-bred** chickens have been produced by **selective breeding**.

a) Suggest two ways in which farm-bred chickens are likely to differ from wild Jungle Fowl.

1. .... 2. ....

b) Suggest how selective breeding in chickens might harm the welfare of the birds.

....

....

Q5 Scientists tried to **genetically modify** some bacteria. They inserted a piece of DNA containing both the human gene for **growth hormone** and a gene for **penicillin resistance** into a bacterium. Afterwards, the bacteria were grown on agar plates containing penicillin.

a) Why were the bacteria grown on plates containing penicillin?

Hint: It's hard to tell by looking if the growth hormone gene has been inserted correctly.

....

....

b) Give **two advantages** of producing growth hormone with bacteria, rather than by other methods.

....

....

Respiration and Exercise

Q1 Tick the correct boxes to show whether the sentences are true or false.

		True	False
a)	Aerobic respiration releases energy.	☐	☐
b)	Respiration usually releases energy from protein.	☐	☐
c)	Aerobic respiration is more efficient than anaerobic respiration.	☐	☐
d)	Respiration takes place in a cell's nucleus.	☐	☐
e)	Aerobic respiration produces carbon dioxide.	☐	☐
f)	Anaerobic respiration happens when there's not enough oxygen available.	☐	☐
g)	Plants use photosynthesis instead of respiration.	☐	☐

Q2 Write the word equations for:

a) Aerobic respiration ....

b) Anaerobic respiration ....

Q3 Jim is a keen runner. He takes part in a 400 metre race. The **graph** below shows Jim's **breathing rate** before and after the race.

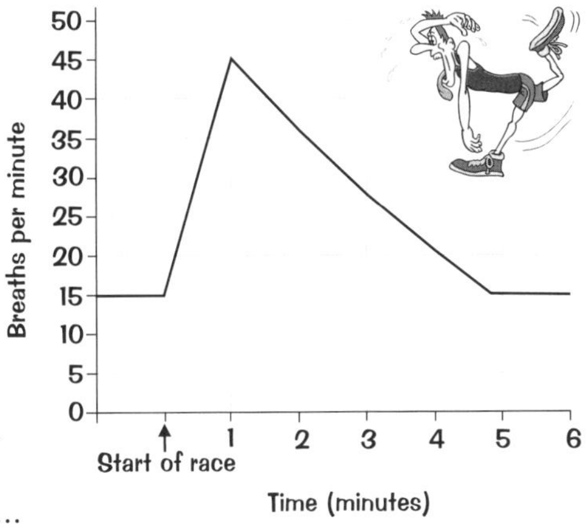

a) How much does Jim's breathing rate go up during the race?

.... **breaths per minute**

b) Explain why Jim's breathing rate increased.

....

....

....

c) Why does Jim's breathing rate not return to normal immediately after the race?

....

....

Q4 Oxygen diffuses into the blood through the walls of the **alveoli** of the lungs.

a) Describe **two** ways in which the structure of the alveoli helps them to exchange oxygen efficiently.

....

....

b) What effect would holding your breath have on the rate of diffusion of oxygen?

....

Enzymes and Digestion

Q1 Fill in the boxes to show how the **three main food groups** are **broken down** during digestion.

a)

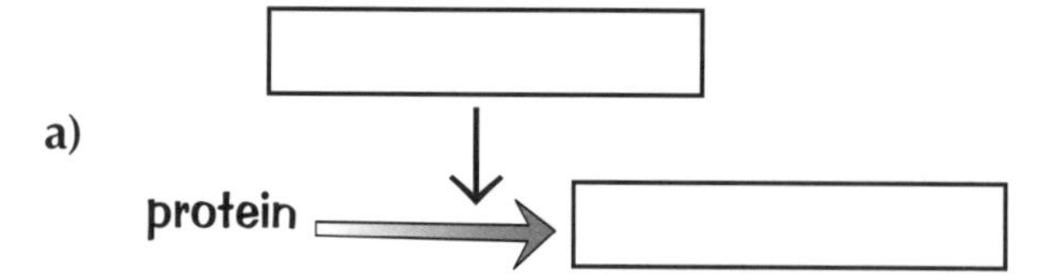

b)

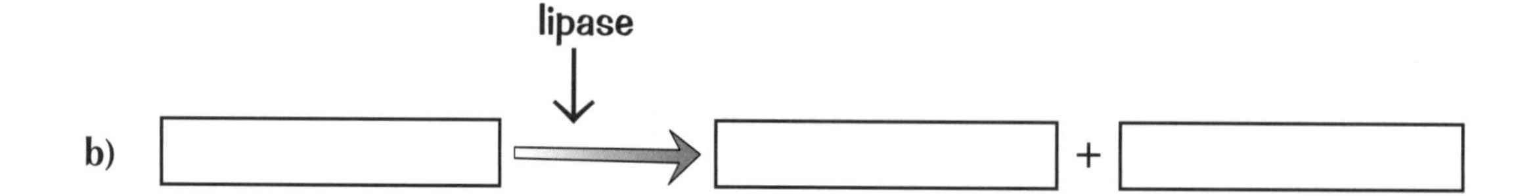

c)

simple sugars

Q2 Choose from the words below to complete the table showing where **amylase**, **protease**, **lipase** and **bile** are made. You may use some words more than once and you might not need some of them.

pancreas liver salivary glands small intestine

large intestine stomach gall bladder kidneys

Amylase	Protease	Lipase	Bile

Q3 a) Circle the correct words to complete this passage about bile.

Bile is stored in the **gall bladder** / **pancreas** before being released into the **liver** / **small intestine**. Bile **acidifies** / **neutralises** the material from the stomach so that it is the optimum pH for the **enzymes** / **microorganisms** in the rest of the digestive system to work. Bile also breaks **fat** / **glycerol** into smaller droplets.

b) Explain how emulsification helps digestion.

....

....

The Digestive System

Q1 Fill in the boxes to label this diagram of the human **digestive system**.

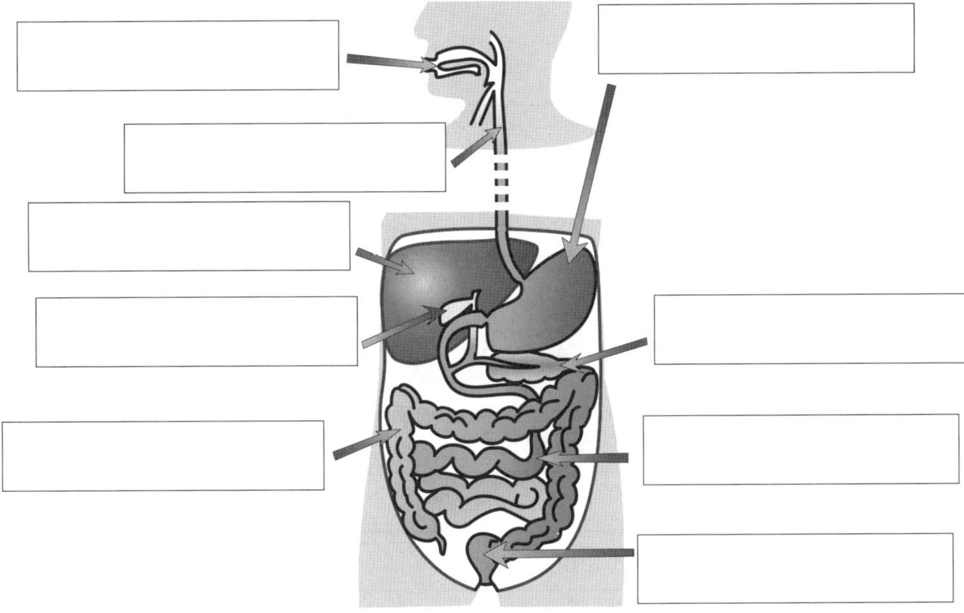

Q2 Describe the role of each of the following in **digestion**:

a) Salivary glands ....

b) Gall bladder ....

c) Pancreas ....

d) Liver ....

e) Large intestine ....

Q3 The **small intestine** is adapted for the absorption of food.

a) Label the diagram below showing part of the **small intestine**.

i) ....

ii) ....

iii) ....

iv) ....

b) Explain how the following aid absorption of food:

i) millions of finger-like projections ....

....

ii) very long length ....

....

Functions of the Blood

Q1 Which of these statements are **true**, and which are **false**? Tick the correct boxes.

		True	False
a)	The function of red blood cells is to fight germs.	☐	☐
b)	White blood cells help to clot blood.	☐	☐
c)	Glucose can be found in the blood.	☐	☐
d)	The liquid part of blood is called urine.	☐	☐
e)	Platelets help to seal wounds to prevent blood loss.	☐	☐

Q2 **Plasma** carries just about everything around the body.

a) For each of the substances listed in the table, state where in the body it is travelling **from** and **to**.

Substance	Travelling from	Travelling to
Urea		
Carbon dioxide		
Glucose		

b) List six other things that are carried by plasma.

1. .... 4. ....

2. .... 5. ....

3. .... 6. ....

oxygen

Q3 Use the words below to complete the passage about the structure of **red blood cells**.

large small nucleus flexible rigid
carbon dioxide oxygen cytoplasm haemoglobin oxyhaemoglobin

Red blood cells are biconcave in shape, which means they have a .... surface area for absorbing oxygen. They have no ...., but their cytoplasm is full of ...., which can combine with .... to form .... Red blood cells are very ...., which means that they can fit easily through capillaries.

Q4 The main role of **white blood cells** is defence against disease.

a) What do they produce to fight microbes? ....

b) What do they produce to neutralise the toxins produced by microbes? ....

c) Explain how white blood cells are able to digest microorganisms.

....

....

Circulatory System: Blood Vessels

Q1 Draw lines to match each of the words below with its correct description.

artery	fatty substance
capillary	hole in the middle of a tube
cholesterol	microscopic blood vessel
lumen	vessel that takes blood towards the heart
vein	vessel that takes blood away from the heart

Q2 Circle the correct word in each of the sentences below.

a) **Arteries / Veins** contain valves to prevent the blood going backwards.

b) **Capillaries / Veins** have walls that are only one cell thick.

c) **Arteries / Capillaries** have smooth muscle in their walls.

d) The blood pressure in the **arteries / veins** is higher than in the **arteries / veins**.

Q3 **Cholesterol** is a fatty substance needed in the body.

a) Why do we need cholesterol in our body? ....

b) Complete the following sentence.

A diet high in .... has been linked to high levels of cholesterol in the blood.

c) Explain what might happen if you have too much cholesterol in your body.

....

....

Q4 Gareth did an experiment to compare the elasticity of **arteries** and **veins**. He dissected out an artery and a vein from a piece of fresh meat. He then took a 5 cm length of each vessel, hung different weights on it, and measured how much it stretched. His results are shown in the table.

weight added (g)	length of blood vessel (mm)	
	artery	vein
0	50	50
5	51	53
10	53	56
15	55	59
20	56	-

a) Suggest one way in which he could have decided which was the artery and which was the vein.

....

....

b) If Gareth plots his results on a graph, which variable should he put on the vertical axis, and why?

....

c) Which vessel stretched more easily? Explain why this was.

....

d) Why did he take both vessels from the same piece of meat?

....

Circulatory System: The Heart

Q1 The diagram below shows the human **heart**, as seen from the front.
The left atrium has been labelled. Complete the remaining labels a) to j).

a) ....

b) ....

c) ....

d) ....

e) ....

f) ....

g) ....

left atrium

h) ....

i) ....

j) ....

Q2 Tick the boxes to say whether each statement below is **true** or **false**.

		True	False
a)	Arteries always carry oxygenated blood.	☐	☐
b)	Blood vessels taking blood to and from the lungs are called pulmonary vessels.	☐	☐
c)	The right side of the heart pumps deoxygenated blood.	☐	☐
d)	Valves prevent blood flowing backwards.	☐	☐

Q3 Mammals have a **double** circulatory system in which blood is pumped by the **heart**.

a) Explain the meaning of the term 'double circulatory' system.

....

b) Explain why the walls of the atria are thinner than the walls of the ventricles.

....

....

c) Explain why the wall of the left ventricle is thicker than the wall of the right ventricle.

....

....

Q4 Complete the passage using some of the words provided below.

artificial	chambers	vena cava	irregular	pacemaker	valves	regular

The rate at which the heart beats is determined by the .... Sometimes, this stops working properly, and the heartbeat becomes .... In this case, an .... unit is fitted. Defective heart .... can also be replaced.

Homeostasis

Q1 Define the word '**homeostasis**'.

....

Q2 a) Name **four** things that the body has to keep at a **constant** level.

1. .... 2. ....

3. .... 4. ....

b) Name **two** waste products that have to be removed from the body.

1. .... 2. ....

Q3 a) Why does the human body need to be kept at around **37 °C**?

....

....

b) Explain how your body **monitors** its internal temperature.

....

....

....

Q4 Fill in this table describing how different parts of the body help to bring your body temperature back to normal if you get **too hot** or **too cold**. One has been done for you.

	Too hot	Too cold
hair	Hairs lie down flat	
sweat glands		
blood vessels		
muscles		

The Kidneys and Homeostasis

Q1 Tick the correct boxes to show whether these sentences are **true** or **false**.

	True	False
a) The kidneys make urea.	☐	☐
b) Breaking down excess amino acids produces urea.	☐	☐
c) Proteins can't be stored in the body.	☐	☐
d) The kidneys monitor blood temperature.	☐	☐
e) The bladder stores urine.	☐	☐

Q2 One of the kidneys' roles is to adjust the **ion content** of the **blood**.

a) Where do the ions in the blood come from?

....

b) What would happen if the ion content of the blood wasn't controlled?

....

c) Excess ions are removed from the blood by the kidneys.
How else can ions be lost from the body?

....

Q3 The kidneys are involved in the control of the body's **water levels**.

a) Name **three** ways that water is lost from the body.

....

b) Complete the table showing how your body maintains a water balance on hot and cold days.

	Do you sweat **a lot** or **a little**?	Is the amount of urine you produce **high** or **low**?	Is the urine you produce **more** or **less** concentrated?
Hot Day			
Cold Day			

c) Sheona ran 25 km. Afterwards she didn't urinate for six hours. When Sheona did urinate, her urine was a very dark colour. Explain why this happened.

....

....

....

Top Tips: You can live with only one kidney and so it is possible for some people with kidney failure to receive a donated kidney from a living member of their family.

Controlling Blood Sugar

Q1 Most people's **blood sugar** levels are controlled by **homeostasis**.

a) Where does the **sugar** in your blood come from?

....

b) Name the **two** main **organs** that are involved in the control of blood sugar levels.

....

c) Name **one hormone** that is involved in the regulation of blood sugar levels.

....

Q2 Complete the flow chart to show what happens when **glucose** levels in the blood get too **high**.

Blood contains too much glucose.

.... is released by the ....

.... makes the .... store glucose.

.... is removed from the ....

Blood glucose level is now ....

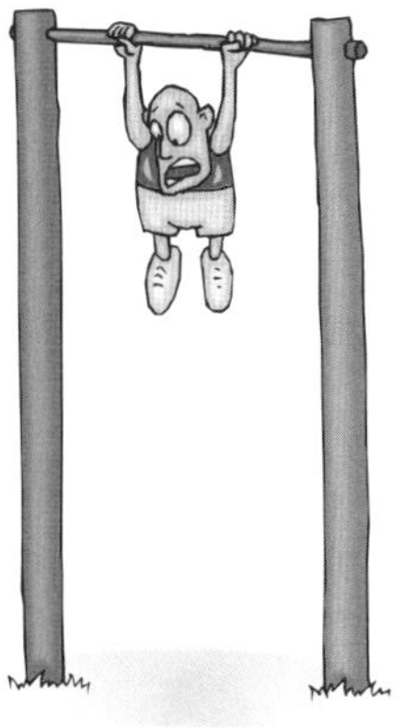

Q3 Approximately **1.8 million** people in the UK have **diabetes**.

a) Explain what type 1 diabetes is.

....

b) How can diabetics **monitor** their blood sugar levels?

....

c) Describe two ways that diabetics can **control** their blood sugar levels.

1. ....

2. ....

Insulin and Diabetes

Q1 Tick the correct boxes to show whether these sentences are true or false.

		True	False
a)	Insulin is often taken as a tablet.	☐	☐
b)	Needle-free devices can deliver insulin.	☐	☐
c)	When diabetics use insulin they can eat as they like of any food.	☐	☐
d)	The livers of diabetic people have stopped making insulin.	☐	☐
e)	Blood glucose levels can vary a lot without causing a problem.	☐	☐

Q2 During the 19th century **Banting** and **Best** researched **diabetes** by experimenting on dogs. In some of their experiments they injected an extract into diabetic dogs.

a) Where did they get the extract from? ....

b) When they injected the extract into a diabetic dog, its blood sugar level changed.

i) Describe how the blood sugar level changed.

....

ii) Which hormone did the extract contain? ....

Q3 Describe the **improvements** that have been made in the treatment of diabetes:

a) The source of the insulin used by diabetics.

....

....

b) The way diabetics take their insulin.

....

....

Q4 Injecting insulin can be **painful** and **inconvenient**.

a) What **surgical** treatment can be used to cure type 1 diabetes? ....

b) Describe some of the **problems** with the treatment you have named.

....

....

c) Scientists are constantly researching new treatments and cures for diabetes.
Name **two** treatments that are currently in development.

1. ....

2. ....

Top Tips: Many diabetics are able to control their blood sugar levels and lead normal lives. Sir Steve Redgrave won a gold medal at the Olympics after being diagnosed with diabetes.

Mixed Questions — Section Three

Q1 The diagram shows substances moving in and out of cells in the body. The cells are respiring **aerobically**.

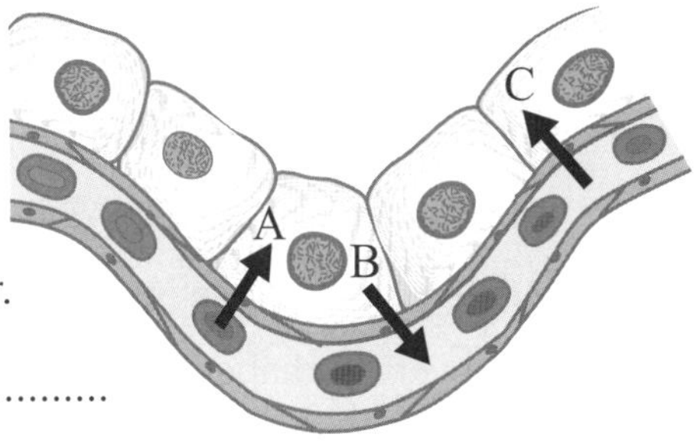

a) Which arrow, A, B or C, represents the uptake of sugar molecules by a cell? Give a reason for your answer.

....

....

b) Complete the following word equation below for aerobic respiration.

[ ] + [ ]

→ [ ] + [ ] + ENERGY

c) Give **two** uses for the energy produced during respiration.

....

Q2 Explain how the following help to maintain a **constant internal temperature**:

a) Blood vessels near the surface of the skin **dilating** and **constricting**.

....

....

b) Raising hairs. ....

c) Sweating. ....

Q3 The diagram below shows how **blood sugar level** is controlled in humans.

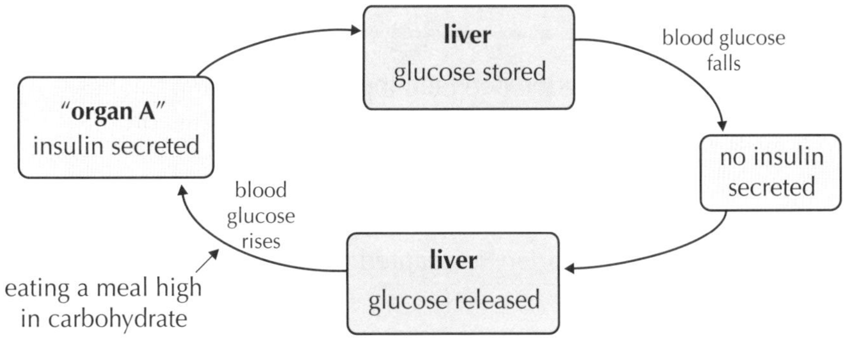

"organ A" insulin secreted → liver glucose stored → blood glucose falls → no insulin secreted → liver glucose released → blood glucose rises → "organ A" insulin secreted

eating a meal high in carbohydrate

a) Why do your cells need a continual supply of glucose?

....

b) Name "organ A" in the diagram above. ....

c) Which hormone brings about the removal of glucose? ....

Mixed Questions — Section Three

Q4 The diagram shows the human digestive system.

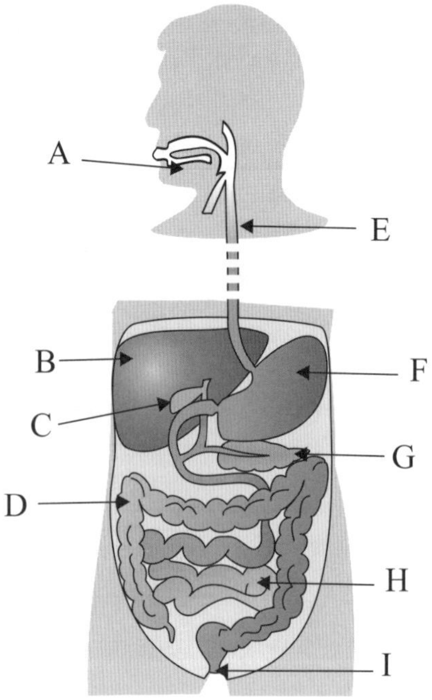

a) Which part(s) labelled A–I:

i) produce(s) the enzyme amylase? ....

ii) produce(s) HCl and the enzyme protease? ....

iii) produce(s) all three groups of enzymes, but is not where digestion takes place? ....

iv) is where the products of digestion are absorbed. ....

v) is where excess water is absorbed. ....

A B C D E F G H I

b) Give **two** functions of the HCl produced in the digestive system.

....

....

c) Due to illness, a patient's body has stopped producing bile. What effects will this have on their digestive system?

....

....

Q5 The diagram shows part of the circulatory system.

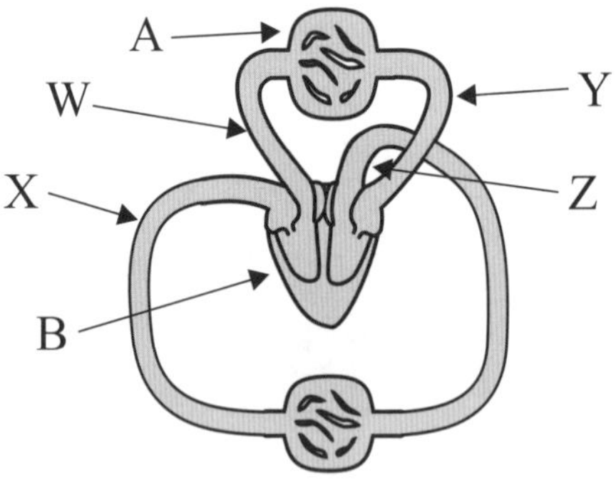

A W Y X Z B

a) Name the blood vessels labelled W, X, Y and Z.

W ....

X ....

Y ....

Z ....

b) State one difference in composition between the blood entering the heart from the vena cava and the blood leaving the heart through the aorta.

....

c) Explain how the structure of an artery is adapted for its function.

....

....

d) **i)** Which type of blood vessel contains valves? ....

ii) What is the function of these valves?

....

Photosynthesis

Q1 **Photosynthesis** is the process that produces 'food' in plants.

a) Use some of the words below to complete the equation for photosynthesis.

oxygen   carbon dioxide   nitrogen   water   glucose   sodium chloride

.... + ... —sunlight / chlorophyll→ .... + ...

b) Draw lines to match each word below to its role in photosynthesis.

chloroplast	a green pigment needed for photosynthesis
chlorophyll	the food that is produced in photosynthesis
sunlight	the structure in a cell where photosynthesis occurs
glucose	supplies the energy for photosynthesis

Q2 Complete the passage using the words from the list below.

convert   fruits   leaves   fructose   cells
cellulose   energy   walls   sucrose   lipids

Plants make glucose in their .... Some of it is used for respiration, which releases .... and allows the plant to .... the rest of the glucose into other substances for storage and to build new .... Some plants combine glucose with another sugar called .... to make .... This is stored in ...., which are eaten by animals. Glucose is also converted into .... to build cell .... Seeds can store glucose in the form of ....

Q3 The rate of photosynthesis in some pondweed was recorded by counting the bubbles produced per minute at equal intervals during the day.

No. of bubbles per minute	Time of day
0	06.00
10	12.00
20	18.00
0	

a) The time for the final reading is missing.
Predict what this time is likely to be and write it on the table.

b) Explain why the rate of photosynthesis is 0 at this time of day.

....

....

c) Suggest where plants get their food from at this time of day.

....

d) Plot a bar graph on the grid on the right to display the results shown on the table.

No. of bubbles per minute

Time of day

Rate of Photosynthesis

Q1 Sunlight contains light of different **wavelengths**, some of which we see as different **colours**. The amount of light absorbed at each wavelength by the green pigment **chlorophyll** is shown below.

a) What wavelengths and colours of light are best absorbed by chlorophyll?

....

....

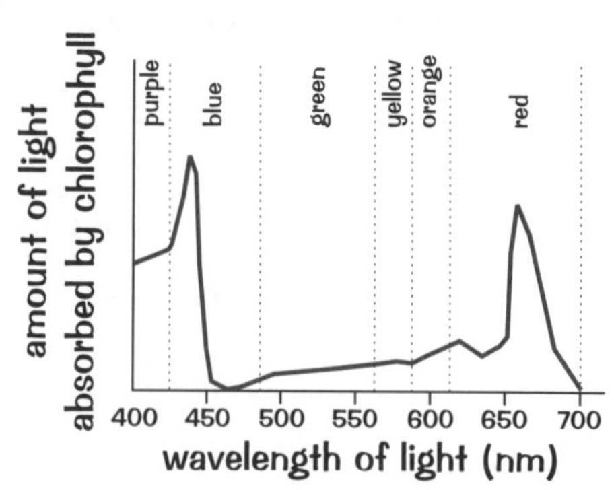

b) Suggest how you could use the information on the graph to increase the growth rate of plants in a greenhouse.

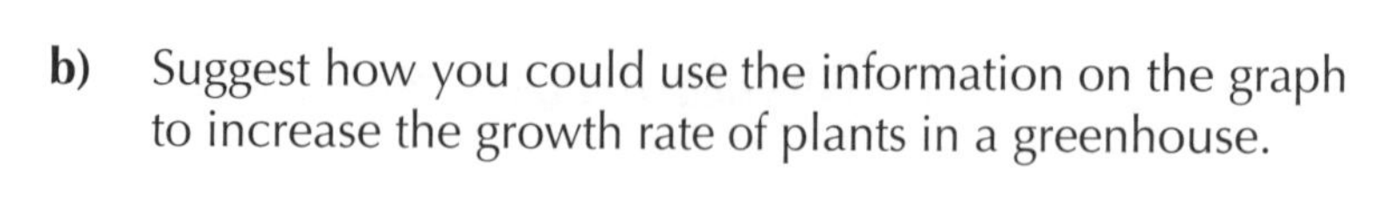

....

....

Q2 The table shows the average daytime summer temperatures in different habitats around the world.

Habitat	Temperature (°C)
Forest	19
Arctic	0
Desert	32
Grassland	22
Rainforest	27

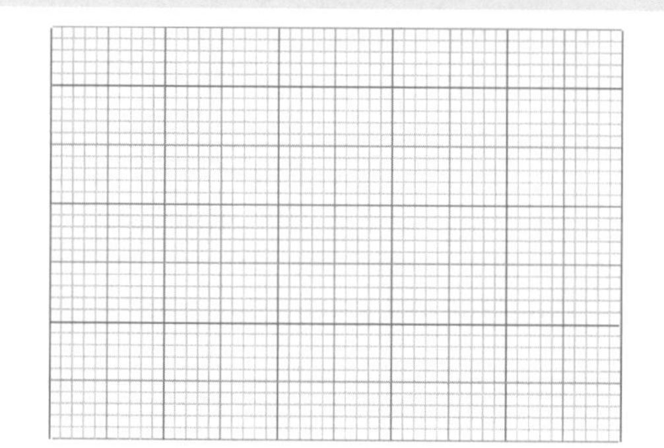

a) Plot a **bar chart** for these results on the grid.

b) From the values for temperature, in which area would you expect fewer plants to grow?

....

c) Suggest a reason for your answer above using the terms **enzymes** and **photosynthesis**.

....

....

Q3 Seth investigated the effect of different concentrations of **carbon dioxide** on the rate of photosynthesis of his Swiss cheese plant. He measured the rate of photosynthesis with increasing light intensity at **three** different CO_2 concentrations. The results are shown on the graph below.

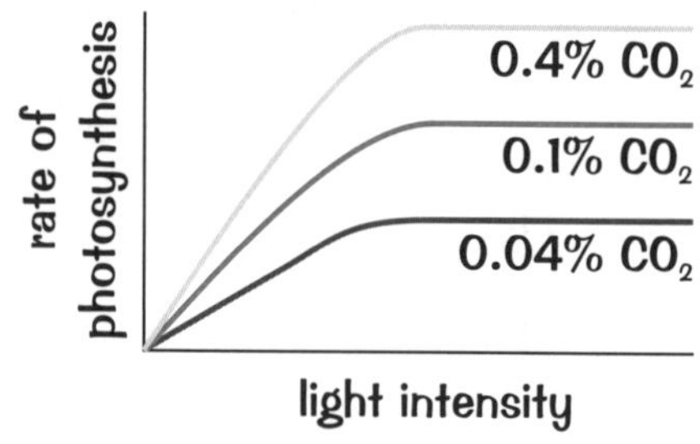

a) What effect does increasing the concentration of CO_2 have on the rate of photosynthesis?

....

....

....

b) Explain why all the graphs level off eventually.

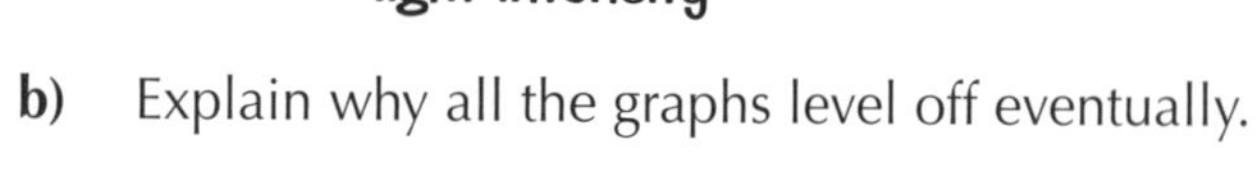

.... Think about the third limiting factor.

....

Leaf Structure

Q1 Name the parts labelled **A – E** to complete the diagram of a **leaf** below.

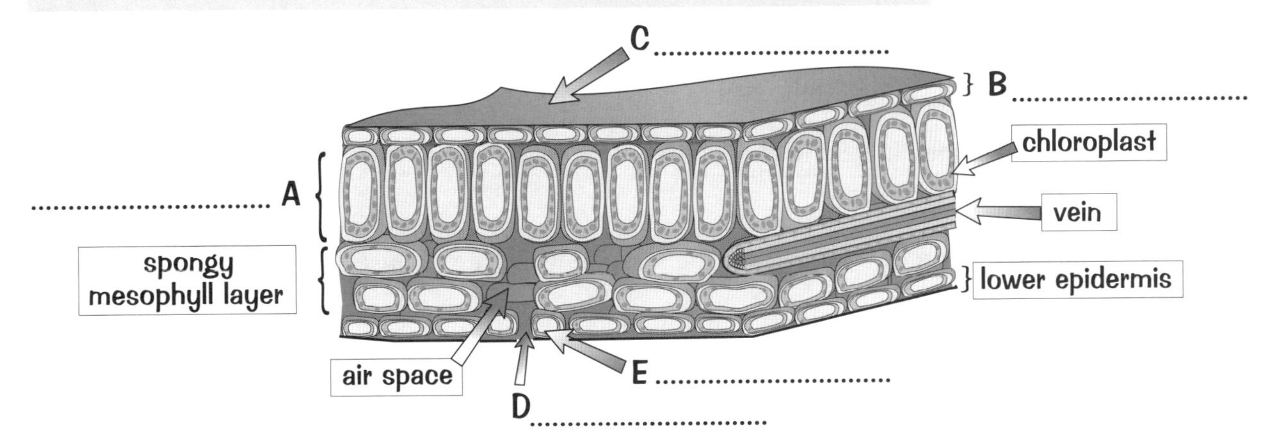

Q2 Answer the following questions about **gas exchange** in leaves.

a) Which process in the leaf uses CO_2 and produces O_2? ....

b) Which process in the leaf uses O_2 and produces CO_2? ....

Q3 A diagram of a cross-section through part of a **leaf** which is **photosynthesising** is shown.

a) Suggest what substance is represented by each of the letters shown on the diagram.

A ....

B ....

C ....

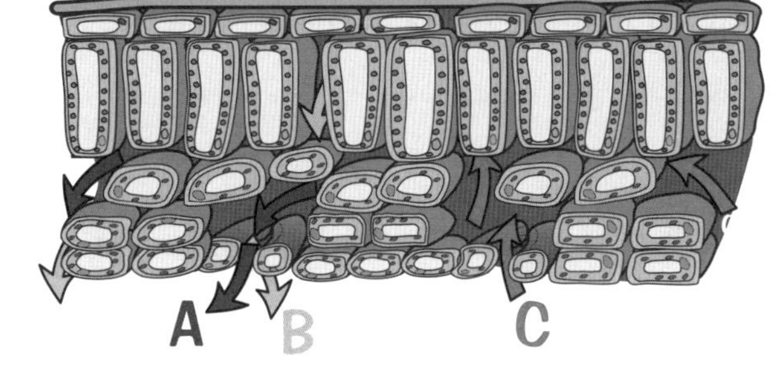

b) What differences would occur at night? Explain your answer.

....

....

Q4 Describe how the following features of leaves help with **photosynthesis**.

a) Air spaces in the mesophyll layer. ....

b) Broad leaves. ....

c) Veins. ....

d) Lots of chloroplasts. ....

Top Tips: Leaves are adapted for efficient diffusion. They help to maximise gas exchange by creating a large surface area and a short distance for diffusion to happen across. They have also adapted to minimise water loss from the plants. The clever little things...

Transpiration

Q1 Complete this diagram of a **plant** according to the instructions given below.

a) Draw an **X** on the diagram to show where water enters the plant.

b) Add **Y**s to the diagram to show where water leaves the plant.

c) Add arrows to the diagram to show how water moves from where it enters to where it leaves.

Q2 Indicate whether each of the following statements is **true** or **false**.

	True	False
a) The transpiration rate decreases as the temperature increases.	☐	☐
b) The more intense the light, the faster the transpiration rate.	☐	☐
c) Transpiration happens more slowly when the air is humid.	☐	☐
d) As the wind speed increases, the rate of transpiration decreases.	☐	☐

Q3 Choose from the following words to complete the passage.

Each word may be used more than once.

osmosis leaves evaporation roots flowers phloem diffusion transpiration xylem stem

Water leaves plants through the .... by the processes of .... and .... This creates a slight shortage of water in the .... which draws water from the rest of the plant through the .... vessels. This causes more water to be drawn up from the .... This whole process is called ....

Q4 Give three ways that transpiration **benefits** plants.

1. ....

2. ....

3. ....

Q5 Stomata are different sizes at different **light intensities.**

a) Would you expect a plant's stomata to be open or closed on a bright sunny morning? Explain your answer.

....

b) What happens to the stomata at night? What is the advantage of this?

....

c) If the supply of water to the roots of a plant dries up, the stomata close. Give one **advantage** and one **disadvantage** of this mechanism for the plant.

....

....

Water Flow in Plants

Q1 Put the following statements under the **correct heading** in the table.

- transport water
- made of living cells
- have end-plates
- have no end-plates
- transport food
- made of dead cells

XYLEM VESSELS	PHLOEM VESSELS

Q2 **Xylem** are designed for transporting substances in plants.

a) Name **two** things that are transported by the xylem. ....

b) Give another function of the xylem, other than transport. ....

c) How is the xylem adapted for this function?

....

Q3 Plant cells look different depending on how much **water** they contain.

a) Use the words in the box below to describe the states of the following cells.

plasmolysed	turgid	normal	flaccid

A .... B .... C .... D ....

b) Explain why plants start to wilt if they don't have enough water.

....

....

c) Explain why the cell in diagram D hasn't totally lost its shape.

....

Q4 Plants need to **balance** water loss with water gain.

a) Give two ways that plants are adapted to reduce water loss from their leaves.

1. ....

2. ....

b) How have plants in hot climates adapted to reduce water loss?

....

Minerals Needed for Healthy Growth

Q1 Draw lines to match the following **minerals** with their **functions** in plants.

MAGNESIUM	for making proteins
POTASSIUM	for making chlorophyll
PHOSPHATES	for making DNA and cell membranes
NITRATES	for helping enzymes to function

Q2 A diagram of a **specialised plant cell** is shown.

a) Name the type of cell shown. ....

b) What is the main **function** of this type of cell?

....

c) How is this type of cell adapted for its function?

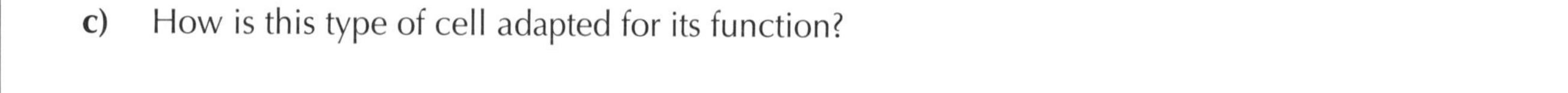

....

d) Explain why minerals are **not** absorbed from the soil by **diffusion**.

....

e) Explain how these specialised cells absorb minerals from the soil.

....

....

Q3 Spring has arrived but Pat has noticed that his **grain crop** has **stunted growth** and **yellow older leaves**. He has grown grain on this field for the last **three years**.

a) Which mineral would you recommend that Pat add to ensure better growth of his crops?

....

Pat has been offered some **manure** for his field. The table shows the mineral content of different manures.

Material	% Nitrogen	% Phosphorus	% Potassium
Bullock manure	0.6	0.1	0.7
Cow manure	0.4	0.1	0.4
Horse manure	0.6	0.1	0.5
Pig manure	0.4	0.1	0.5
Poultry manure	1	0.4	0.6
Sheep manure	0.8	0.1	0.7

b) Which type of manure would you recommend that Pat use? Explain your answer.

....

Top Tip: Whatever you do, **don't** say in an exam that minerals enter the root by diffusion. That would be **impossible**, because there are only a **few** minerals in the soil but a **lot** inside the root. It's **active transport**, which uses energy to drag those minerals kicking and screaming in the wrong direction.

Pyramids of Number and Biomass

Q1 Place a **tick** in the correct column to say whether each feature applies to pyramids of **numbers** or **biomass**. For each feature, you might need to tick one column, both, or neither.

Feature	Pyramid of numbers	Pyramid of biomass
Values for mass are shown at each level.		
Nearly always a pyramid shape.		
Each bar represents a step in a food chain.		
Always starts with a producer.		
Can only have 3 steps.		
Numbers are shown at each step.		

Q2 A single **robin** has a mass of 15 g and eats caterpillars. Each robin eats 25 **caterpillars** that each have a mass of 2 g. The caterpillars feed on 10 **stinging nettles** that together have a mass of 500 g. Study the pyramid diagrams shown then answer the questions that follow.

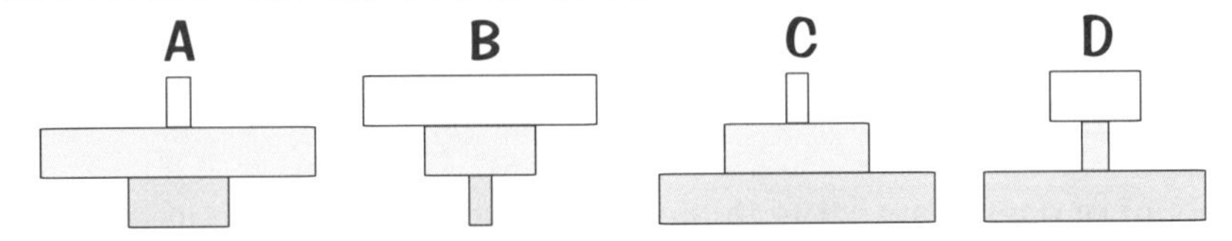

a) Which diagram is most likely to represent a pyramid of **numbers** for these organisms? ....

b) Which is most likely to represent a pyramid of **biomass** for these organisms? ....

c) Explain how you decided on your answer to part b) above.

....

Q3 **Ladybirds** feed on **aphids** which feed from an **oak tree**.

a) Draw a pyramid of number for the food chain in the box.

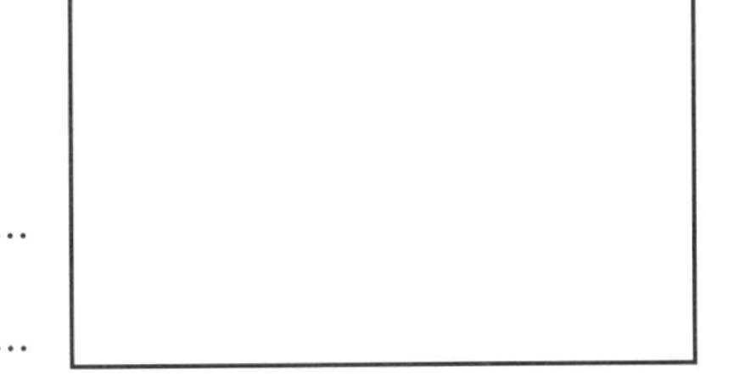

b) Explain the unusual shape of this pyramid.

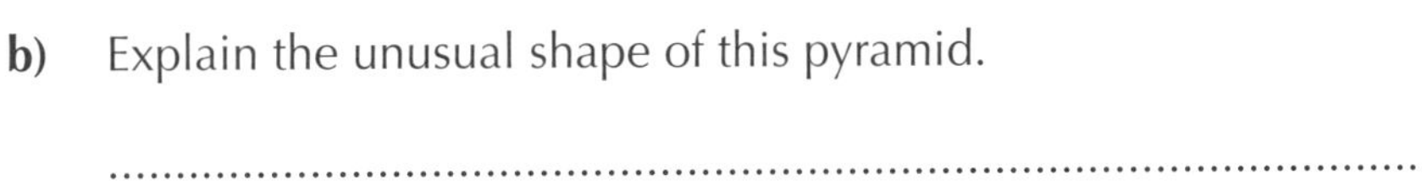

....

....

Q4 Study the food web shown before answering the following questions.

If there was a sudden increase in the number of gazelle, explain what may happen to the population of:

a) lions ....

....

b) zebras ....

....

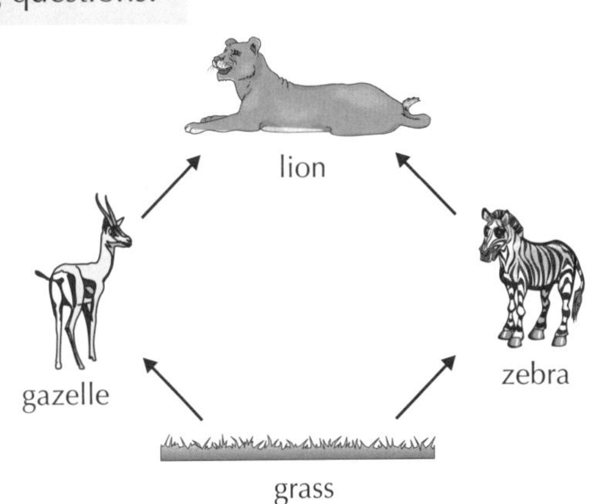

Energy Transfer and Energy Flow

Q1 Complete the sentences below by circling the correct words.

a) Nearly all life on Earth depends on **food / energy** from the Sun.

b) **Plants / Animals** can make their own food by a process called **photosynthesis / respiration**.

c) To obtain energy animals must **decay / eat** plant material or other animals.

d) Animals and plants release energy through the process of **photosynthesis / respiration**.

e) Some of the energy released in animals is **gained / lost** through **growth / movement** before it reaches organisms at later steps of the food chain.

f) Some energy is lost between steps of a food chain because it's used to make **edible / inedible** materials such as **hair / flesh**.

Q2 An **aquatic food chain** is shown.

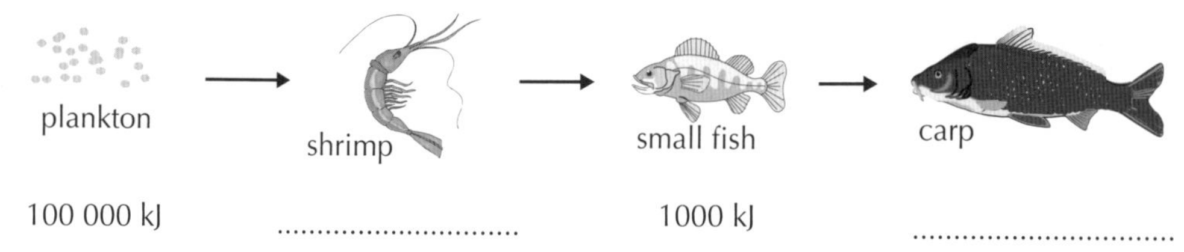

100 000 kJ .... 1000 kJ ....

a) 90 000 kJ is lost at the first transfer.

i) Write the amount of energy available in the shrimp for the small fish in the space provided.

ii) Calculate the **efficiency** of energy transfer from the plankton to the **shrimp**.

....

b) The energy transfer from the small fish to the carp is **5%** efficient.

i) Write the amount of **energy** passed on to the **carp** in the space provided.

ii) How much energy is **lost** from the food chain at this stage?

....

Q3 Study the diagram of **energy transfer** shown.

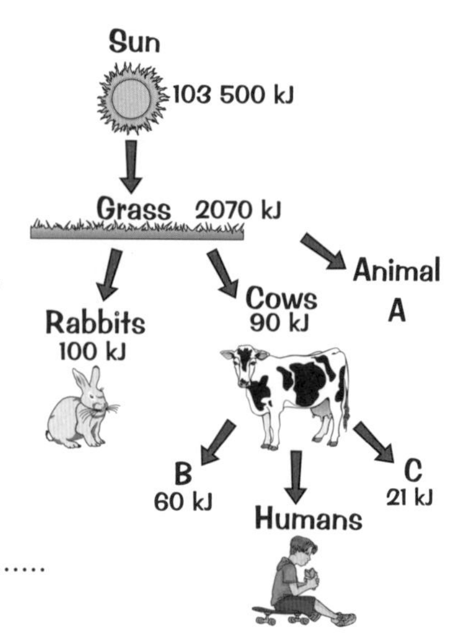

a) Using the figures shown on the diagram, work out the percentage of the Sun's energy that is passed to the grass.

....

b) Only 10% of the energy in the grass reaches the next trophic level. Work out how much energy from the grass passes to animal A.

....

c) **B** and **C** are processes that represent energy loss. Suggest what these processes might be.

....

d) Why do food chains rarely have more than five trophic levels?

....

....

Biomass and Fermentation

Q1 Give four ways that **energy** stored as **biomass** can be released for human use.

1. .... 2. ....

3. .... 4. ....

Q2 Are the following statements about fermenters **true** or **false**?

		True	False
a)	The culture medium is a solid.	☐	☐
b)	The food for the microorganisms is contained in the air.	☐	☐
c)	The pH inside the fermenter must be carefully monitored.	☐	☐
d)	It doesn't matter what temperature it is inside the fermenter.	☐	☐
e)	Air is piped in to supply carbon dioxide to the microorganisms.	☐	☐

Q3 Answer the following questions about **biofuels**.

a) Explain why burning fast-growing trees need **not** contribute to global warming.

....

b) What piece of equipment is used to make biogas?

....

c) How is biogas used?

....

Q4 The diagram below shows a **fermenter** that can be used for producing **mycoprotein**.

a) What is mycoprotein?

....

b) Give two advantages of using microorganisms to make food.

....

....

c) Explain the purpose of each of the following:

i) the water jacket ....

ii) the air supply ....

iii) the paddles ....

Top Tip: Not all microorganisms used in fermenters need oxygen — it depends on whether they respire aerobically or anaerobically to produce the useful product.

Managing Food Production

Q1 Tick the correct boxes to show whether the following statements are true or false.

		True	False
a)	Fish farms decrease the amount of energy that's lost in a food chain.	☐	☐
b)	Fish kept in fish farms are more prone to disease.	☐	☐
c)	Organic meat comes from animals that have been intensively farmed.	☐	☐

Q2 Three different **food chains** are shown here.

Grass → Cattle → Human

Pondweed → Small fish → Salmon → Human

Wheat → Human

a) Circle the food chain that shows the most **efficient** production of **food** for **humans**.

b) Explain your choice.

....

....

Q3 Give a **disadvantage** of the following methods of improving the efficiency of food production.

a) Animals are crowded together. ....

....

b) Animals are given antibiotics. ....

....

c) Animals are kept warm. ....

....

Q4 Emma compared two ecosystems. **Ecosystem A** was carefully controlled — the fish were kept in large cages and fed a special diet. Pesticides were used to kill unwanted pests. **Ecosystem B** was kept as natural as possible, with no cages, special diet or pest control. Emma's observations are recorded in the table below.

Time (months)	Number of fish		Average size of fish (mm)		Comments	
	A	B	A	B	A	B
0	200	200	362	348	200 fish introduced.	200 fish introduced.
2	189	191	368	392	A few initial losses due to change in habitat.	A few initial losses due to change in habitat. Initial growth rate seems fast.
4	188	152	374	423	Numbers have stabilised. Water quality good.	High numbers of fish lice. Adults still growing well.
6	277	136	436	426	Breeding looks successful. Fish growth increasing.	Fish lice levels still high. Breeding has started. Growth rate decreasing.
8	349	172	359	372	End of breeding season. Adult fish growing well.	Breeding season. Fish numbers stabilising. Water pH 8.
10	338	184	401	382	Very few of the new fish have been lost.	Breeding season now over. Growth has slowed.
12	336	179	443	393	Population seems stable. Large, healthy fish.	Population stabilising. Water pH improved at 7.5.

a) Suggest why the **average size** of fish drops so much in both ecosystems at 8 months.

....

....

b) What factors may have affected the **growth rate** and **number** of fish in Ecosystem B?

....

....

c) What conclusions could Emma draw from her investigation?

....

....

Pesticides and Biological Control

Q1 a) What are **pesticides** and why are they used?

....

....

b) Give one problem that can be caused by the use of pesticides.

....

Q2 **Cockroaches** were sprayed with a **pesticide** to control the size of their population.

Explain what effect this could have on the rest of the food web shown.

cockroach → frog → fox
rabbit → fox

....

....

....

Q3 **Biological control** is an alternative to using pesticides.

a) What is biological control?

....

b) Give two examples of biological control.

1. ....

2. ....

c) Give an **advantage** and a **disadvantage** of using biological control.

Advantage: ....

Disadvantage: ....

Q4 **Pesticides** that were being sprayed onto fields near to a bird of prey's habitat were found in the birds in **toxic** levels.

Birds of prey only eat other animals and fish.

a) Suggest how pesticide that was sprayed onto crops was found in the birds.

....

b) The amount of pesticide sprayed onto the field was carefully controlled to keep the concentration below the toxic level. Suggest why the birds contained such large amounts of the pesticide.

....

....

Alternatives to Intensive Farming

Q1 **Hydroponics** is an **alternative method** of growing plants.

a) What are the plants grown in? ....

b) Give an example of a plant that is grown in this way. ....

c) Are the following features of hydroponics an **advantage** or a **disadvantage** of the technique?

i) Amount of land required. ....

ii) The cost. ....

iii) Amount of weeding required. ....

iv) Ability to grow plants in places with poor soil. ....

v) Support needed by the plants. ....

vi) Special soluble nutrients are needed. ....

Q2 For each of the substances used in **intensive farming** below suggest an **organic farming alternative** and give one **advantage** of the alternative.

a) **Insecticides:** alternative — ....

Advantage: ....

b) **Herbicides:** alternative — ....

Advantage: ....

c) **Chemical fertilisers:** alternative — ....

Advantage: ....

Q3 Comment on the **cost**, amount of **labour** needed and effect on the **environment** for a farmer considering using **manure and compost** instead of chemical fertilisers and **weeding** instead of herbicides.

a) **Cost** ....

....

....

b) **Amount of labour** ....

....

....

c) **Effect on the environment** ....

....

....

Recycling Nutrients

Q1 Complete the diagram below as instructed to show part of the **carbon cycle**.

CO_2 in the air

plant **animal**

a) Add an arrow or arrows labelled **P** to represent **photosynthesis**.

b) Add an arrow or arrows labelled **R** to represent **respiration**.

c) Add an arrow or arrows labelled **F** to represent **feeding**.

Q2 The sentences below describe how **elements** are **recycled** in a food chain. Sort them into the correct order by numbering them 1 to 5. The first one has been done for you.

☐ **Materials are recycled and returned to the soil by decay.**

1 **Plants take up minerals from the soil.**

☐ **Plants use minerals and the products of photosynthesis to make complex nutrients.**

☐ **Nutrients in plants are passed to animals through feeding and used in respiration to provide energy.**

☐ **Waste and dead tissues are decayed by microorganisms.**

Q3 **Carbon** is a very important element that is constantly being recycled.

a) How is carbon removed from the atmosphere? ....

b Why is carbon so important to living things?

....

c) How is this carbon passed on through the food chain?

....

d) By what process do **all** living organisms return carbon to the air? ....

Q4 Complete the following table about two types of organism that are important in decay.

Type of organism involved in decay	Example	How they help in decay
Detritivores	....	....
....	Bacteria / fungi	....

Recycling Nutrients

Q5 Circle the correct word or phrase to complete the following sentences.

a) Nitrogen is need to make **protein / carbohydrate / fat**.

b) The percentage of the air that is nitrogen is **100% / 21% / 78%**.

c) Nitrogen is **a reactive gas / an unreactive gas / an unreactive liquid**.

Q6 Match up each type of **organism** below with the way that it obtains **nitrogen**.

Organism	Way of obtaining nitrogen
Plants	By breaking down dead organisms and animal waste
Animals	From nitrates in the soil
Bacteria	By eating other organisms

Q7 Explain the role of each of the following types of **bacteria** in the nitrogen cycle.

a) Decomposers ....

b) Nitrifying bacteria ....

c) Denitrifying bacteria ....

d) Nitrogen-fixing bacteria ....

Q8 Below is a diagram of the **nitrogen cycle**. Explain what is shown by the arrows labelled:

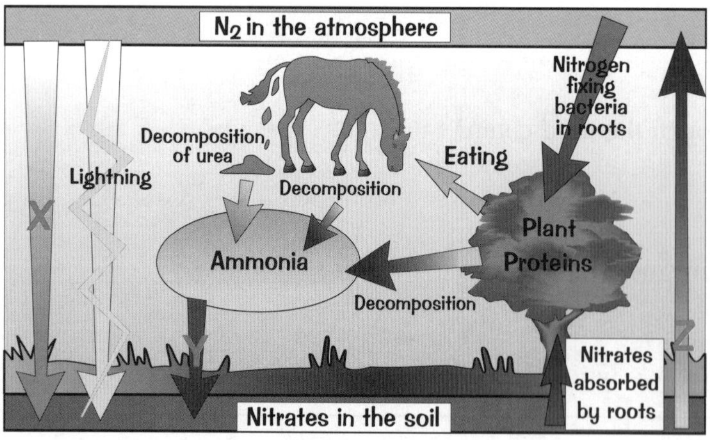

a) X ....

....

....

b) Y ....

....

....

c) Z ....

....

....

Q9 A farmer was told that if he planted **legume plants** his soil would be more **fertile**. Explain how the legume plants would increase the fertility of the soil.

....

....

Air Pollution

Q1 Draw lines to link the correct parts of these sentences.

The main cause of acid rain is	acid rain.
Acid rain kills trees and	sulfuric acid.
Limestone buildings and statues are affected by	acidifies lakes.
In clouds sulfur dioxide reacts with water to make	sulfur dioxide.

Q2 Use the words and phrases below to complete the paragraph.

nitric **sulfur dioxide** **the greenhouse effect** **sulfuric** **nitrogen oxides** **acid rain**

When fossil fuels are burned carbon dioxide is produced. The main problem caused by this is .... The gas .... is also produced. This comes from sulfur impurities in the fuel. When it combines with moisture in the air .... acid is produced. This falls as acid rain. In the high temperatures inside a car engine nitrogen and oxygen from the air react together to produce .... These react with moisture to produce .... acid, which is another cause of acid rain.

Q3 **Exhaust** fumes from cars and lorries often contain **carbon monoxide** (CO).

a) Why is CO more likely to be formed in **engines** than if the fuel was burnt in the open air?

....

b) Why is carbon monoxide **dangerous**?

....

Q4 Look at the graph and then answer the questions below.

a) Describe the **trend** shown by the graph.

....

....

b) What is the main cause of this trend?

....

c) What effect do many scientists believe the trend shown in the graph is having on the Earth's average temperature?

....

Water Pollution

Q1 State four possible causes of **water pollution**.

1. ....
2. ....
3. ....
4. ....

Q2 Number the following stages 1 – 6 to describe the process of **eutrophication**.

☐ The amounts of nitrates and phosphates in the water increases.

☐ Plants die because they don't receive enough light.

☐ There's a rapid growth of plants and algae.

☐ Fish and other living organisms start to die.

☐ Excess fertiliser washes off fields into rivers and streams.

☐ Decomposers feed off the dead plants using up all the oxygen in the water.

Q3 A farmer uses too much **DDT** on his land and the rain washes it into a nearby lake. DDT is a chemical that has been used as a **pesticide** to kill insects such as mosquitoes and lice.

Explain why DDT is passed along food chains.

....

....

Q4 Mayfly larvae and sludge worms are often studied to see how much **sewage** is in water.

a) Is this a direct or indirect measure of water pollution? ....

Juanita recorded the number of each species in water samples taken at three different distances away from a sewage outlet. Her results are shown on the right.

Distance (km)	No. of mayfly larvae	No. of sludge worms
1	3	20
2	11	14
3	23	7

b) Give one thing that she would have to do to make this experiment a fair test.

....

c) What can you conclude about the two organisms from these results?

....

....

d) Suggest why sewage may decrease the number of mayfly larvae.

....

....

Pollution Indicators

Q1 The level of pollution can be monitored using **non-living indicators**.

a) Name two **direct** non-living indicators. ....

b) Name two **indirect** non-living indicators. ....

Q2 Michael wanted to investigate the amount of **pollution** around his home town, Brightchester. He recorded the number of different **lichen species** at 5 different sites around the town.

a) What type of pollution are lichen sensitive to?

....

Site Number	Distance from the town centre (miles)	Number of different lichen species found on trees
1	0	3
2	0.5	5
3	1.0	6
4	1.5	12
5	2.0	16

b) Describe the trend in the data.

....

....

c) Suggest an explanation for these results. ....

....

Q3 An indicator of air pollution is the number of cases of **skin cancer**.

a) Circle the correct words to complete the paragraph.

> Skin cancer in the UK has rapidly **increased / decreased** in recent years.
> This is thought to be partly due to the **increase / decrease** of ozone in the ozone layer.
> Ozone absorbs harmful UV radiation from the Sun. The **less / more** ozone there is the **less / more** UV radiation reaches the Earth's surface where it can cause skin cancer.
> When **air / water** is polluted with CFCs, the CFCs react with the ozone molecules in the atmosphere and **destroy them / cause them to multiply**.

b) Describe the trend shown in the graph.

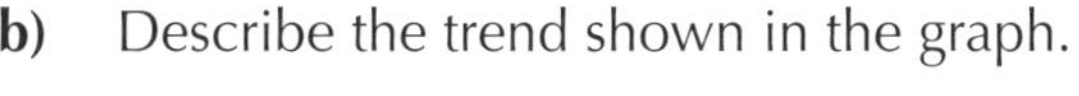

....

c) Does the graph prove that ozone depletion causes skin cancer?

....

Top Tips: Don't jump to conclusions — always look at evidence suspiciously. Think about what else might have caused the effect. Take skin cancer for example — it's increased over the last 30 years, during which time the ozone layer has been thinning. But this doesn't mean that there's definitely a link. There have been lots of lifestyle changes too, and some of these may be responsible.

Conservation and Recycling

Q1 Decide whether each of the following statements are **true** or **false**.

		True	False
a)	Recycling could help to slow the increase in greenhouse gas levels.	☐	☐
b)	Paper can only be recycled a limited number of times.	☐	☐
c)	Plastics can be recycled over and over again.	☐	☐
d)	Recycling costs nothing and has huge benefits for the environment.	☐	☐
e)	Recycling causes more land to be used for landfill sites.	☐	☐

Q2 Match the following methods of woodland conservation to their descriptions.

coppicing	replanting trees that have been cut down in the past
reforestation	new trees are replanted at the same rate that others are cut down
replacement planting	cutting trees down to just above ground level

Q3 **Recycling** helps to conserve our natural resources.

a) What is recycling? ....

....

b) Give **three** examples of things that can be recycled.

....

c) Does recycling usually use more or less energy than extracting the material from scratch?

....

Q4 Rainforests contain many different **species**. If we destroy rainforests we risk making species extinct and **reducing biodiversity**.

a) What is meant by '**reducing biodiversity**'?

....

b) Suggest an implication for humans that reducing biodiversity might have.

....

Q5 Describe how **conservation** measures and **recycling** help us to sustain resources for future use.

....

....

....

Mixed Questions — Section Four

Q1 Pieces of blue cobalt chloride paper were stuck to the **upper** and **lower** surfaces of a leaf. Cobalt chloride turns pink as it becomes **moist**.

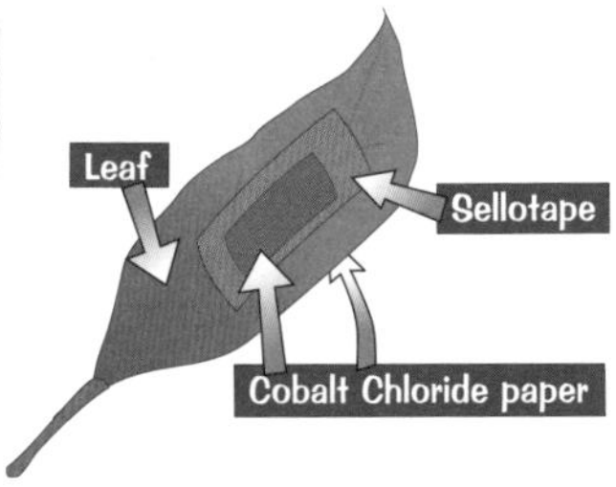

Leaf
Sellotape
Cobalt Chloride paper

a) Which surface will turn the cobalt chloride paper pink first? Explain your answer.

....

....

b) What do we call the process by which water is lost from the leaf? ....

c) From where did the plant obtain the water that is lost from the leaf? ....

d) Give one environmental condition that slows down water loss from leaves.

....

Q2 The graph below shows the **oxygen** and **carbon dioxide** exchanged by a plant. The concentration of each gas was measured next to the leaves as light intensity increased.

a) Which gas is oxygen and which is carbon dioxide?

Gas A is ....

Gas B is ....

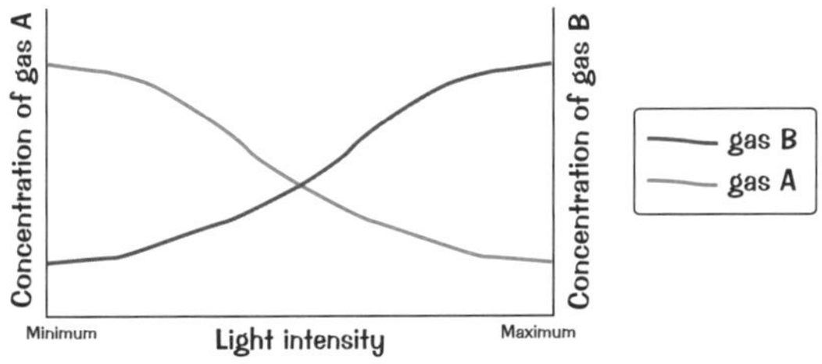

Concentration of gas A
Concentration of gas B
Light intensity
Minimum
Maximum
gas B
gas A

b) Explain how you decided.

....

....

Q3 A lot of farmers use **chemical pesticides** and **fertilisers** on their crops.

a) Explain why farmers use these chemicals.

....

....

b) Describe **three** ways in which these chemicals can cause problems for the environment.

....

....

....

c) Suggest **two** ways that organic farming can be helpful in conserving endangered species.

....

....

....

Mixed Questions — Section Four

Q4 The diagram on the right shows the fate of **energy** captured by photosynthesis in **barley plants**, as it passes through **pigs** on its way to **humans** in a food chain.

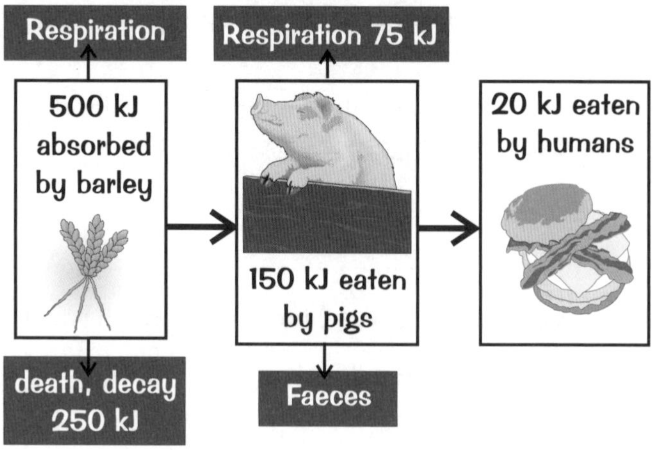

Respiration
500 kJ absorbed by barley
death, decay 250 kJ
Respiration 75 kJ
150 kJ eaten by pigs
Faeces
20 kJ eaten by humans

a) Work out how much energy is lost from the barley plants by respiration.

....

b) Work out how much energy is lost from the pigs in their faeces.

....

c) If the amount the pigs respired could be reduced, more energy would pass to the humans. Suggest **two** ways that the amount they respire could be reduced and explain your answer.

....

....

d) Apart from reducing the various types of energy loss that occur throughout this food chain, what could be done to the food chain that would mean more energy passing to humans?

....

Q5 **Legumes** are plants which have nodules on their roots containing **nitrogen-fixing bacteria**.

a) Suggest why some farmers rotate their crops, alternating between cereals and legumes in a field.

....

....

b) Explain why plants need nitrogen and how an insufficient intake of nitrogen affects them.

....

....

Q6 An investigation was carried out into which organisms are found along a stream. A **sewage outflow pipe** was located midway along the study site. The graph shows the numbers of different species found.

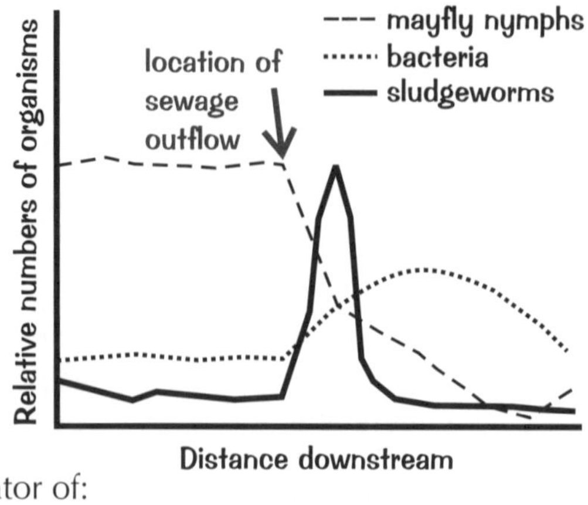

Relative numbers of organisms
Distance downstream
location of sewage outflow
--- mayfly nymphs
······ bacteria
— sludgeworms

a) Explain the change in bacteria levels as you move downstream from the outflow pipe.

....

....

b) Which species in the investigation would be a good indicator of:

i) polluted water .... **ii)** clean water ....

Atoms

Q1 **Complete** the following sentences.

a) Neutral atoms have a ....neutral.... charge.

b) A charged atom is called an ....ion.....

c) A neutral atom has the same number of ....protons.... and ....electrons.....

d) If an electron is added to a neutral atom, the atom becomes ....negatively.... charged.

Q2 Complete this table:

Particle	Mass	Charge
Proton	1	+1
Neutron	1	0
Electron	$\frac{1}{2000}$	–1

Q3 **What am I?**

Choose from: **nucleus** **proton** **electron** **neutron**

a) I am in the centre of the atom. I contain protons and neutrons. ....Nucleus....

b) I move around the nucleus in a shell. ....Electron....

c) I am the lightest. ....electron....

d) I am a positively-charged particle. ....Proton....

e) I have no charge. ....Neutron....

f) In a neutral atom there are as many of me as there are electrons. ....Protons....

Q4 Elements have a **mass number** and an **atomic number**.

a) What does the **mass number** of an element tell you about its atoms?

....The number of protons and electrons in an atom....

b) What does the **atomic number** of an element tell you about its atoms?

....The number of protons....

c) Fill in this table using a periodic table.

Element	Symbol	Mass Number	Number of Protons	Number of Electrons	Number of Neutrons
Sodium	Na		11		
		16	8	8	8
Neon			10	10	10
	Ca			20	20

Elements, Compounds and Isotopes

Q1 a) Correctly label the following diagrams as either '**element**' or '**compound**'.

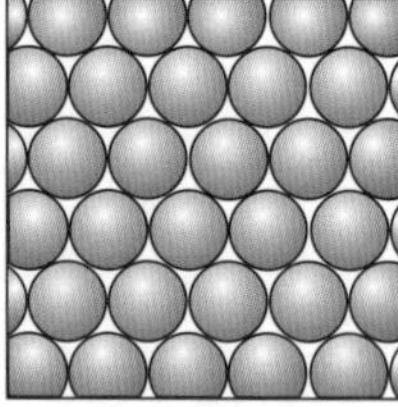

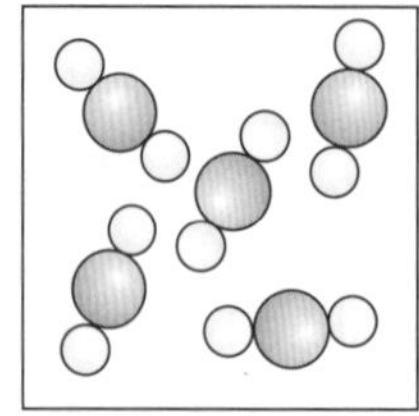

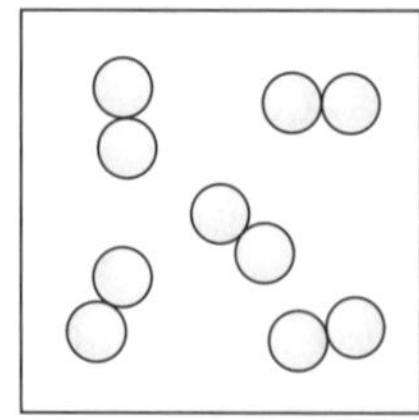

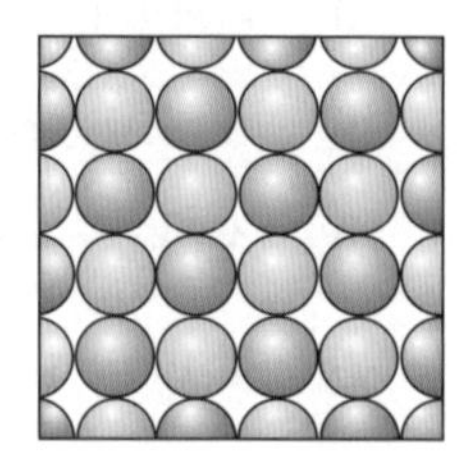

A = Element B = Compound C = Element D = Compound

b) Suggest which diagram (A, B, C or D) could represent:

i) oxygen C **ii)** sodium A **iii)** sodium chloride D **iv)** carbon dioxide B

Q2 Circle the **correct words** in these sentences.

a) **Compounds / Atoms** are formed when two or more elements react together.

b) The properties of compounds are **exactly the same as / completely different to** the original elements.

c) It is **easy / difficult** to separate the elements in a compound.

d) Carbon dioxide is **a compound / an element**, whereas iron is **a compound / an element**.

e) The number of **neutrons / electrons** determines the chemistry of an element.

Q3 Choose the correct words to **complete** this paragraph.

electrons	element	isotopes	protons	compound	neutrons

Isotopes are different atomic forms of the same element which have the same number of protons but a different number of neutrons.

Q4 Which of the following atoms are **isotopes** of each other? Explain your answer.

W $^{12}_{6}C$ **X** $^{4}_{2}He$ **Y** $^{14}_{6}C$ **Z** $^{14}_{7}N$

Answer W and Y

Explanation They're atomic numbers are the same, therefore their protons are the same.

Q5 Chlorine exists as two isotopes: **chlorine-35** and **chlorine-37**. Would you expect atoms of these isotopes to react in the same way as each other? Explain your answer.

Electrons determine chemistry of an atom; isotopes of the same element have same number of electrons

The Periodic Table

Q1 Select from these **elements** to answer the following questions.

iodine nickel silicon sodium radon krypton calcium

a) Which two are in the same group? Sodium .... and calcium ....

b) Name an alkali metal. Sodium ....

c) Name a transition metal. Nichel ....

d) Name an element with seven electrons in its outer shell. ....

e) Name a non-metal which is not in group 0. ....

Q2 **True** or **false**?

	True	False
a) Elements in the same **group** have the same number of electrons in their outer shell.	☐	☐
b) The periodic table shows the elements in order of ascending **atomic mass**.	☐	☐
c) Each **column** in the periodic table contains elements with similar properties.	☐	☐
d) The periodic table is made up of all the known compounds.	☐	☐
e) There are more than 100 known elements.	☐	☐

Q3 Elements in the same group undergo **similar reactions**.

a) Tick the pairs of elements that would undergo similar reactions.

A potassium and rubidium ☐ **C** calcium and oxygen ☐

B helium and fluorine ☐ **D** calcium and magnesium ☐

b) Explain why fluorine and chlorine undergo similar reactions.

....

....

Q4 Complete the following table.

	Alternative Name for Group	Number of Electrons in Outer Shell
Group 1	Alkali metals	
Group 7		7
Group 0		*

* excluding helium

Electron Shells

Q1 Tick the boxes to show whether each statement is **true** or **false**.

	True	False
a) Electrons occupy shells in atoms.	☐	☐
b) The highest energy levels are always filled first.	☐	☐
c) Atoms are most stable when they have partially filled shells.	☐	☐
d) Noble gases have a full outer shell of electrons.	☐	☐
e) Reactive elements have full outer shells.	☐	☐

Q2 Write out the **electron configurations** for the following elements.

a) Beryllium ....

b) Oxygen ....

c) Silicon ....

d) Calcium ....

e) Aluminium ....

f) Argon ....

Q3 Do the following groups of elements contain **reactive** or **unreactive** elements? Explain your answers in terms of **electron shells.**

a) Noble gases ....

....

b) Alkali metals ....

....

Q4 **Chlorine** has an atomic number of 17.

a) What is its electron configuration? ....

b) Draw the electrons on the shells in the diagram. →

Cl

c) Why does chlorine react readily?

....

Q5 Draw the **full electron configurations** for these elements.

C — **Carbon**

Mg — **Magnesium**

K — **Potassium**

Top Tips: Once you've learnt the 'electron shell rules', drawing electron configurations are pretty easy — the first shell only takes 2 electrons, and the second and third shells a maximum of 8.

Ionic Bonding

Q1 Use the **diagram** to answer the following questions.

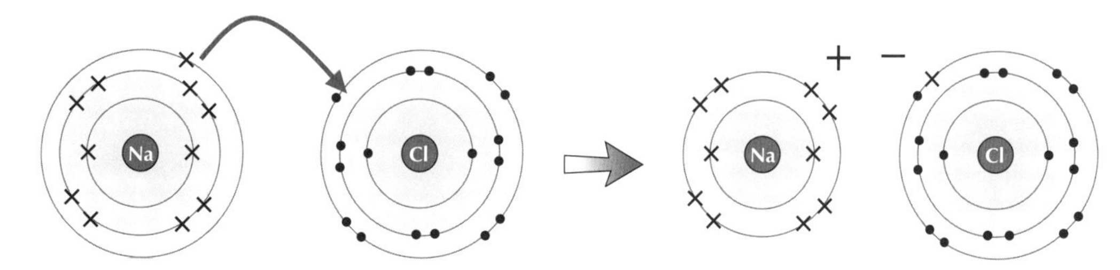

a) Which **group** of the periodic table does **sodium** belong to? ....

b) How many **electrons** does **chlorine** need to gain to get a full outer shell of electrons? ....

c) What is the **charge** on a **sodium ion**? ....

d) What is the chemical formula of **sodium chloride**? ....

Q2 Elements react in order to get a **full outer shell** of electrons.

a) How many electrons does magnesium need to **lose** to get a full outer shell? ....

b) How many electrons does oxygen need to **gain** to get a full outer shell? ....

c) Draw a 'dot and cross' diagram to show what happens to the outer shells of electrons when magnesium and oxygen react.

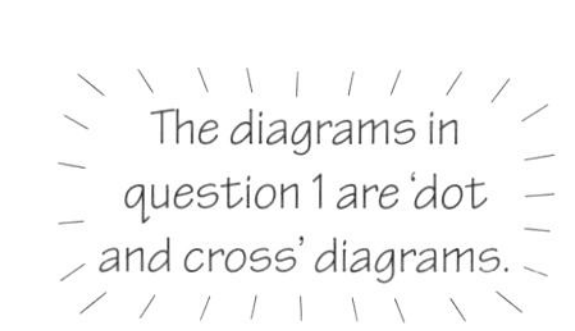

d) What is the chemical formula of magnesium oxide? ....

e) What type of **structure** would you expect magnesium oxide to have? ....

Q3 **Giant ionic structures** usually have certain properties in common.

a) Circle the correct words to explain why sodium chloride (salt) has a high melting point.

> Salt has very **strong** / **weak** chemical bonds between the **negative** / **positive** sodium ions and the **negative** / **positive** chlorine ions. This means that it needs a **little** / **large** amount of energy to break the bonds.

b) Mike conducts an experiment to find out if **calcium chloride** conducts electricity. He tests the compound when it's solid, when it's dissolved in water and when it's molten.

i) Complete this table of results.

ii) Explain your answers to part b)i).

....

....

....

	Conducts electricity?
When solid	
When dissolved in water	
When molten	

Electron Shells and Ions

Q1 Complete the following sentences by circling the correct words.

a) Atoms that have lost or gained electrons are called **isotopes / ions**.

b) Elements in Group 1 **readily / rarely** form ions.

c) Elements in Group 0 **readily / rarely** form ions.

d) Positive ions are called **anions / cations**.

Q2 Atoms can **gain** or **lose** electrons to get a full outer shell.

a) How many **electrons** do the following elements need to **lose** in order to get a **full outer shell**?

i) Lithium .... **ii)** Calcium .... **iii)** Potassium ....

b) How many **electrons** do the following elements need to **gain** in order to get a **full outer shell**?

i) Oxygen .... **ii)** Chlorine .... **iii)** Fluorine ....

Q3 Write the **electron configurations** for the following ions and draw the **electrons** on the shells. (The first one's been done for you.)

+ Na

− Cl

Na^+ Na [2,8]$^+$ ....

a) Cl^- ....

+ + Mg

− − O

b) Mg^{2+} ....

c) O^{2-} ....

Q4 What are the **electron configurations** of the following ions?

a) K^+ ....

b) Ca^{2+} ....

c) F^- ....

d) Be^{2+} ....

Reactivity Trends

Q1 **Fluorine** and **chlorine** are both halogens.

a) Draw 'dot and cross' diagrams of a fluorine atom and a chlorine atom in the space provided.

b) Give **one similarity** and **one difference** between the electronic structures of these two atoms.

Similarity: ....

Difference: ....

c) When these atoms react to form ions, how does their electronic structure change?

....

d) State which of these two atoms will be more reactive and explain why.

....

....

Q2 **Sodium**, **potassium** and **lithium** are all alkali metals.

a) When these atoms react to form ions how does their electronic structure change?

....

b) Put these three alkali metals in order of increasing reactivity.

least reactive .... **most reactive**

c) Explain the trend in reactivity down Group 1.

....

....

Q3 Neon is **unreactive**.

a) Draw the electronic structure of neon in the space on the right.

b) Explain why neon is so unreactive.

....

....

Top Tips: If you make sure you **understand** why these reactivity trends exist, then it'll be far easier for you to remember which way round they go. In fact, it'll all start to make much more sense.

Covalent Bonding

Q1 Indicate whether each statement is **true** or **false**.

		True	False
a)	Covalent bonding involves sharing electrons.	☐	☐
b)	Atoms react to gain a full outer shell of electrons.	☐	☐
c)	Some atoms can make both ionic and covalent bonds.	☐	☐
d)	Hydrogen can form two covalent bonds.	☐	☐
e)	Carbon can form four covalent bonds.	☐	☐

Q2 **Complete** the following table to show how many electrons are needed to **fill up** the **outer shell** of these atoms.

Atom	Carbon	Chlorine	Hydrogen	Nitrogen	Oxygen
Number of electrons needed to fill outer shell					

Q3 Complete the following diagrams by adding the **electrons**. Only the outer shells are shown.

a) Hydrogen chloride (HCl)

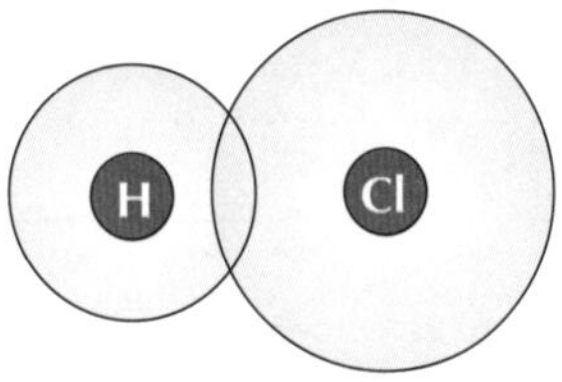

H Cl

b) Oxygen (O_2)

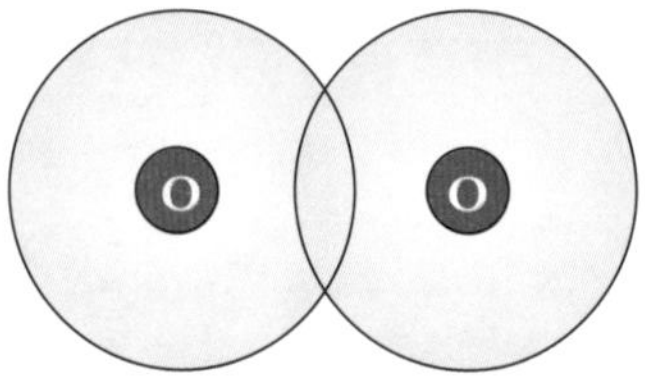

O O

c) Water (H_2O)

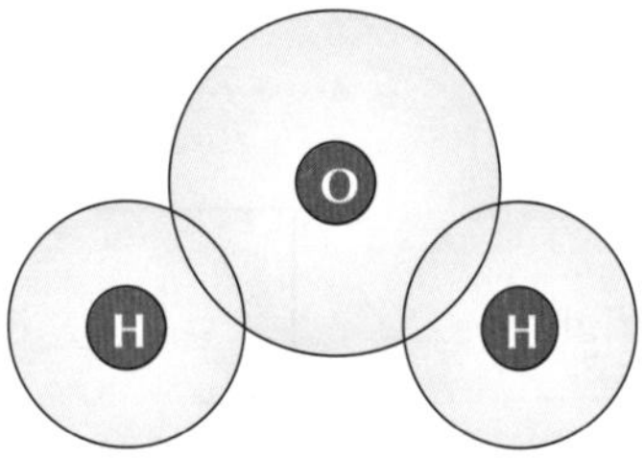

O H H

d) Ammonia (NH_3)

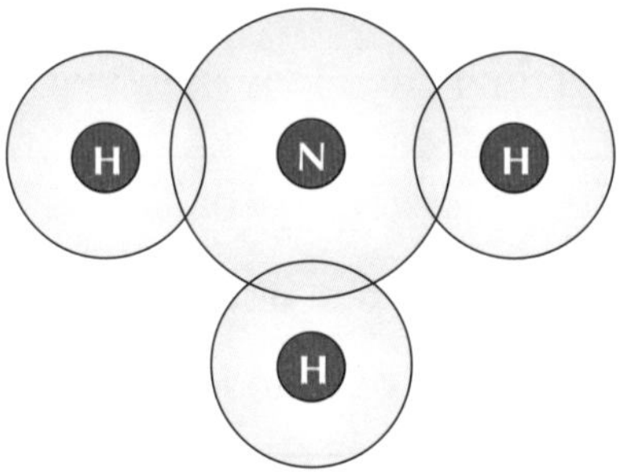

H N H H

e) Methane (CH_4)

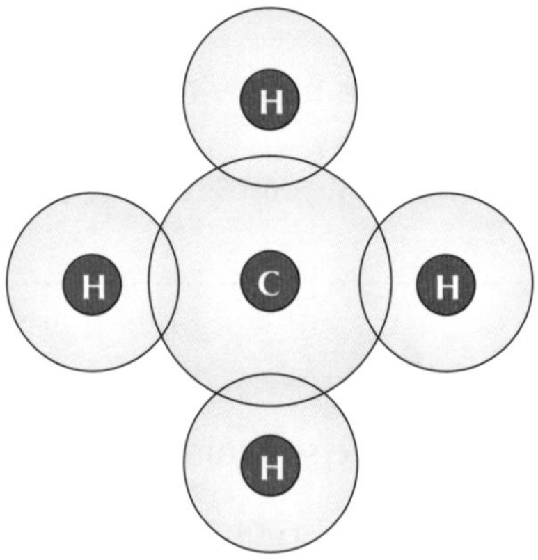

H H C H H

Q4 Why do some atoms **share** electrons?

....

....

Covalent Substances: Two Kinds

Q1 Which am I — **diamond**, **graphite** or **silicon dioxide** (silica)?

Match up the statements to the drawings.

I am used in jewellery.

I am used to make glass.

I am the hardest natural substance.

I have layers which move over one another.

I am used in pencils.

Diamond

Graphite

Silicon dioxide

I am the only non-metal which is a good conductor of electricity.

Sand is made from me.

I am not made from carbon.

My carbon atoms form three covalent bonds.

My carbon atoms form four covalent bonds.

Q2 Circle the correct words to complete the following paragraph.

Giant covalent structures contain **charged ions** / **uncharged atoms**. The covalent bonds between the atoms are **strong** / **weak**. Giant covalent structures have **high** / **low** melting points, they usually **do** / **don't** conduct electricity and they are usually **soluble** / **insoluble** in water.

Q3 Hydrogen and chlorine share electrons to form a molecule called **hydrogen chloride**.

Predict two physical properties hydrogen chloride will have.

1. ....

2. ....

Q4 **Graphite** and **diamond** are both entirely made from **carbon**, but have different properties.

a) Explain why graphite is a good conductor of electricity.

....

....

b) Explain why diamond's structure makes it hard.

....

....

Molecular Substances: The Halogens

Q1 Draw lines to match each halogen to its **description**.

chlorine	dense green gas
iodine	orange liquid
bromine	dark grey solid

Hubba hubba

Q2 Say whether these statements are **true** or **false**.

		True	False
a)	Chlorine gas is made up of molecules which each contain three chlorine atoms.	☐	☐
b)	The atoms of the halogens get bigger as you go down the group.	☐	☐
c)	Halogens with larger atoms have lower melting and boiling points.	☐	☐
d)	There are stronger attractions between bromine molecules than between chlorine molecules.	☐	☐

Q3 The melting and boiling points of halogens **increase** down the group. Explain why this is.

....

....

Q4 Equal volumes of **bromine water** were added to two test tubes, each containing a different **halogen salt solution**. The results are shown in the table below.

SOLUTION	RESULT
potassium chloride	no change
potassium iodide	colour change

a) Explain these results.

....

....

b) Write a **symbol equation** for the reaction which caused the colour change in the iodide solution.

....

Q5 **Sodium** was reacted with **bromine gas** using the equipment shown. White crystals of a new solid were formed during the reaction.

a) Name the white crystals.

....

b) Write a balanced symbol equation for the reaction.

....

Metallic Structures

Q1 Draw a diagram in the space below to show the arrangement of the atoms in a typical **metal**. Label the **atoms** and the **free electrons**, and show any relevant charges.

Q2 Explain how **heat** and **electricity** are conducted through metals.

....

....

Q3 Transition metals and their compounds make good **catalysts**.

a) Circle the **transition metals** below. You might need to use a periodic table to help you.

silicon iron nickel sodium vanadium calcium copper manganese

b) Name two transition metal catalysts and give a process that each one catalyses.

Transition metal: .... **Process:** ....

Transition metal: .... **Process:** ....

Q4 Under normal conditions, **all** metals have **electrical resistance**.

a) What happens to wires as electricity flows through them, and why is this usually a waste?

....

b) Explain what a **superconductor** is, and say how you can make some metals superconduct.

....

Q5 Scientists are still working to try and **improve superconductors**.

a) Give **two** possible uses of superconductors.

....

b) What is the **main problem** with today's superconductors?

....

New Materials

Q1 **Buckminsterfullerene** is made up of 60 carbon atoms.

a) What is the **molecular formula** of buckminsterfullerene? ....

b) How many covalent bonds does each carbon atom form? ....

c) Can buckminsterfullerene conduct electricity? Explain your answer.

....

....

Q2 **Smart materials** have some really weird properties.

a) What are **smart materials**?

....

b) Choose from the words below to complete the paragraph.

gases	liquids	solid	dyes	contract	temperature	evaporate

Smart materials include .... that change colour depending on the ...., ... that turn .... when you place them in a magnetic field, and other materials that expand or .... when you put an electric current through them.

c) Nitinol is a smart material known as a '**shape memory alloy**'. Explain what this means.

....

....

Q3 **Nanoparticles** are really tiny particles, between 1 and 100 nanometres across.

a) How many nanometres are there in **1 mm**? ....

b) Explain how nanoparticles are useful in producing industrial **catalysts**.

1 nm = 0.000 001 mm

....

....

c) Nanoparticles can be made by **molecular engineering**. What is molecular engineering?

....

....

d) Fullerenes can be joined together to make **nanotubes**. Give two uses of nanotubes.

....

Top Tips: Scientists have made nanostructures from DNA that look like smiley faces — each one a thousandth of the width of a human hair. They've also made a nanomap of the Americas.

Mixed Questions — Section Five

Q1 Three forms of the element carbon are shown in the diagram.

R S T

○ carbon atoms

a) Identify the different forms by name.

R .... **S** .... **T** ....

b) The **properties** of four substances are given below.

i) Which substances in the table could be **R** and **S** above?

R: ....

S: ....

Substance	Melting Point (°C)	Good Electrical Conductor?
A	2000	Only when molten and dissolved
B	3550	No
C	20	No
D	3652	Yes

ii) What **type of structure** is substance **A** likely to have? ....

iii) Identify the substance in the table that is **likely** to have a **simple molecular** structure. Justify your answer.

....

Q2 **Calcium** is a reactive metal in **Group 2** of the periodic table.

a) Give the electron arrangements in a calcium **atom** and a calcium **ion**, Ca^{2+}.

Electron arrangement in a Ca atom ....

Electron arrangement in a Ca^{2+} ion ....

b) The **mass number** of the main isotope of calcium is 40.
Use the periodic table to determine the number of **neutrons** in the nucleus of this isotope.

....

c) Name an element which has similar chemical properties to calcium. ....

Q3 **Hydrogen gas** reacts explosively with **oxygen gas** to form **water**.

a) Complete the diagram to show the electron arrangement in an oxygen **molecule**.
One oxygen **atom** has been drawn for you.

b) A water molecule contains two single covalent bonds, as shown in the diagram:
Carefully explain what is meant by a single covalent bond.

O
H H

....

....

Mixed Questions — Section Five

Q4 **Lithium** is a metallic element in **Group 1** of the periodic table.

a) Draw a diagram to show the electron arrangement in a lithium atom.

Use the periodic table to help you.

b) Explain how lithium forms ions.

....

c) **Fluorine** is in **Group 7** of the periodic table. It reacts with lithium to form a **compound**.

i) Define the term '**compound**'.

....

ii) Give the chemical formula for the compound that forms between lithium and fluorine.

....

iii) What would you expect to happen if you added chlorine to a solution of the substance you named in part c)ii). Explain your answer.

....

....

d) Would you expect the reaction between lithium and fluorine to be faster or slower than:

i) the reaction between **lithium and bromine**? Explain your answer using the idea of **shielding**.

....

....

ii) the reaction between **sodium and fluorine**? Explain your answer using the idea of **shielding**.

....

....

Maximus wished he'd revised shielding more thoroughly.

Q5 **New materials** are being developed continually.

a) Describe the main advantage of superconductors. ....

....

b) Give two useful properties of **nanotubes**.

....

c) i) What metals is the shape memory alloy **nitinol** made from? ....

ii) What name is given to these metals and others in the same block of the periodic table as them?

....

Balancing Equations

Q1 Atoms form **ions** with various charges. Write down the ions formed by the following elements:

a) lithium .... b) oxygen .... c) iron(III) .... d) chlorine ....

Q2 Give the **formulas** of the following:

a) methane ....

b) silver nitrate ....

c) lithium oxide ....

d) sodium carbonate ....

e) potassium hydroxide ....

f) aluminium chloride ....

Q3 A book describes a reaction as follows: "**methane** (CH_4) can be burnt in **oxygen** (O_2) to form **carbon dioxide** (CO_2) and **water** (H_2O)".

a) What are the **reactants** and the **products** in this reaction?

Reactants: .... Products: ....

b) Write the **word equation** for this reaction.

....

c) Write the **balanced symbol equation** for the reaction.

....

Don't forget, the oxygen ends up in both products.

Q4 Add **one** number to each of these equations so that they are **correctly balanced**.

a) $CuO + HBr \rightarrow CuBr_2 + H_2O$

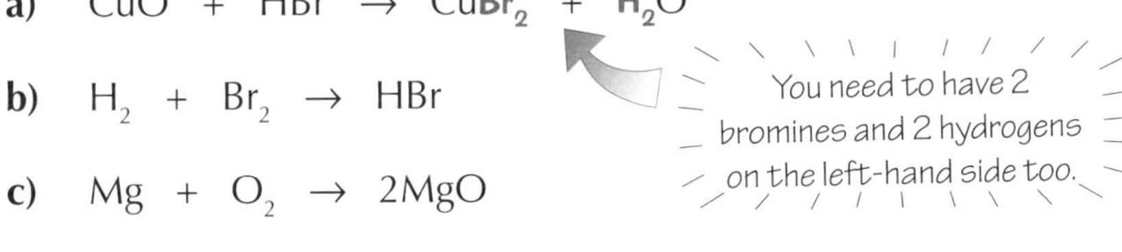

b) $H_2 + Br_2 \rightarrow HBr$

c) $Mg + O_2 \rightarrow 2MgO$

d) $2NaOH + H_2SO_4 \rightarrow Na_2SO_4 + H_2O$

Q5 **Balance** these equations.

a) $NaOH + AlBr_3 \rightarrow NaBr + Al(OH)_3$

b) $FeCl_2 + Cl_2 \rightarrow FeCl_3$

c) $N_2 + H_2 \rightarrow NH_3$

d) $Fe + O_2 \rightarrow Fe_2O_3$

e) $NH_3 + O_2 \rightarrow NO + H_2O$

$Fe_2O_3 + 3CO \rightarrow 2Fe + 3CO_2$

Top Tips: The most important thing to remember with balancing equations is that you can't change the **little numbers** — if you do that, you'll change the substances into completely different things. Just take your time and work through everything logically.

Relative Formula Mass

Q1 a) What is meant by the **relative atomic mass** of an element?

....

b) Give the **relative atomic masses (A_r)** of the following:

i) magnesium .... **iv)** hydrogen .... **vii)** K ....

ii) neon .... **v)** C .... **viii)** Ca ....

iii) oxygen .... **vi)** Cu .... **ix)** Cl ....

Q2 Identify the elements A, B and C.

Element A has an A_r of 4.
Element B has an A_r 3 times that of element A.
Element C has an A_r 4 times that of element A.

Element A is ....

Element B is ....

Element C is ....

Q3 a) Explain how the **relative formula mass** of a **compound** is calculated.

....

b) Give the **relative formula masses (M_r)** of the following:

i) water (H_2O) ....

ii) potassium hydroxide (KOH) ....

iii) nitric acid (HNO_3) ....

iv) sulfuric acid (H_2SO_4) ....

v) ammonium nitrate (NH_4NO_3) ....

Q4 The equation below shows a reaction between element X and water.
The total M_r of the products is **114**. What is substance X?

$$2X + 2H_2O \rightarrow 2XOH + H_2$$

....

....

Top Tips: The periodic table really comes in useful here. There's no way you'll be able to answer these questions without one (unless you've memorised all the elements' relative atomic masses — and that would just be silly). And lucky for you, you'll get given one in your exam. Yay!

Two Formula Mass Calculations

Q1 a) Write down the **formula** for calculating the **percentage mass** of an element in a compound.

b) Calculate the percentage mass of the following elements in ammonium nitrate, NH_4NO_3.

i) Nitrogen ....

ii) Hydrogen ....

iii) Oxygen ....

Q2 **Nitrogen monoxide**, NO, reacts with oxygen, O_2, to form **oxide R**.

a) Calculate the percentage mass of nitrogen in **nitrogen monoxide**.

....

b) Oxide R has a percentage composition by mass of **30.4% nitrogen** and **69.6% oxygen**. Work out its empirical formula.

....

....

....

Q3 1.48 g of a **calcium compound** contains 0.8 g of calcium, 0.64 g of oxygen and 0.04 g of hydrogen.

Work out the empirical formula of the compound.

....

....

....

Q4 a) Calculate the percentage mass of **oxygen** in each of the following compounds.

A Fe_2O_3 **B** H_2O **C** $CaCO_3$

b) Which compound has the **greatest** percentage mass of oxygen? ....

Calculating Masses in Reactions

Q1 Anna burns **10 g** of **magnesium** in air to produce **magnesium oxide** (MgO).

a) Write out the **balanced equation** for this reaction.

....

b) Calculate the mass of **magnesium oxide** that's produced.

....

....

....

Q2 What mass of **sodium** is needed to make **2 g** of **sodium oxide**? $4Na + O_2 \rightarrow 2Na_2O$

....

....

....

Q3 **Aluminium** and **iron oxide** (Fe_2O_3) react together to produce **aluminium oxide** (Al_2O_3) and **iron**.

a) Write out the **balanced equation** for this reaction.

....

b) What **mass** of iron is produced from **20 g** of iron oxide?

....

....

....

Q4 When heated, **limestone** ($CaCO_3$) decomposes to form **calcium oxide** (CaO) and **carbon dioxide**.

How many **kilograms** of limestone are needed to make **100 kilograms** of **calcium oxide**?

....

....

The calculation is exactly the same — just use 'kg' instead of 'g'.

....

....

Top Tips: You'll get nowhere with this type of calculation if you don't look at the **balanced equations**. These tell you how many moles of one thing react with how many moles of another thing. And they tell you how many moles of product will be made using those quantities of reactants.

The Mole

Q1 a) **Complete** the following sentence.

One mole of atoms or molecules of any substance will have a .... in grams equal to the .... for that substance.

b) How many **moles** are there in each of the following?

i) 20 g of calcium. ....

ii) 112 g of sulfur. ....

iii) 200 g of copper oxide (CuO). ....

c) Calculate the **mass** of each of the following.

i) 2 moles of sodium. ....

ii) 0.75 moles of magnesium oxide (MgO). ....

Q2 What **volume** is occupied by the following gases at room temperature and pressure?

a) 4.5 moles of oxygen. ....

b) 0.48 moles of hydrogen. ....

Q3 A one **molar solution** (1M) contains one mole per litre.

There are 1000 cm^3 in 1 litre.

a) Calculate the number of moles in:

i) 50 cm^3 of a 2M solution. ....

ii) 250 cm^3 of a 0.5M solution. ....

b) **200 cm^3** of a solution contains **0.25 moles** of iron hydroxide. Calculate its **molar concentration**.

....

c) What **volume** of a 1.5M solution of calcium hydroxide contains **2 moles** of calcium hydroxide?

....

Q4 Danni adds **0.6 g** of magnesium to sulfuric acid. Magnesium sulfate and hydrogen form. All the magnesium reacts.

a) Write a **balanced symbol equation** for this reaction. ....

b) What **volume** of hydrogen was produced?

....

c) Calculate the **mass** of magnesium sulfate produced.

....

....

Atom Economy

Q1 **Copper oxide** can be reduced to copper by heating it with carbon.

copper oxide + carbon → copper + carbon dioxide

$2CuO + C \rightarrow 2Cu + CO_2$

a) What is the useful product in this reaction? ....

b) Calculate the atom economy.

$$\text{atom economy} = \frac{\text{total } M_r \text{ of useful products}}{\text{total } M_r \text{ of reactants}} \times 100$$

....

....

c) What percentage of the starting materials are wasted?

....

Q2 It is important in industry to find the **best atom economy**.

a) Explain why. ....

....

....

b) What types of reaction have the highest atom economy? Give an example.

....

Q3 **Titanium** can be reduced from titanium chloride ($TiCl_4$) using magnesium or sodium.

a) Work out the atom economy for each reaction.

With magnesium: $TiCl_4 + 2Mg \rightarrow Ti + 2MgCl_2$ ....

....

With sodium: $TiCl_4 + 4Na \rightarrow Ti + 4NaCl$ ....

....

b) Which one has the better atom economy? ....

Q4 **Chromium** can be extracted from its oxide (Cr_2O_3) using **aluminium**. **Aluminium oxide** and **chromium** are formed.

Calculate the atom economy of this reaction.

....

....

Percentage Yield

Q1 James wanted to produce **silver chloride** (AgCl). He added a carefully measured mass of silver nitrate to an excess of dilute hydrochloric acid. An **insoluble white salt** formed.

a) Write down the formula for calculating the **percentage yield** of a reaction.

b) James calculated that he should get 2.7 g of silver chloride, but he only got 1.2 g. What was the **percentage yield**?

....

....

Q2 Explain how the following factors reduce the percentage yield.

a) Reversible reactions ....

....

b) Filtration (when you want to keep the liquid) ....

....

c) Transferring liquids ....

....

d) Unexpected reactions ....

....

Q3 Aaliya and Natasha mixed together barium chloride ($BaCl_2$) and sodium sulfate (Na_2SO_4) in a beaker. An **insoluble** substance formed. They **filtered** the solution to obtain the solid substance, and then transferred the solid to a clean piece of **filter paper** and left it to dry.

a) Aaliya calculated that they should produce a yield of **15 g** of barium sulfate. However, after completing the experiment they found they had only obtained **6 g**.

Calculate the **percentage yield** for this reaction.

....

....

b) Suggest **two** reasons why their actual yield was lower than their predicted yield.

1. ....

2. ....

Mixed Questions — Section Six

Q1 Here is the equation for the production of carbon **monoxide** from a poorly ventilated charcoal flame. It is **not** balanced correctly.

$$C + O_2 \rightarrow CO$$

Circle the **correctly balanced** version of this equation.

$C + O_2 \rightarrow CO_2$ $\qquad$ $C + O_2 \rightarrow 2CO$ $\qquad$ $2C + O_2 \rightarrow 2CO$

Q2 Ali adds **13 g** of zinc to **50 cm³** of hydrochloric acid. All the zinc reacts.

$$Zn + 2HCl \rightarrow ZnCl_2 + H_2$$

a) How many moles of zinc were added? ....

b) How many moles of hydrochloric acid reacted? ....

Look at the symbol equation.

Q3 **Iron oxide** is reduced to **iron** inside a blast furnace using carbon. There are **three** stages involved.

Stage A	$C + O_2 \rightarrow CO_2$
Stage B	$CO_2 + C \rightarrow 2CO$
Stage C	$3CO + Fe_2O_3 \rightarrow 2Fe + 3CO_2$

a) If **10 g** of **carbon** is used in stage B, and all the carbon monoxide produced gets used in stage C, what **mass** of CO_2 is produced in **stage C**?

Work out the mass of CO at the end of stage B first.

....

....

....

b) Suggest how the CO_2 might be used after stage C.

....

Q4 **Sodium sulfate** (Na_2SO_4) is made by reacting **sodium hydroxide** (NaOH) with **sulfuric acid** (H_2SO_4). **Water** is also produced.

a) Write out the **balanced equation** for this reaction. ....

b) What mass of **sodium hydroxide** is needed to make **75 g** of **sodium sulfate**?

....

....

....

c) Sodium sulfate is the useful product in this reaction. Calculate the **atom economy**.

....

....

Mixed Questions — Section Six

Q5 Orwell found that 1.4 g of silicon reacted with 7.1 g of chlorine to produce the reactive liquid silicon chloride.

a) Work out the **empirical formula** of the silicon chloride.

....

....

b) Calculate the **percentage mass** of chlorine in silicon chloride.

....

....

c) What **volume** would be occupied by 7.1 g of chlorine gas at room temperature and pressure?

....

d) Write down the balanced chemical equation for the reaction.

....

e) **i)** Orwell predicted he would obtain 8.5 g of silicon chloride, however he only obtained 6.5 g. Calculate the **percentage yield** for this reaction.

....

ii) The reaction was not reversible, nor was there any filtration involved. Suggest two reasons why the yield was still not 100%.

....

....

f) Does this reaction have a **high atom economy**? Explain your answer.

....

Q6 Magnesium reacts with nitric acid (HNO_3) to form magnesium nitrate ($Mg(NO_3)_2$).

a) Work out the **relative formula mass** of magnesium nitrate.

....

b) When 0.12 g of magnesium reacted with excess acid, 0.74 g of magnesium nitrate was formed.

i) Calculate the **number of moles** of magnesium and magnesium nitrate.

....

ii) The total volume of the solution formed was 0.2 dm^3. Work out the **concentration** of magnesium nitrate in this solution using your answer from part i).

....

c) If 0.025 moles of nitric acid was used, what **mass** of nitric acid was this?

....

Rates of Reaction

Q1 The five statements below are about **rates of reaction**. Circle the correct words to complete the sentences.

a) The **higher** / **lower** the temperature the faster the rate of reaction.

b) A **higher** / **lower** concentration will reduce the rate of reaction.

c) If the reactants are **gases** / **liquids**, the higher the pressure the **faster** / **slower** the rate of reaction.

d) A smaller particle size **increases** / **decreases** the rate of reaction.

e) A catalyst changes the rate of reaction but **is** / **isn't** used up.

Q2 In an experiment, **different sizes** of marble chips were reacted with excess hydrochloric acid. The **same mass** of marble was used each time. The graph below shows how much **gas** was produced when using large marble chips (X), medium marble chips (Y) and small marble chips (Z).

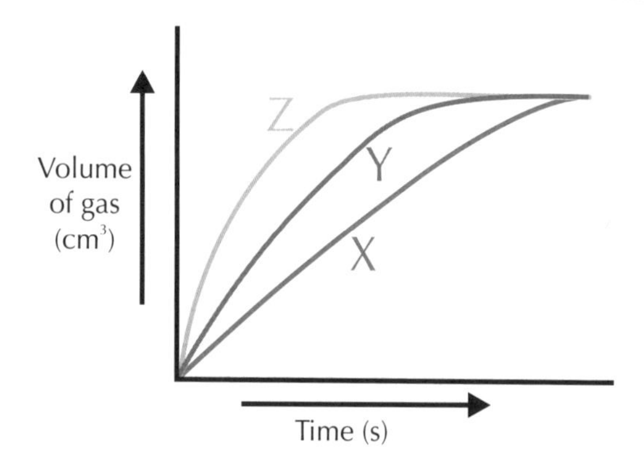

a) i) Which curve (X, Y or Z) shows the **fastest** reaction? Circle the correct answer.

X **Y** **Z**

ii) How can you tell this by looking at the graph?

....

....

b) Why is an **excess** of acid used? ....

c) Why do all the reactions produce the **same** volume of gas?

....

d) On the graph, draw the curve you would expect to see if you used **more** of the small marble chips. Assume that all the other conditions are the same as before.

Q3 Another experiment investigated the **change in mass** of the reactants during a reaction in which a **gas** was given off. The graph below shows the results for three experiments carried out under different conditions.

a) Does the mass of the reactants **increase** or **decrease**?

....

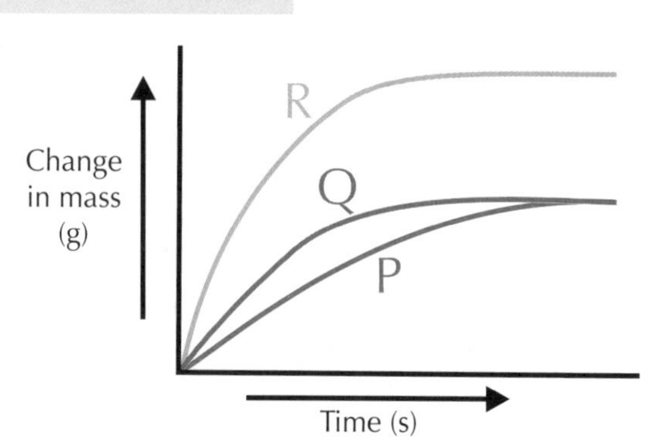

b) Suggest **why** reaction R has a greater change in mass than reactions P and Q.

....

....

c) Suggest what might have caused the difference between reaction P and reaction Q.

....

Measuring Rates of Reaction

Q1 Charlie was comparing the rate of reaction of 5g of magnesium ribbon with 20 ml of **five different concentrations** of hydrochloric acid. Each time he measured how much **gas** was produced during the **first minute** of the reaction. He did the experiment **twice** for each concentration of acid and obtained these results:

Concentration of HCl (mol/dm^3)	Experiment 1 — volume of gas produced (cm^3)	Experiment 2 — volume of gas produced (cm^3)	Average volume of gas produced (cm^3)
2	92	96	
1.5	63	65	
1	44	47	
0.5	20	50	
0.25	9	9	

a) **Fill in** the last column of the table.

b) Circle the **anomalous** result in the table.

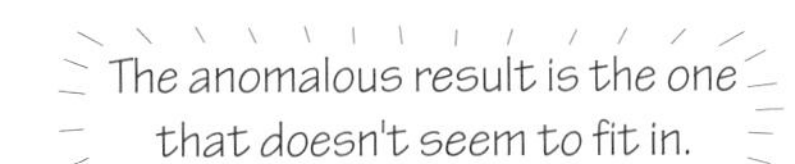

c) Which concentration of hydrochloric acid produced the fastest rate of reaction? ....

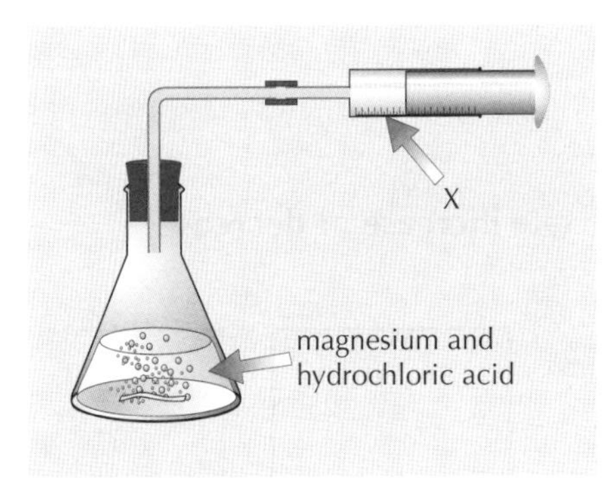

d) A diagram of the **apparatus** used in the experiment is shown on the left.

i) What is the object marked **X** called?

....

ii) Name one other key piece of apparatus needed for this experiment (not shown in the diagram).

....

e) **Sketch** a graph of the average volume of gas produced from this investigation against the concentration of HCl and **label** the axes. Do not include the anomalous result.

You don't need to plot the values, just draw what the graph would look like.

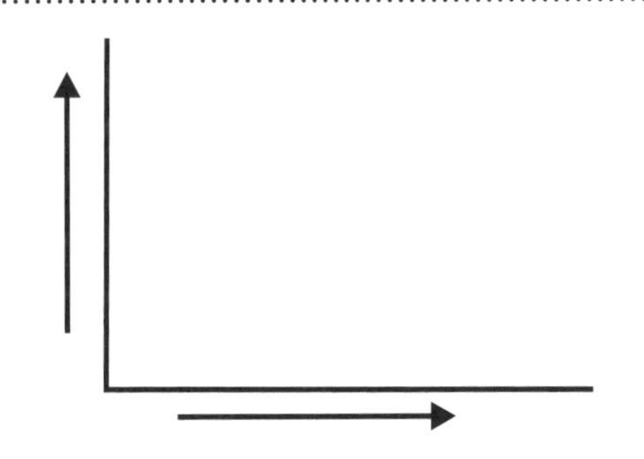

f) Why did Charlie do each measurement twice and calculate the average volume?

....

g) How might the **anomalous** result have come about?

....

h) Suggest **two changes** Charlie could make to improve his results if he repeated his investigation.

1. ....

2. ....

Collision Theory

Q1 Draw lines to match up the changes with their effects.

increasing the temperature

decreasing the concentration

adding a catalyst

increasing the surface area

lowers the activation energy and may provide a surface for particles to stick to

makes the particles move faster, so they collide more often

gives particles a bigger area of solid reactant to react with

means fewer particles of reactant are present, so fewer collisions occur

Q2 Circle the correct words to complete the sentences.

a) If you heat up a reaction mixture, you give the particles more **energy / surface area**.

b) This makes them move **faster / slower** so there is **more / less** chance of successful collisions.

c) So, increasing the temperature increases the **concentration / rate of reaction**.

Q3 Gases are always under **pressure**.

a) i) If you increase the pressure of a gas reaction, does the rate **increase** or **decrease**? ....

ii) Explain your answer.

....

....

b) In the boxes on the right draw two diagrams — one showing particles of two different gases at low pressure, the other showing the same two gases at high pressure.

low pressure | high pressure

Q4 Here are four statements about **surface area** and rates of reaction. Tick the appropriate boxes to show whether they are true or false.

		True	False
a)	Breaking a larger solid into smaller pieces decreases its surface area.	☐	☐
b)	A larger surface area will mean a faster rate of reaction.	☐	☐
c)	A larger surface area decreases the number of useful collisions.	☐	☐
d)	Powdered marble has a larger surface area than an equal mass of marble chips has.	☐	☐

Q5 **Catalysts** affect particle collisions in a different way from changes in concentration and surface area. Do catalysts **increase** or **decrease** the number of **successful** collisions?

....

Catalysts

Q1 To get a reaction to **start**, you have to give the particles some **energy**.

a) What is this energy called? Circle the correct answer.

potential energy activation energy chemical energy

b) The diagram opposite shows two identical reactions — one with a catalyst and one without. Which line shows the reaction **with** a catalyst — A or B? ....

c) On this diagram, draw and label arrows to show the activation energy for the reaction without a catalyst and the activation energy for the reaction with a catalyst.

Energy
B
A
Reactants
Products
Progress of Reaction

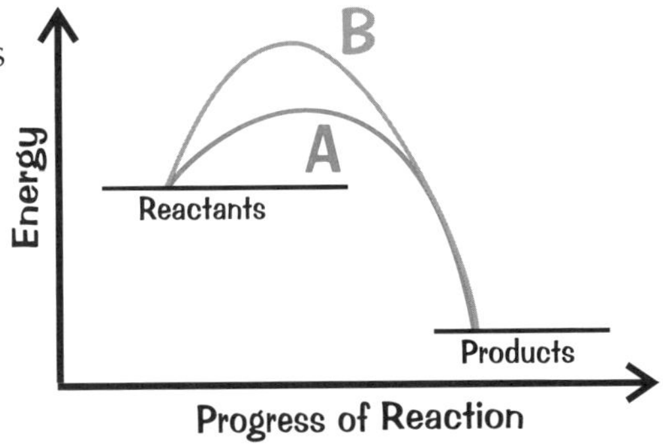

Q2 Solid catalysts come in **different forms**. Two examples are **pellets** and **fine gauze**.

a) Name another form of solid catalyst. ....

b) Explain why solid catalysts are used in forms such as these.

....

c) How do catalysts help particles to react?

....

d) Suggest one potential problem associated with using catalysts in industrial processes.

....

Q3 Industrial catalysts are often **metals**.

You find them in the middle of the periodic table.

a) Which type of metal is commonly used? ....

b) Give an example of a catalyst and say which industrial process it is used in.

....

Q4 Modern cars have a '**catalytic converter**' in the exhaust system. It contains a platinum and rhodium **catalyst**. The catalyst converts highly toxic carbon monoxide (CO) in the exhaust gases into non-toxic carbon dioxide (CO_2). Exhaust gases pass through the exhaust system very quickly.

Under normal conditions CO reacts with air to form CO_2, so why is a catalyst needed?

....

....

Energy Transfer in Reactions

Q1 Circle the correct words in this paragraph about **exothermic** reactions.

Exothermic reactions **take in** / **give out** energy, usually in the form of **heat** / **sound**.

This is often shown by a **fall** / **rise** in **temperature** / **mass**.

Q2 Two examples of exothermic reactions are **burning fuels** and **neutralisation reactions.**

a) Write **B** for burning fuel or **N** for neutralisation reaction next to each of the following reactions.

☐ sulphuric acid + sodium hydroxide → sodium sulphate + water

☐ methane + oxygen → carbon dioxide + water

☐ potassium hydroxide + hydrochloric acid → potassium chloride + water

☐ ethanol + oxygen → carbon dioxide + water

b) Give another word for 'burning'. ....

c) Give **one** reaction in part a) which is also an oxidation reaction.

....

Q3 Fill in the missing words in this paragraph about **endothermic** reactions to make it correct.

Endothermic reactions .... energy, usually in the form of .... This is often shown by a .... in ....

Q4 Limestone (**calcium carbonate**, $CaCO_3$) decomposes when heated to form quicklime (calcium oxide, CaO) and carbon dioxide.

a) Write a balanced symbol equation for this reaction.

....

b) The reaction requires a large amount of heat.

i) Is it **exothermic** or **endothermic**? ....

ii) Explain your answer. ....

c) Decomposing 1 tonne (1000 kg) of $CaCO_3$ requires about 1 800 000 kJ of heat energy.

i) How much heat energy would be needed to make **1 kg** of $CaCO_3$ decompose?

....

ii) How much $CaCO_3$ could be decomposed by **90 000 kJ** of heat energy?

....

Reversible Reactions

Q1 Use words from the list below to complete the following sentences about **reversible reactions**.

escape reactants catalysts closed products react balance

a) In a reversible reaction, the .... of the reaction can themselves .... to give the original ....

b) In an equilibrium, the amounts of reactants and products reach a ....

c) To reach equilibrium the reaction must happen in a .... system, where products and reactants can't ....

The reaction going from left to right is called the forward reaction. The reaction going from right to left is called the backward reaction.

Q2 Look at this diagram of a **reversible reaction**.

A + B —1→ AB

A + B ←2— AB

a) For the forward reaction:

i) give the reactant(s) ....

ii) give the product(s) ....

b) i) Here are two labels:

X product splits up

Y reactants combine

Which of these labels goes in position 1 — X or Y? ....

ii) Which label goes in position 2 — X or Y? ....

c) Write the equation for the reversible reaction. ....

d) Complete the sentence by circling the correct phrase.
In a dynamic equilibrium, the forward and backward reactions are happening
at different rates / at zero rate / at the same rate.

Q3 a) In this reaction: $2SO_{2(g)} + O_{2(g)} \rightleftharpoons 2SO_{3(g)}$

i) Which reaction, forward or backward, is accompanied by a **decrease** in volume? Explain your answer.

....

ii) How will increasing the pressure affect the position of the equilibrium in this reaction?

....

b) What does adding a catalyst to a reversible reaction do?
Circle the letter next to the correct answer.

A It moves the equilibrium position towards the products.

B It makes the reaction achieve equilibrium more quickly.

C It moves the equilibrium position towards the reactants.

D It causes a decrease in pressure.

The Haber Process

Q1 The Haber process is used to make **ammonia**.

a) The equation for the reaction is:

$$N_2(g) + 3H_2(g) \rightleftharpoons 2NH_3(g)$$

i) Name the reactants in the forward reaction ....

ii) Which side of the equation has more molecules? ....

b) Name a **useful substance** that can be made from ammonia.

....

Q2 The **industrial conditions** for the Haber process are carefully chosen.

a) What conditions are used? Tick one box.

☐ 1000 atmospheres, 450 °C	☐ 200 atmospheres, 1000 °C	☐ 450 atmospheres, 200 °C	☐ 200 atmospheres, 450 °C

b) Give two reasons why the pressure used is chosen.

1. ....

2. ....

Q3 In the Haber process reaction, the forward reaction is **exothermic**.

a) What effect will raising the temperature have on the position of the equilibrium?

....

b) Explain why a high temperature is used industrially.

....

c) What happens to the leftover nitrogen and hydrogen? ....

Q4 The Haber process uses an **iron catalyst**.

a) What effect does this have on the % yield? ....

b) Iron catalysts are relatively cheap. What effect does using one have on the **cost** of producing the ammonia? Explain your answer.

....

....

Top Tips: Changing the conditions in a reversible reaction to get more product sounds great, but don't forget that these conditions might be too difficult or expensive for factories to produce, or they might give a reaction that's too slow to be profitable.

Acids and Alkalis

Q1 a) Complete the equation below for the reaction between an acid and a base.

acid + base → .... + ...

b) Circle the correct term for this kind of reaction.

decomposition   oxidation   neutralisation

Q2 Ants' stings hurt because of the **formic acid** they release. The pH measurements of some household substances are given in the table.

SUBSTANCE	pH
lemon juice	4
baking soda	9
caustic soda	14
soap powder	11

a) Describe how you could test the formic acid to find its pH value.

....

....

b) Suggest a substance from the list that could be used to relieve the discomfort of an ant sting. Explain your answer.

....

....

Q3 Joey wanted to test whether some antacid tablets really do **neutralise acid**.

He added a tablet to some hydrochloric acid, stirred it until it dissolved and tested the pH of the solution. Further tests were carried out after dissolving a second, third and fourth tablet. His results are shown in the table below.

Number of Tablets	pH
0	1
1	2
2	3
3	7
4	9

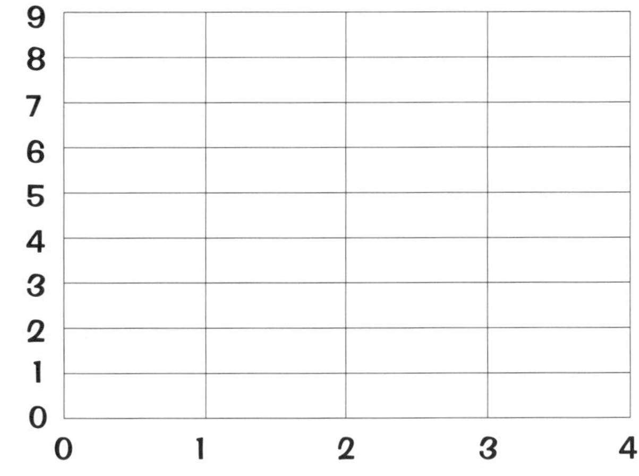

a) i) Plot a graph of the results.

ii) Describe how the pH changes when antacid tablets are added to the acid.

....

iii) How many tablets were needed to neutralise the acid?

....

b) Joey tested another brand of tablets and found that **two** tablets neutralised the same volume of acid. On the graph, sketch the results you might expect for these tablets.

Acids Reacting with Metals

Q1 The diagram below shows **aluminium** reacting with **sulfuric acid**.

a) Label the diagram with the names of the chemicals.

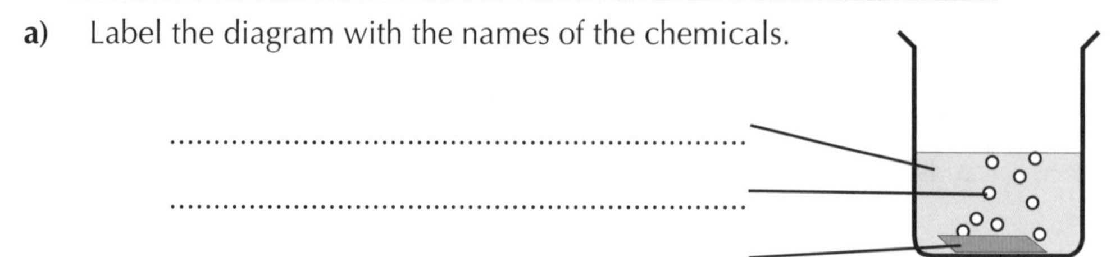

b) Complete the word equation for this reaction:

aluminium + ... → **aluminium sulfate +** ....

c) Write a balanced symbol equation for this reaction.

....

The formula of aluminium sulfate is $Al_2(SO_4)_3$.

Q2 Fill in the blanks using some of the words given below.

reactive silver nitric more hydrogen less chlorides
sulfuric carbon dioxide non-metals nitrates metals

Acids react with most .... **to form salts and** .... **gas. Metals like copper and** ....**, which are less** .... **than hydrogen, don't react with acids. The** .... **reactive the metal, the more vigorously the bubbles of gas form. Hydrochloric acid forms** .... **and** .... **acid produces sulfates. However, the reactions of metals with** .... **acid don't follow this simple pattern.**

Q3 a) Write out **balanced** versions of the following equations.

i) $Ca + HCl \rightarrow CaCl_2 + H_2$ ....

ii) $Na + HCl \rightarrow NaCl + H_2$ ....

iii) $Li + H_2SO_4 \rightarrow Li_2SO_4 + H_2$ ....

b) Hydrobromic acid reacts with magnesium as shown in the equation below:

$$Mg + 2HBr \rightarrow MgBr_2 + H_2$$

i) Name the salt formed in this reaction. ....

ii) Write a balanced symbol equation for the reaction between aluminium and hydrobromic acid. (The formula of aluminium bromide is $AlBr_3$.)

....

Neutralisation Reactions

Q1 Fill in the blanks to complete the word equations for **acids** reacting with **metal oxides** and **metal hydroxides**.

a) hydrochloric acid + lead oxide → .... chloride + water

b) nitric acid + copper hydroxide → copper .... + water

c) sulfuric acid + zinc oxide → zinc sulfate + ...

d) hydrochloric acid + ... oxide → nickel .... + ...

e) .... acid + copper oxide → .... nitrate + ...

Q2 **Acids** react with **metal carbonates** in neutralisation reactions.

a) Complete and balance the following symbol equations.

i) .... $HCl + CaCO_3 \rightarrow CaCl_2 +$ .... $+ CO_2$

ii) $H_2SO_4 +$ .... $\rightarrow Na_2SO_4 +$ .... + ...

iii) .... + ... $\rightarrow Ca(NO_3)_2 + H_2O + CO_2$

iv) .... $+ Na_2CO_3 \rightarrow$ .... $NaCl +$ .... + ...

b) Keith wants to confirm that the gas released when he reacts calcium carbonate with hydrochloric acid is **carbon dioxide**. Outline an **experimental procedure** he could use to test the gas.

....

....

Q3 **Ammonia** can be neutralised by **nitric acid** to form a salt.

a) Fill in the blanks in the passage below using some of the words from the list.

proteins solid gas fertilisers acidic nitrogen liquid salts alkaline

> Ammonia is a .... at room temperature which dissolves in water to form an .... solution. Ammonia contains .... which plants need to produce ...., so it is used to make ammonium .... which are widely used as ....

b) Write down the word equation for making **ammonium nitrate**.

....

c) Why is ammonium nitrate a particularly good fertiliser?

....

Making Salts

Q1 Complete the following sentences by circling the correct word from each pair.

a) Most chlorides, sulfates and nitrates are **soluble / insoluble** in water.

b) Most oxides, hydroxides and carbonates are **soluble / insoluble** in water.

c) Soluble salts can be made by reacting acids with **soluble / insoluble** bases until they are just **neutralised / displaced**.

d) Insoluble salts are made by **precipitation / electrolysis**.

e) Salts can be made by displacement, where a **more / less** reactive metal is put into a salt solution of a **more / less** reactive metal.

Q2 **A, B, C** and **D** are symbol equations for reactions in which **salts** are formed.

A $CuO(s) + H_2SO_4(aq) \rightarrow CuSO_4(aq) + H_2O(l)$

B $2NaOH(aq) + H_2SO_4(aq) \rightarrow Na_2SO_4(aq) + 2H_2O(l)$

C $Zn(s) + 2AgNO_3(aq) \rightarrow Zn(NO_3)_2(aq) + 2Ag(s)$

D $Pb(NO_3)_2(aq) + H_2SO_4(aq) \rightarrow PbSO_4(s) + 2HNO_3(aq)$

Which equation (A, B, C or D) refers to the formation of a salt:

a) in an acid/alkali reaction? ....

b) from an insoluble base? ....

c) by precipitation? ....

d) by displacement? ....

Q3 **Nickel sulfate** (a soluble salt) was made by adding insoluble **nickel carbonate** to **sulfuric acid** until no further reaction occurred.

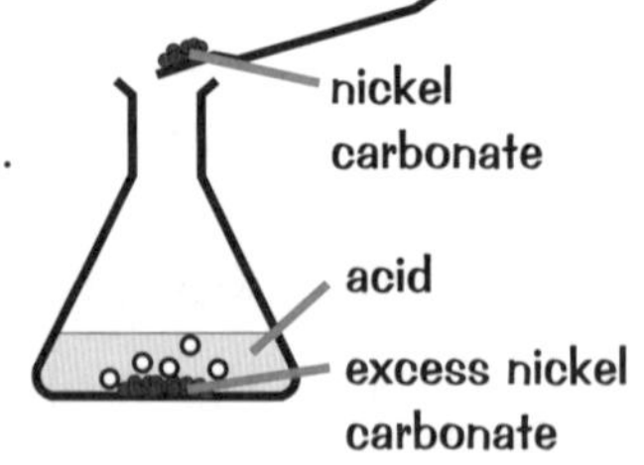

a) State two observations that would tell you that the reaction was complete.

1. ....

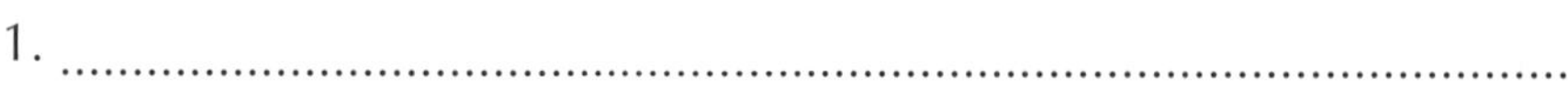

2. ....

Once the reaction was complete, the excess nickel carbonate was separated from the nickel sulfate solution using the apparatus shown.

b) Label the diagram which shows the separation process.

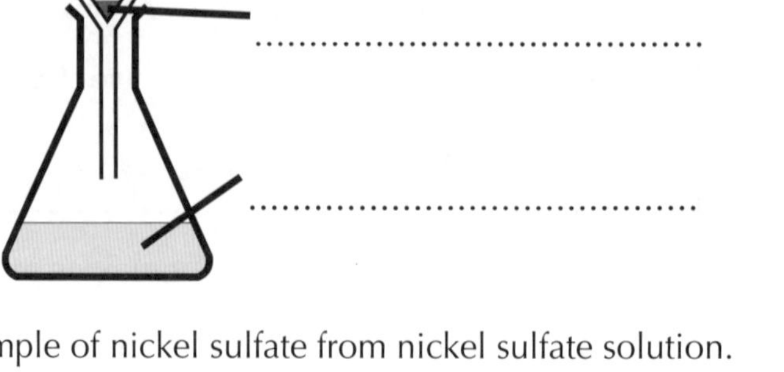

c) What is this method of separation called?

....

d) Describe how you could produce a solid sample of nickel sulfate from nickel sulfate solution.

....

....

Electrolysis and the Half-Equations

Q1 Explain why a substance needs to be in a **liquid state** for electrolysis to work.

....

Q2 The diagram shows the electrolysis of a **salt solution**.

Cathode (-ve)
Anode (+ve)
C
D
A
B
NaCl Solution

a) Identify the ions and molecules labelled A, B, C and D on the diagram. Choose from the options in the box below.

Na^+	H^+	Cl_2	H_2
Cl^-	Na_2	H_2O	

A .... B ....

C .... D ....

b) Write **balanced** half-equations for the processes that occur during the electrolysis of this salt solution.

Cathode: ....

Anode: ....

Make sure the charges balance.

Q3 **Lead bromide** is an ionic substance. It doesn't easily dissolve in water.

a) How could lead bromide be made into a liquid for electrolysis?

....

b) Write **balanced** half-equations for the processes that you would expect to occur at the cathode and anode during the electrolysis of lead bromide.

Cathode: ....

Anode: ....

Remember, when bromide ions lose electrons they pair up to become bromine molecules (Br_2).

Q4 After electrolysing a salt solution, Englebert noticed that the laboratory had a similar smell to his local **swimming pool**.

a) Suggest why this was. ....

....

b) Explain why this could be a safety issue. ....

c) Suggest what could be done in future to make this experiment safer.

....

Top Tips: Half-equations just show what's going on at the cathode and anode in terms of electrons — a positive ion gains electrons (and a negative ion loses electrons) to make neutral atoms.

Crude Oil

Q1 Write a short paragraph summarising why crude oil is the most **common source** of fuel even though **alternatives** are available.

....

....

....

....

Q2 The processing of crude oil is a major industry.

a) Name three products of the crude oil industry other than fuels.

1. ....
2. ....
3. ....

b) What property of carbon atoms makes them versatile enough to form the basis of life?

....

Q3 Cracking is an industrial process used to turn long-chain hydrocarbons into shorter molecules.

a) Explain why this process is important.

....

....

....

b) Cracking is a form of thermal decomposition. What does this mean?

....

c) Dodecane ($C_{12}H_{26}$) is a long-chain hydrocarbon found in the naphtha fraction.

i) Write a balanced equation for the cracking of dodecane to form octane (C_8H_{18}) and ethene (C_2H_4).

....

ii) What family of molecules does the product ethene belong to?

....

Alkanes and Alkenes

Q1 Cracking crude oil results in a mixture of saturated and unsaturated hydrocarbons.

a) Explain in terms of bonds what is meant by:

i) a saturated hydrocarbon ....

ii) an unsaturated hydrocarbon ....

b) Ethane (C_2H_6) is a saturated hydrocarbon. Draw the structure of a molecule of ethane, showing all the bonds.

c) Ethene (C_2H_4) is an unsaturated hydrocarbon. Draw the structure of a molecule of ethene, showing all the bonds.

d) Describe a simple test that would distinguish between ethane and ethene.

....

....

....

Q2 The general formula for **alkanes** is C_nH_{2n+2}. The general formula for **alkenes** is C_nH_{2n}. Use the general formulas to write down the formulas of these molecules.

a) pentene (5 carbons) ....

b) heptane (7 carbons) ....

c) octene (8 carbons) ....

d) pentane (5 carbons) ....

e) hexene (6 carbons) ....

f) decane (10 carbons) ....

g) nonane (9 carbons) ....

h) dodecene (12 carbons) ....

Q3 Ethanol (C_2H_5OH) can be made industrially from ethene.

a) What is the name of this type of reaction? ....

b) Write a balanced symbol equation to show the reaction.

....

c) Circle the three correct industrial conditions from the options below:

high pressure vacuum 20 °C 300 °C 8000 °C nickel catalyst phosphoric acid catalyst

Vegetable Oils

Q1 Match each label below to a fatty acid structure.

Saturated animal fat

Polyunsaturated grape seed oil

Monounsaturated olive oil

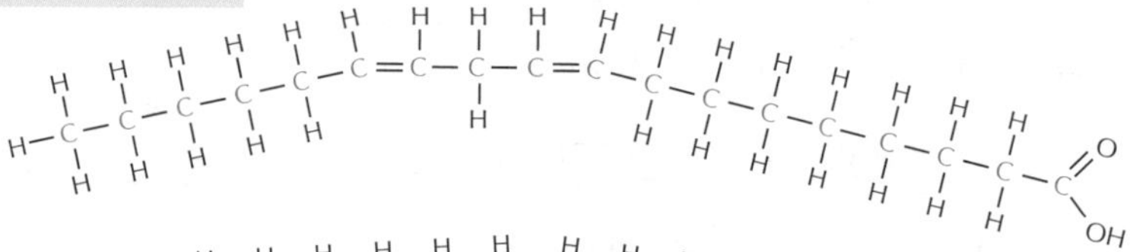

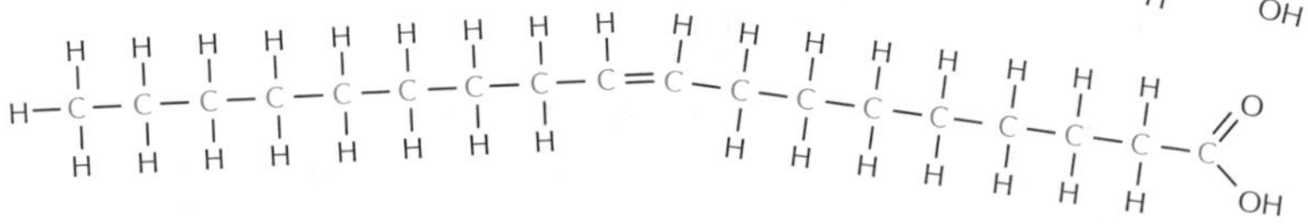

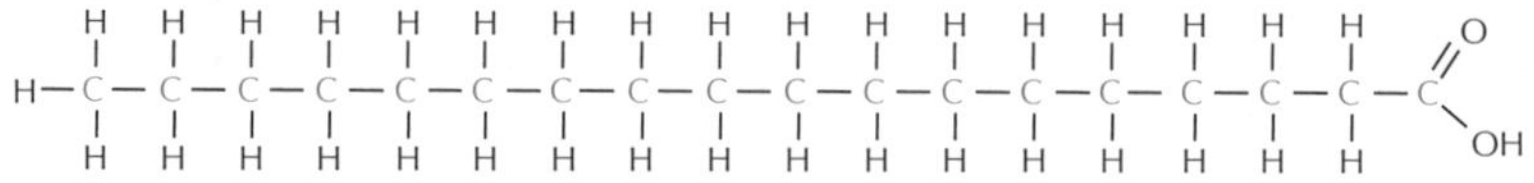

Q2 Margarine is usually made from partially hydrogenated vegetable oil.

a) Describe the process of hydrogenation.

b) How does hydrogenation affect the melting points of vegetable oils?

c) Explain your answer to b) in terms of the structure of saturated and unsaturated oils.

Q3 This table shows the **fat content** of two different butter substitute spreads.

TYPE OF FAT	PERCENTAGE IN SPREAD A	PERCENTAGE IN SPREAD B
Saturated	10	50
Monounsaturated	35	31
Polyunsaturated	54	15
Trans fatty acids	1	4

The packaging of one of the spreads says it is 'proven to reduce cholesterol levels'.
Which spread do you think this is? Explain your answer.

Plastics

Q1 The diagram below shows the polymerisation of ethene to form **polyethene**.

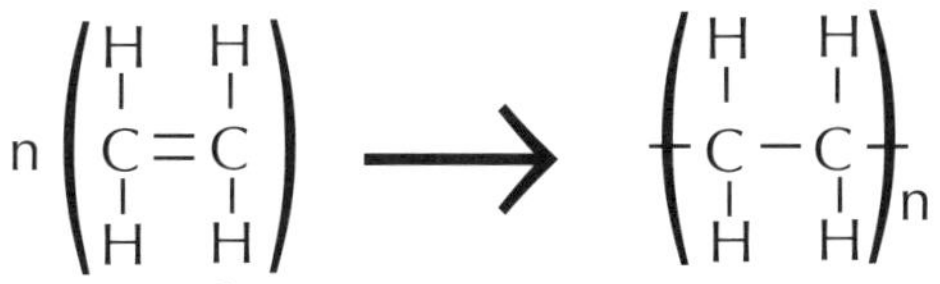

$$n\begin{pmatrix} H & & H \\ | & & | \\ C & = & C \\ | & & | \\ H & & H \end{pmatrix} \longrightarrow \begin{pmatrix} H & & H \\ | & & | \\ -C & - & C- \\ | & & | \\ H & & H \end{pmatrix}_n$$

many ethene molecules → polyethene

A similar molecule called **chloroethene** polymerises in the same way. Draw a diagram in the box below to show the polymerisation of chloroethene to form **polychloroethene**.

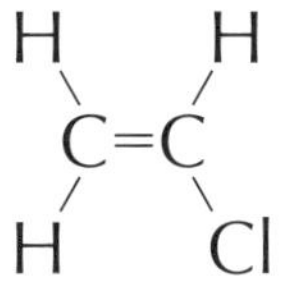

$$\begin{matrix} H & & H \\ & \diagdown\;\diagup & \\ & C=C & \\ & \diagup\;\diagdown & \\ H & & Cl \end{matrix}$$

chloroethene

Q2 This question is about how to dispose of **non-biodegradable** plastics.

a) Lots of plastic is buried in landfill sites. Suggest one problem with this method.

....

b) Another disposal method is to burn the waste plastic. Why might this not be safe?

....

c) Recycling plastics avoids the problems of disposal. What is the main problem with this solution?

....

Q3 Two rulers, made from **different plastics**, were investigated by bending and heating them. The results are shown in the table.

	RESULT ON HEATING	RESULT ON BENDING
Ruler 1	Ruler becomes soft and then melts	Ruler bends easily and springs back into shape
Ruler 2	Ruler doesn't soften and eventually turns black	Ruler snaps in two

a) Which ruler is made from a polymer that has strong forces between its molecules? ....

b) The atoms in both types of plastic are held together with the same strong covalent bonds. Explain why one type of plastic melts and bends more easily than the other.

....

....

Chemical Production

Q1 Suggest whether **continuous** or **batch** production would be used to make the following chemicals.

a) Perfumes ....

b) Sulfuric acid ....

c) Ammonia ....

d) Paints ....

Q2 Widely used chemicals are often produced by **continuous production**.

a) Circle the correct words to complete the following sentences.

> Continuous production is often used for the **small-scale / large-scale** production of chemicals. It's **highly automated / labour-intensive**, which means that there are **low / high** labour costs. Continuous production means that products of a **high / low** consistency can be produced with a **high / low** risk of contamination.

b) State two **disadvantages** of continuous production.

1. ....

2. ....

c) Why are **pharmaceutical drugs** usually manufactured using batch production?

....

Q3 Compounds used in pharmaceutical drugs are often extracted from **plants**.

a) Describe the following steps in the extraction process.

A B C

Step A ....

Step B ....

Step C ....

b) New drugs may be tested on animals before being sold.

i) Give one argument for and one against testing new drugs on **animals**.

For ....

Against ....

ii) After animal testing, why are **human trials** of drugs also necessary?

....

....

Detergents and Dry-Cleaning

Q1 Match the following terms to their correct descriptions.

solvent — A substance that's dissolved in a liquid.

solution — A liquid mixture made from dissolving one substance in another.

solute — A liquid that can dissolve a substance.

Q2 The diagram shows a detergent molecule.

a) Complete the diagram by labelling the **hydrophilic** and **hydrophobic** sections of the molecule.

....

b) Which section of the molecule is attracted to:

i) water molecules? ....

ii) grease and oil? ....

Q3 Fill in the blanks using the appropriate words below.

water stain intermolecular dissolve
intramolecular pull grease sugar react

Detergents work by helping dirt to .... in water. Normally oil or .... stains do not mix with water. The hydrophobic tail of the detergent molecule attaches to the fat molecules in the stain with .... forces. The hydrophilic head is surrounded by .... molecules outside the stain. The movement of the washing machine helps the detergent molecules to .... away droplets of oil into the water.

Q4 Felicity works for a chemical company that is developing a new washing powder. She tests five different powders and records their cleaning effectiveness at different temperatures and against a range of different stains. She uses a scale of 1 (poor) to 10 (excellent).

a) Which powder is best at cleaning grass stains?

....

b) Which powders could be biological detergents? Give a reason for your answer.

....

....

....

		Washing powder				
		A	B	C	D	E
Effectiveness	at 40 °C	9	3	5	7	7
	at 60 °C	3	3	9	8	4
	Against tomato stains (at 40 °C)	8	1	5	4	10
	Against grass stains (at 40 °C)	8	4	5	7	3

Water Purity

Q1 There are limited water resources in the UK.

a) Which of the following water resources contains 'groundwater'? Circle your answer.

reservoirs aquifers rivers lakes

b) Name three important uses of water in **industrial processes**.

1. ....

2. ....

3. ....

Q2 Suggest how water could be **conserved** by:

a) a water company

....

b) domestic water users

....

Q3 Water is **treated** before it reaches our homes.

a) Number the following stages to show the correct order of the processes in a **water treatment** plant.

☐ Sedimentation ☐ Filtration through sand beds

☐ Chlorination ☐ Filtration through a wire mesh

b) Why are two filtration processes needed? ....

....

c) Name a chemical used in the sedimentation process. ....

d) Why are the purification processes unable to remove impurities such as ammonium nitrate?

....

e) What happens in the final stage of the purification process?

....

Q4 Helen's house has an **old plumbing system**. She's concerned about **pollutants** in the tap water.

a) What form of pollution in the tap water could be caused by the plumbing system?

....

b) Helen's water supply comes from a reservoir located in an area of intensive agriculture.
Suggest **two** other forms of pollutant which could be present in the tap water.

....

Water Purity

Q5 **Sodium sulfate** reacts with **barium chloride** in a precipitation reaction.

a) What is a **precipitation reaction**?

....

b) Complete the word equation for this reaction.

sodium sulfate + barium chloride → barium .... + ...

c) Complete and balance the symbol equation for this reaction.

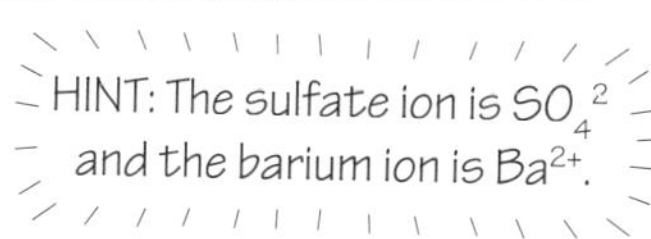

K_2SO_4 + ... → .... + ...KCl

Q6 Sam creates a flow chart as a key to help her identify **halide anions** present in a sample of water.

a) Finish the flow chart by completing the empty boxes.

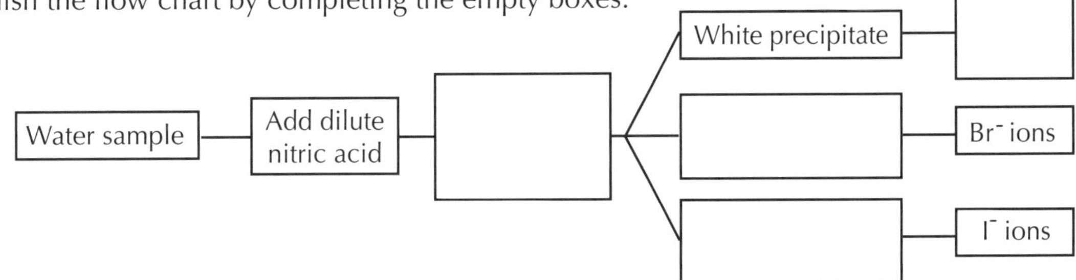

b) Complete the following symbol equations involved in testing for halide ions.

i) $AgNO_3 + KCl \rightarrow$ .... $+ KNO_3$

ii) .... + ... $\rightarrow AgI + NaNO_3$

iii) $Ag^+ + Br^- \rightarrow$ ....

Q7 People in developing countries often can't get **clean water**.

a) How can drinking dirty water make you ill?

....

....

b) Suggest how developing countries can help ensure everyone has a supply of clean water.

....

....

Q8 Some countries get fresh water by **distilling** seawater.

a) Give **one** advantage of this method.

....

b) Give **two** disadvantages of this method.

....

....

Mixed Questions — Section Seven

Q1 Several factors affect **how quickly** chemical reactions occur.

a) Name four factors that can **increase** the rate of a reaction.

....

....

b) Explain **one** of your answers to a) using collision theory.

....

c) Briefly describe two **experimental methods** used to measure reaction rates.

i) ....

ii) ....

Q2 The Haber process is a **reversible reaction.**

a) Write a **balanced symbol equation** for the reaction. ....

b) The Haber process uses an **iron catalyst**.

i) Complete the paragraph about catalysts by circling the correct words.

> Some catalysts give reacting particles a surface to stick to. They **increase / decrease** the number of successful collisions by **lowering / raising** the activation energy of a reaction. Catalysts are often used in industry to save money because they allow a **lower / higher** temperature to be used.

ii) Catalysts are often used in a **powdered** form. Explain why.

....

....

c) The forward reaction of the Haber process is **exothermic**. If you **increase** the temperature will you increase or decrease the amount of ammonia produced?
Circle the correct answer: **increase** **decrease**

Q3 Rose added a piece of **magnesium** to some **HCl** and watched what happened.

a) Complete and **balance** the chemical equation for the reaction.

.... Mg + ... HCl → .... + ...

b) Explain how the **pH** would change after the magnesium was added.

....

c) Name the salt formed by magnesium and **sulfuric acid**. ....

Mixed Questions — Section Seven

Q4 Aluminium is extracted from its ore by **electrolysis.**

a) The aluminium ions are attracted to the **negative** electrode.

i) Explain what happens to the aluminium ions at the negative electrode.

....

ii) Complete the balanced half-equation for the reaction: Al^{3+} + ... → ....

b) **Oxygen** ions are attracted to the **positive** electrode.
Complete the balanced half-equation for the reaction: $2O^{2-}$ → .... + ...

Q5 Propene (C_3H_6) is an unsaturated hydrocarbon.

a) Draw the structure of propene (its displayed formula).

b) Explain what an **unsaturated** hydrocarbon is.

....

c) Propene can be **polymerised** to form a plastic.

i) Write an equation for the polymerisation of propene, using displayed formulas.

ii) Why are waste plastics difficult to dispose of safely?

....

....

Q6 A chemical company is testing three new solvents for dry-cleaning.

a) Which solvent would you expect to form the strongest intermolecular forces with paint molecules? Explain your answer.

....

....

	Solvent		
	A	B	C
Cost per 100 g (£)	0.40	0.15	0.20
Solubility of paint (g per 100 g of solvent)	12.1	0.1	10.3

b) Which solvent would you choose to buy if you were a buyer for a dry-cleaning company? Explain your choice.

....

....

Velocity and Acceleration

Q1 A pulse of laser light takes 1.3 seconds to travel from the Moon to the Earth. The speed of light is approximately 3×10^8 m/s.

You'll need to rearrange the speed formula.

How far away is the Moon from the Earth? Give your answer in km.

....

Q2 An egg is dropped from the top of the Eiffel tower. It hits the ground after 8 seconds, at a speed of 80 m/s.

a) Calculate the egg's acceleration. ....

b) How long did it take for the egg to reach a velocity of 40 m/s?

....

Q3 Ealing is about 12 km west of Marble Arch. It takes a tube train 20 minutes to get to Marble Arch from Ealing.

Only **one** of the following statements is true. Circle the appropriate letter.

A The average speed of the train is 60 m/s.

B The average velocity of the train is 10 m/s.

C The average velocity of the train is 60 m/s due east.

D The average speed of the train is 10 m/s.

E The average velocity of the train is 10 m/s due west.

Q4 Paolo and some friends want to order a takeaway. Paolo writes down what they know about the two nearest takeaways:

Ludo's Pizza	Moonlight Indian Takeaway
• Time taken to cook the food is 1/4 hour	• Time taken to cook the food is 1/2 hour
• Distance to the house is 6.5 km	• Distance to the house is 4 km
• Deliver on scooters with average speed of 30 km/h	• Delivery van has average speed of 40 km/h

Remember to add on the time taken to cook the food.

Which takeaway should they order from to get their food the **quickest**?

....

Q5 A car accelerates at 2 m/s². After 4 seconds it reaches a speed of 24 m/s.

How fast was it going before it started to accelerate?

....

....

D-T and V-T Graphs

Q1 Steve walked to football training only to find that he'd left his boots at home. He turned round and walked back home, where he spent 30 seconds looking for them. To make it to training on time he had to run back at twice his walking speed.

Below is an incomplete **distance-time graph** for Steve's journey.

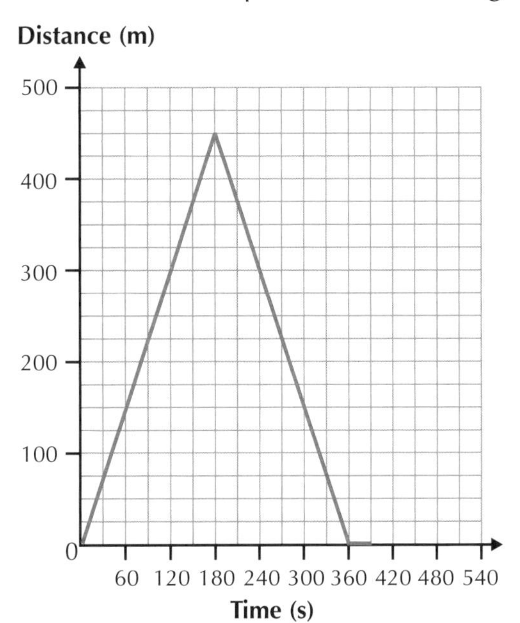

a) How long did it take Steve to walk to training?

....

b) Calculate Steve's speed (in m/s) as he walked to training.

....

....

c) Complete the graph to show Steve's run back from his house to training (with his boots).

Q2 The speed limit for cars on motorways is 70 mph (31 m/s). A motorist was stopped for speeding as she joined the motorway from a service station.

The distance-time graph on the right shows the car's acceleration. The motorist denied speeding. Was she telling the truth?

....

....

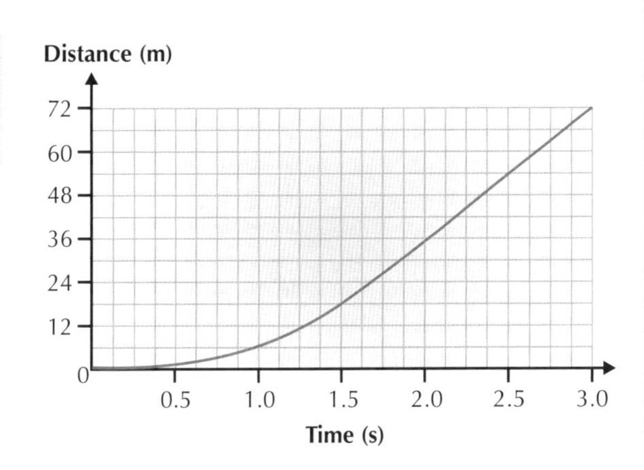

Q3 A motorist saw a kitten asleep on the road 25 m in front of him. It took him 0.75 seconds to react and slam on the brakes. The velocity-time graph below shows the car's deceleration.

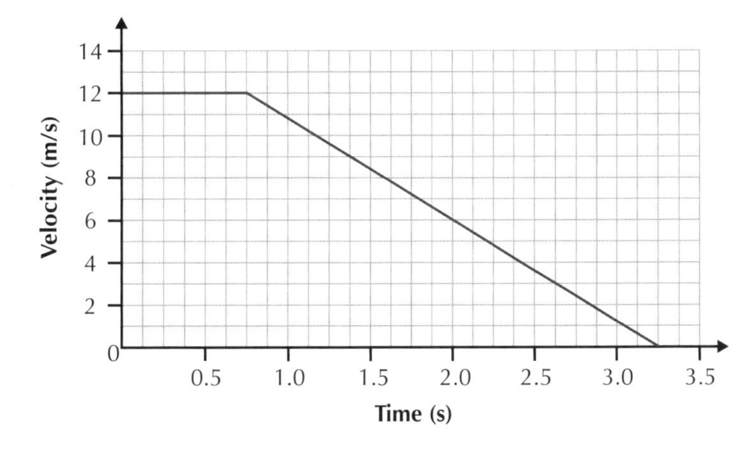

It helps to split the graph up into two smaller shapes.

Use the graph to work out whether the motorist stopped before hitting the kitten.

....

....

....

Mass, Weight and Gravity

Q1 Which is the correct explanation for why the Moon orbits the Earth? Tick the appropriate box.

- ☐ There is an attractive force between the weights of the Earth and Moon.
- ☐ They attract each other as they have masses caused by them having weight.
- ☐ The weight of the Moon acts downwards.
- ☐ There is an attractive force between the masses of the Earth and Moon.
- ☐ The mass of the Moon acts downwards.

Q2 Two mad scientists are planning a trip to Mars.

a) Professor White tells Professor Brown —

"We won't need so much fuel for the return trip — the rocket will have less mass on Mars."

Is Professor White's reasoning correct? Explain your answer.

....

b) Professor Brown wants to investigate gravity on Mars. He takes a small fire extinguisher to Mars which weighs 50 N on Earth. He also takes his bathroom scales.

On Mars, Professor Brown weighs the fire extinguisher.
The scales read **1.9 kg**.
Calculate the **acceleration due to gravity** on Mars.

Find the mass of the fire extinguisher first.

1.90

....

....

....

Q3 A space probe lands on the icy surface of Europa, a moon of Jupiter. It weighs a set of known masses. The results are shown below.

Mass (kg)	0.1	0.2	0.3	0.4	0.5
Weight (N)	0.15	0.30	0.36	0.55	0.68

Weight (N): 0, 0.1, 0.2, 0.3, 0.4, 0.5, 0.6, 0.7
Mass (kg): 0.1, 0.2, 0.3, 0.4, 0.5

a) **i)** Plot a graph of this data on the axes given.

ii) Use your graph to estimate the gravitational field strength at Europa's surface.

....

....

b) Suggest why several masses were weighed, not just one.

....

Friction Forces and Terminal Speed

Q1 Choose from the words supplied to fill in the blanks in the paragraph below about a skydiver.

decelerates decrease less balances increase constant greater accelerates

When a skydiver jumps out of a plane, his weight is .... than his air resistance, so he .... downwards. This causes his air resistance to .... until it .... his weight. At this point, his velocity is .... When his parachute opens, his air resistance is .... than his weight, so he .... This causes his air resistance to .... until it .... his weight. Then his velocity is .... once again.

Q2 Which of the following will **reduce** the drag force on an aeroplane? Tick all appropriate boxes.

- ☐ flying higher (where the air is thinner)
- ☐ carrying less cargo
- ☐ flying more slowly
- ☐ making the plane more streamlined

Q3 A scientist plans to investigate gravity by dropping a hammer and a feather from a tall building. Three onlookers predict what will happen. Say whether each is right or wrong, and explain why.

Paola: "They will land at the same time — gravity is the same for both."

Guiseppe: "The feather will reach its terminal velocity before the hammer."

Raphael: "The hammer will land first — it has less drag compared to its weight than the feather does."

a) Paola is **right** / **wrong** because ....

....

b) Guiseppe is **right** / **wrong** because ....

....

c) Raphael is **right** / **wrong** because ....

....

Q4 Mavis is investigating **drag** by dropping balls into a measuring cylinder full of oil and timing how long they take to reach the bottom. She does the experiment with a **golf ball**, a **glass marble** and a **ball bearing**.

From this experiment, can Mavis draw any conclusions about the effect of size on drag? Explain your answer.

....

....

Top Tips: When objects move through the air at high speed, the air resistance is proportional to the object's **velocity squared**. That's why, for skydivers, air resistance soon balances their weight and they reach terminal velocity. It's also why **driving** very fast is very **inefficient**.

The Three Laws of Motion

Q1 Use the words below to fill in the blanks.

proportional	force	reaction	stationary	accelerates	opposite
constant	resultant	inversely	balanced		

Newton's 1st law: If the forces on an object are ...., it's either .... or moving at .... speed.

Newton's 2nd law: If an object has a .... force acting on it, it .... in the direction of the ....
The acceleration is .... to the force and .... to the mass.

Newton's 3rd law: For every action there is an equal and ....

Q2 Otto is driving the school bus at a **steady speed** along a level road.
Tick the boxes next to any of the following statements which are **true**.

- ☐ The driving force of the engine is bigger than the friction and air resistance combined.
- ☐ The driving force of the engine is equal to the friction and air resistance combined.
- ☐ There are no forces acting on the bus.
- ☐ No force is required to keep the bus moving.

Q3 State whether the **forces** acting on these objects are **balanced** or **unbalanced**. Explain your answers.

a) A **cricket ball** slowing down as it rolls along the outfield.

....

b) A **car** going round a roundabout at a steady 30 mph.

....

c) A **vase** knocked off a window ledge.

....

d) A **satellite** orbiting over a fixed point on the Earth's surface.

....

e) A **bag of rubbish** which was ejected from a spacecraft in empty space.

....

The Three Laws of Motion

Q4 The table below shows the **masses** and **maximum accelerations** of four different antique cars.

Car	Mass (kg)	Maximum acceleration (m/s^2)
Disraeli 9000	800	5
Palmerston 6i	1560	0.7
Heath TT	950	3
Asquith 380	790	2

Write down the names of the four cars in order of increasing driving force.

....

Q5 Jo and Brian have fitted both their scooters with the same engine.
Brian's scooter has a mass of 110 kg and an acceleration of 2.80 m/s^2.
Jo's scooter only manages an acceleration of 1.71 m/s^2.

a) What **force** can the engine exert?

....

b) Calculate the mass of Jo's scooter.

....

Q6 A spacecraft launches a probe at a constant speed. A day later, the probe returns at the same speed.

Did the probe have to burn any fuel? Explain your answer.

....

....

Q7 Maisie drags a **1 kg** mass along a table with a newton-meter so that it accelerates at **0.25** m/s^2.
The newton-meter reads **0.4 N**. Calculate the force of friction between the mass and the table.

....

....

Q8 Which of the following statements correctly explains what happens when you walk?
Circle the appropriate letter.

A Your feet push the ground backwards, so the ground pushes you forwards.

B The force in your muscles overcomes the friction between your feet and the ground.

C The ground's reaction can't push you backwards because of friction.

D Your feet push forwards, and the ground's reaction is upwards.

Stopping Distances

Q1 **Stopping distance** and **braking distance** are not the same thing.

a) What is meant by 'braking distance'?

....

b) Use the words in the box to complete the following word equations.

braking	speed	reaction time	thinking

i) Thinking distance = ... × ....

ii) Stopping distance = ... distance + ... distance.

Q2 Will the following factors affect **thinking** distance, **braking** distance or **both**? Write them in the relevant columns of the table.

tiredness alcohol road surface tyres weather brakes speed load

Thinking Distance	Braking Distance

Q3 A car joins a motorway and changes speed from 30 mph to 60 mph. Which one of the following statements is **true**? Tick the appropriate box.

☐ The total stopping distance will double.

☐ The braking distance will double.

☐ Thinking distance will double and braking distance will more than double.

☐ Both thinking and braking distance will more than double.

Q4 A car has just driven through a deep puddle, making the brakes wet. Explain why this will increase the stopping distance of the car.

....

....

Momentum and Collisions

Q1 Place the following four trucks in order of increasing momentum.

Truck A
speed = 30 m/s
mass = 3000 kg

Truck B
speed = 10 m/s
mass = 4500 kg

Truck C
speed = 20 m/s
mass = 4000 kg

Truck D
speed = 15 m/s
mass = 3500 kg

....

....

(lowest momentum) .... , ... , ... , ... (highest momentum)

Q2 A skateboarder with a mass of 60 kg is moving at 5 m/s. He skates past his bag, picks it up from the floor and slows down to 4.8 m/s. Assuming no friction, find the mass of the skater's bag.

You might find it helpful to draw a diagram showing the masses and velocities involved.

....

....

....

Q3 A rocket is stationary in empty space. It is then propelled forwards by quickly releasing exhaust gases in the opposite direction. Indicate which of the following statements are **true**.

- ☐ The velocity of the exhaust gas is equal and opposite to the rocket's velocity.
- ☐ The momentum of the exhaust gas is equal and opposite to the rocket's momentum.
- ☐ The velocity of the exhaust gas is greater than the rocket's velocity.
- ☐ The momentum of the exhaust gas is greater than the rocket's momentum.

Q4 A 750 kg car is travelling at 30 m/s along the motorway. It crashes into the barrier of the central reservation and is stopped in a period of 1.2 seconds.

a) Find the size of the **average force** acting on the car to stop it.

....

....

b) Explain in terms of the forces acting why the occupants of the car are likely to be less severely injured if they are wearing seat belts made of slightly **stretchy** material.

....

....

Car Safety

Q1 A car travels along a level road and brakes to avoid hitting a cat.

a) What type of **energy** does the moving car have?

....

b) Explain how energy is **conserved** as the brakes slow down the car.

....

....

Q2 Modern cars are fitted with many **safety features**.

a) Why are car safety features often designed to **slow** the car and passengers down over a **long time**?

....

....

b) How do the following features achieve this?

i) Crumple zones ....

ii) Airbags ....

c) How do seat belts **absorb** energy to slow down a passenger?

....

....

Q3 Use the words supplied to fill in the blanks in the passage below.

crashes	skidding	safety	steering	lock	power	interact	control

Many modern cars have active .... features. These .... with the way the car is driven to help avoid ....

These features include .... assisted steering and traction ....

ABS brakes stop the car .... by making sure the wheels don't .... and so the driver can always control the .... of the car.

Q4 **Roads** themselves can be designed to be safer.

Explain how **crash barriers** keep passengers safer in a collision.

....

....

Work and Potential Energy

Q1 Circle the correct words to make the following sentences true.

a) Work involves the transfer of **force** / **heat** / **energy**.

b) To do work **a force** / **an acceleration** acts over a **distance** / **time**.

c) Work is measured in **watts** / **joules**.

Q2 Indicate whether the following statements are **true** or **false**.

	True	False
a) Work is done when a toy car is pushed along the ground.	☐	☐
b) No work is done if a force is applied to an object which does not move.	☐	☐
c) Gravity does work on an apple that is not moving.	☐	☐
d) Gravity does work on an apple that falls out of a tree.	☐	☐

Q3 An elephant exerts a constant force of **1200 N** to push a donkey along a track at a steady 1 m/s.

a) Calculate the work done by the elephant if the donkey moves **8 m**.

....

b) From where does the elephant get the energy to do this work? ....

c) Into what form(s) is this energy transferred when work is done on the donkey?

....

Q4 Ben's mass is 60 kg. He climbs a ladder. The rungs of the ladder are 20 cm apart.

20 cm

a) What force(s) is Ben doing work **against** as he climbs?

....

b) As he climbs, what happens to the **energy** supplied by Ben's muscles?

....

....

c) How much work does Ben do when he climbs **10 rungs**? (Ignore any 'wasted' energy.) Assume that g = 10 N/kg.

....

....

d) How many rungs of the ladder must Ben climb before he has done **15 kJ** of work? (Ignore any 'wasted' energy.) Assume that g = 10 N/kg.

....

....

Kinetic Energy

Q1 Find the **kinetic energy** of a 200 kg tiger running at a speed of 9 m/s.

....

....

Q2 A golf ball is hit and given 9 J of kinetic energy.
The ball's velocity is 20 m/s. What is its **mass**?

....

....

Q3 A 4 g bullet is fired from a rifle with a kinetic energy of 2 kJ.
What is the **speed** of the bullet when it leaves the rifle?

....

....

Q4 The **braking distance** for a car travelling at **30 mph** is approximately **14 m**.
At **50 mph** the braking distance is about **38 m**.

Explain, in terms of kinetic energy, why the braking distance more than doubles when the car's speed is less than doubled.

....

....

Q5 A skier with a mass of 70 kg rides a chairlift up a ski slope to a height of 20 m.
She then skis back down to the bottom of the chairlift.

a) Calculate the **work done** against gravity by the chairlift in carrying the skier up the slope. (Assume that g = 10 N/kg.)

....

....

b) Find the skier's **maximum speed** when she reaches the bottom of the chairlift.

....

....

Top Tips: Kinetic energy's all about moving — the bigger something's mass and the faster it's going, the larger the kinetic energy. Get comfy working with the formulas as they crop up everywhere, especially in energy conservation questions. It's pretty simple stuff — so get learning.

Roller Coasters

Q1 A roller coaster carriage and passengers are stationary at the top of a ride. At this point they have a gravitational potential energy of **300 kJ**.

a) Draw lines to connect each stage of the roller coaster with the correct energy statement.

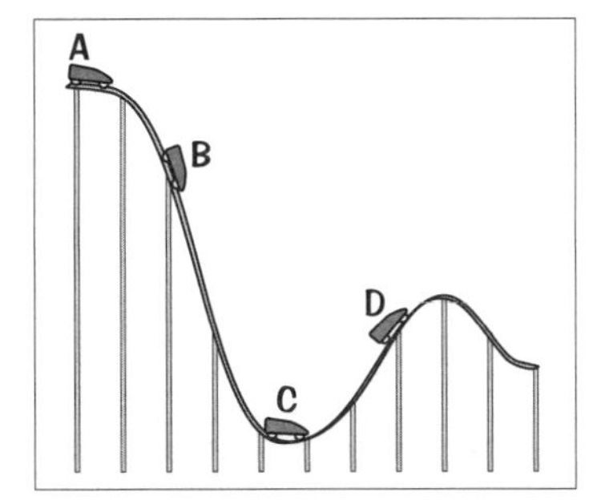

A
B
C
D

minimum P.E., maximum K.E.

K.E. is being converted to P.E.

P.E. is being converted to K.E.

maximum P.E.

K.E. = kinetic energy
P.E. = gravitational potential energy

b) **i)** When the carriage has dropped to half its original height, what is the maximum **kinetic energy** it could have?

....

ii) Explain why in real life the kinetic energy is **less** than this.

....

c) Chris thinks that a **heavier** roller coaster carriage will go **faster** downhill than a lighter one. Is he right? Give a reason for your answer.

....

Q2 On the planet Greldar, a full roller coaster carriage has a mass of **1500 kg**.

a) If **g = 15 N/kg**, calculate the **weight** of a full carriage.

....

b) At the start of the ride, the roller coaster rises up to its highest point of **25 m**.

i) What is its gain in gravitational **potential energy**?

....

ii) How much **work** does the motor need to do to get the roller coaster to the top of the ride?

....

c) The first drop of the roller coaster takes the carriage from a height of 25 m to a height of 7 m.

i) What is its change in gravitational **potential energy**?

....

ii) Assuming no friction, how fast is the carriage going at the bottom of the dip?

....

....

Power

Q1 Tom likes to build model boats. His favourite boat is the Carter which has a motor power of **150 W**.

a) How much **energy** does the Carter's motor transfer in **10 minutes**?

....

b) If the petrol for the boat's motor contains **30 kJ/ml**, how much is used up in **10 minutes**?

....

c) Tom decides to get a model speed boat which transfers **120 kJ** in the same 10 minute journey. What is the **power** of the engine?

....

Q2 Josie runs home after school so she can watch her favourite TV programme. She has a mass of **60 kg** and her school bag weighs **5 kg**.

a) At the start of her run, she accelerates from **0** to **8 m/s** in **6 seconds** whilst carrying her bag. Calculate her power output for this part of her run.

....

b) Josie gets to her house, puts **down** her school bag, and then runs up the stairs to her room. It takes her **4 seconds** to get to the top of the stairs where she is **5 m** above ground level. How much power does she generate getting up the stairs?

....

Q3 Andy loves running and wants to improve his starts in sprint races. He uses a timing gate to measure his maximum speed and how long the start takes him. He has a mass of **70 kg**.

Sprint number	Time taken (s)	Maximum speed (m/s)
1	3.2	8.0
2	3.1	8.2
3	3.3	7.9
4	4.6 *	7.2
5	3.2	7.9

*** He slips because his shoes don't grip properly.**

a) The information from one of the sprints should be ignored. Which one?

....

b) Calculate the **power** output for both the fastest and slowest reliable starts.

....

....

....

....

c) Andy's friend Peter has a **mass of 80 kg**. If he ran a sprint with the same time and maximum speed as Andy, would his **power output** be higher or lower than Andy's?

....

Mixed Questions — Section Eight

Q1 Scott water-skis over a 100 m course. A forcemeter on the tow rope registers a force of 475 N. When he reaches the end of the course, Scott lets go of the tow rope.

a) Calculate the **energy** needed to pull Scott over the course.

....

b) Scott completed the course in 27 seconds. Calculate the power output of the tow boat.

....

c) The graph below shows how Scott's velocity changed over the course.
Describe his **acceleration**:

i) between 0 and 5 seconds,

....

ii) between 5 and 22 seconds,

....

iii) after 30 seconds.

....

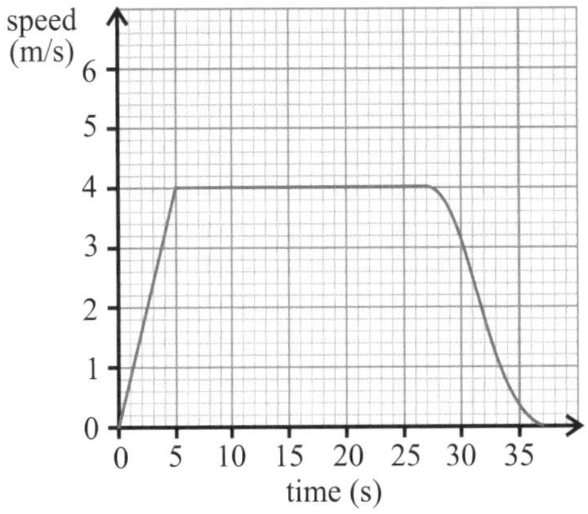

speed (m/s)
6
5
4
3
2
1
0
0 5 10 15 20 25 30 35
time (s)

d) Scott's mass is 75 kg. Find his kinetic energy 20 seconds after he started water-skiing.

....

....

e) How far did Scott travel in the first 20 seconds?

....

Q2 Paul sets off from a junction on his scooter which produces a thrust of 270 N. The total mass of Paul and his scooter is 180 kg.

a) Calculate the initial acceleration of Paul's scooter.

....

b) Calculate the size of the force produced when Paul applies his brakes and decelerates at 5 m/s^2.

....

c) State two factors that would affect Paul's braking distance.

1. .... 2. ....

d) Explain why the total stopping distance would be increased if Paul were tired.

....

....

Mixed Questions — Section Eight

Q3 At the start of a race a motorcyclist accelerates to a speed of 90 km per hour in 5 seconds and then rides three laps at that speed. The total mass of the motorbike and rider is 200 kg.

a) Calculate the force needed to accelerate the motorbike during the first five seconds of the race.

....

b) A competitor on a better bike rides the same three laps at 135 km/h. Which bike would you expect to have consumed **more fuel** during the three laps? Explain your answer.

....

....

c) Explain why the motorbikes' tyres are likely to leave black skid marks on the track if the riders brake suddenly.

....

....

Q4 The diagram shows Karl jumping between two stationary boats.

West
A
B
East

a) When Karl leaps to the east from boat A, boat A moves west. Explain why, using Newton's third law of motion.

....

....

b) Karl has a mass of 80 kg and jumps with a velocity of 3 m/s east. Boat A has a mass of 100 kg. What is its velocity just after Karl jumps?

....

....

....

c) Boat B has a mass of 112 kg. Calculate boat B's velocity just after Karl lands in it.

....

....

....

Static Electricity

Q1 Fill in the gaps in these sentences with the words below.

electrons	positive	static	friction	insulating	negative

.... electricity can build up when two .... materials are rubbed together. The .... moves .... from one material onto the other. This leaves a .... charge on one of the materials and a .... charge on the other.

Q2 **Circle** the pairs of charges that would attract each other and **underline** those that would repel.

positive and positive   positive and negative   negative and positive   negative and negative

Q3 A **Van de Graaff generator** is a machine which is used to generate static electricity. One type of Van de Graaff generator works like this:

1. The bottom comb is positively charged and attracts electrons away from the rubber belt.
2. The rubber belt loses electrons and becomes positively charged.
3. As the positive charge on the belt passes the top comb, electrons are attracted from the metal dome onto the belt.
4. The dome loses electrons and builds up a positive charge.

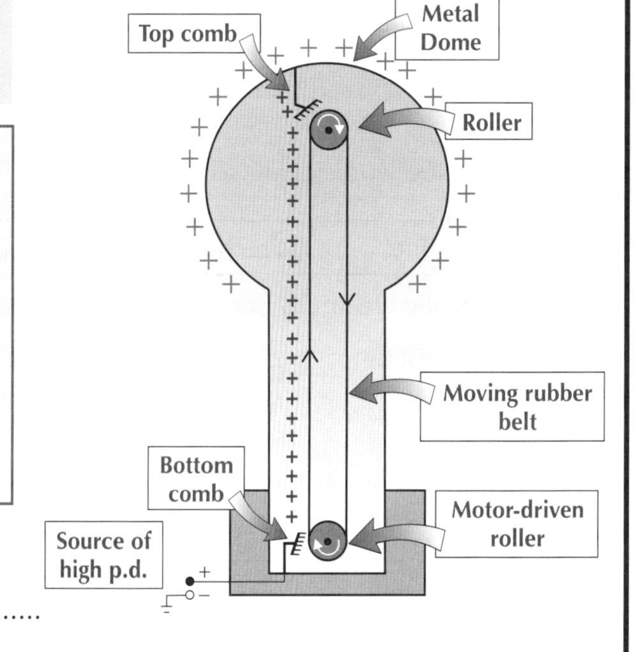

a) Why is the belt made of rubber?

....

b) The top comb needs to be a **conductor**. Explain why.

....

....

c) Nadia is doing an experiment with a Van de Graaff generator. Her teacher tells her that if she touches the generator, she will become charged. When Nadia touches the generator, her hair starts to stand on end.

Use your knowledge of electrostatic charges to **explain why** Nadia's hair stands on end.

....

....

Static Electricity

Q4 Three friends are talking about static electricity on their clothes.

Answer their questions in the spaces below.

Lisa: ....

....

Sara: ....

....

Tim: ....

....

Q5 Use the words below to fill in the gaps.

fuel	grain chutes	paper rollers	sparks	explosion	earthed

Static electricity can be dangerous when refuelling cars. If too much static builds up, there might be .... which can set fire to the .... This could lead to an .... To prevent this happening, the nozzle is .... so the charge is conducted away. There are similar safety problems with .... and ....

Q6 Match up these phrases to describe what happens in a **thunderstorm**.
Write out your complete sentences below in the correct order.

If the voltage gets big enough...

... the voltage gets higher and higher.

The bottoms of the clouds become negatively charged...

... and electrons move between them.

As the charge increases...

... there is a huge spark (a flash of lightning).

Raindrops and ice bump together...

... because they gain extra electrons.

1. ....
2. ....
3. ....
4. ....

Uses of Static Electricity

Q1 Choose from the words below to fill in the gaps.

defibrillator	earthed	shock	precipitator	sparks	paddles	insulated

The beating of your heart is controlled by tiny little electrical pulses, so an electric .... to a stopped heart can make it start beating again. This is done with a machine called a .... The machine uses two .... connected to a power supply.
It's important that only the patient receives a ...., so the operator holds .... handles.

Q2 A **smoke precipitator** stops smoke particles from escaping up a chimney.

Explain why:

a) the smoke is made to pass through a wire grid with a high negative charge.

....

b) the metal collection plates are also charged up.

....

c) the smoke particles stick to the metal plates.

....

Q3 In a **photocopier**, the image plate is **positively** charged.

a) Why do some parts of the image plate lose their charge?

....

....

b) Explain why the black powder sticks to the image plate.

....

c) Describe what would happen if the paper wasn't charged.

....

Top Tips: Static electricity's responsible for many of life's little annoyances — bad hair days, and those little shocks you get from touching car doors. Still, it has its uses too.

Circuits — The Basics

Q1 Use the words in the box to fill in the gaps. Use each word once only.

more
voltage
resistance
less
current
force

a) The flow of electrons round a circuit is called the ....

b) .... is the .... that pushes the current round the circuit.

c) If you increase the voltage, ... current will flow.

d) If you increase the ...., ... current will flow.

Q2 Match up these items from a standard test circuit with the **correct description** and **symbol**.

ITEM	DESCRIPTION	SYMBOL
Cell	The item you're testing.	(A)
Variable Resistor	Provides the voltage.	variable resistor symbol
Component	Used to alter the current.	cell symbol
Voltmeter	Measures the current.	(V)
Ammeter	Measures the voltage.	resistor symbol

World's Strongest Current

Q3 Write down:

a) the **unit** of:

i) current .... **ii)** voltage .... **iii)** resistance ....

b) two ways of **decreasing** the current in a standard test circuit:

1. ....

2. ....

Q4 Indicate whether these statements are **true** or **false**.
Write out a **correct version** of the false statements.

		True	False
a)	Current flows from positive to negative.	☐	☐
b)	An ammeter should be connected in parallel with a component.	☐	☐
c)	Items that are in series can be in any order.	☐	☐
d)	A voltmeter should be connected in series with a component.	☐	☐

....

....

....

....

Measuring AC

Q1 Choose from the words below to fill in the gaps.

changing AC hertz DC volts direct
alternating ohms frequency amps direction

In the United Kingdom the mains electrical supply is about 230 ....
The supply is .... current (.........) which means that the
.... of the current is constantly ....
The supply has a .... of 50 ....

Q2 Answer the following:

a) What does "CRO" stand for?

....

b) What does the trace on a CRO screen show?

....

c) Give the names of the two main dials on the front of a CRO.

....

Q3 The diagram shows three traces on the same CRO. The settings are the same in each case.

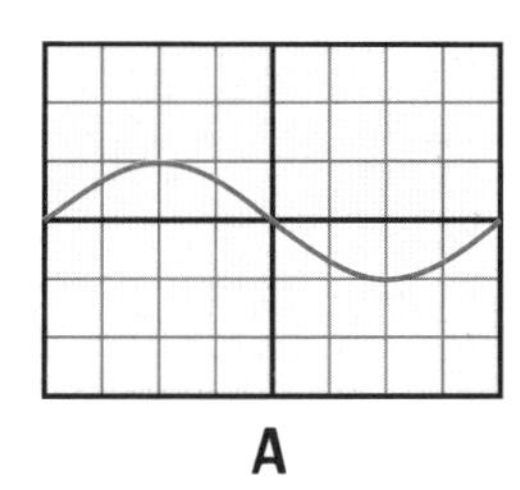

A

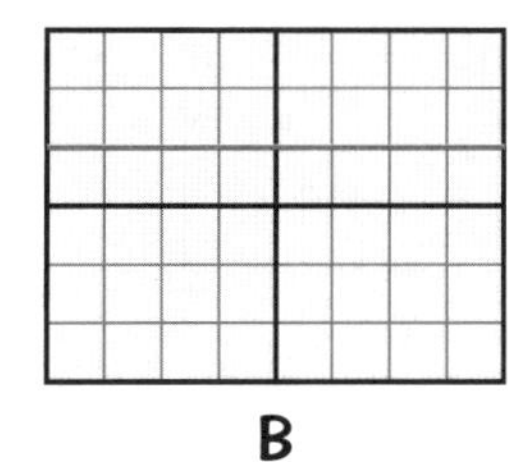

B

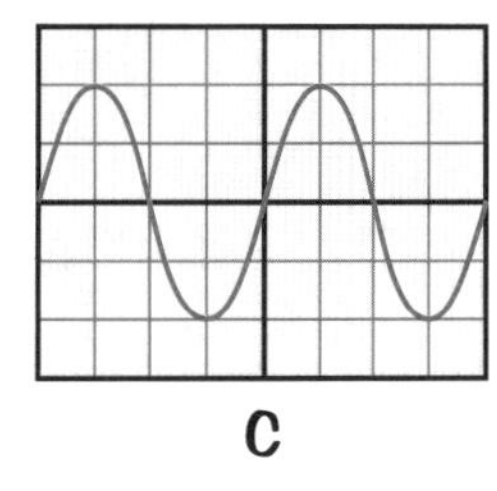

C

Write down the **letter** of the trace that shows:

a) the highest frequency AC ...., **b)** direct current ...., **c)** the lowest AC voltage ....

Q4 The diagram shows a trace on a CRO screen. The **timebase** is set to 10 ms per division, and the **gain** to 1 volt per division.

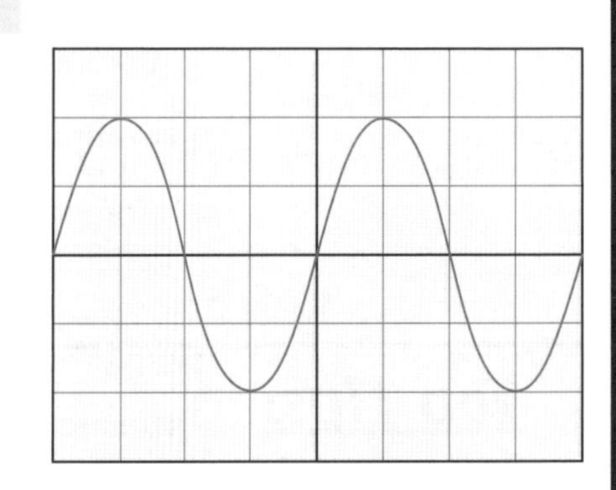

a) What is the peak voltage? ....

b) What is the time period?

....

c) Calculate the frequency of the supply.

....

Resistance and V = I × R

Q1 Fill in the missing values in the table below.

Use the formula triangle to help.

Voltage (V)	Current (A)	Resistance (Ω)
6	2	
8		2
	3	3
4	8	
2		4
	0.5	2

Q2 Peter tested **three components** using a standard test circuit. The table below shows his results.

Voltage (V)	–4.0	–3.0	–2.0	–1.0	0.0	1.0	2.0	3.0	4.0
Component **A** current (A)	–2.0	–1.5	–1.0	–0.5	0.0	0.5	1.0	1.5	2.0
Component **B** current (A)	0.0	0.0	0.0	0.0	0.0	0.2	1.0	2.0	4.5
Component **C** current (A)	–4.0	–3.5	–3.0	–2.0	0.0	2.0	3.0	3.5	4.0

a) Draw a **V-I graph** for each component on the axes below.

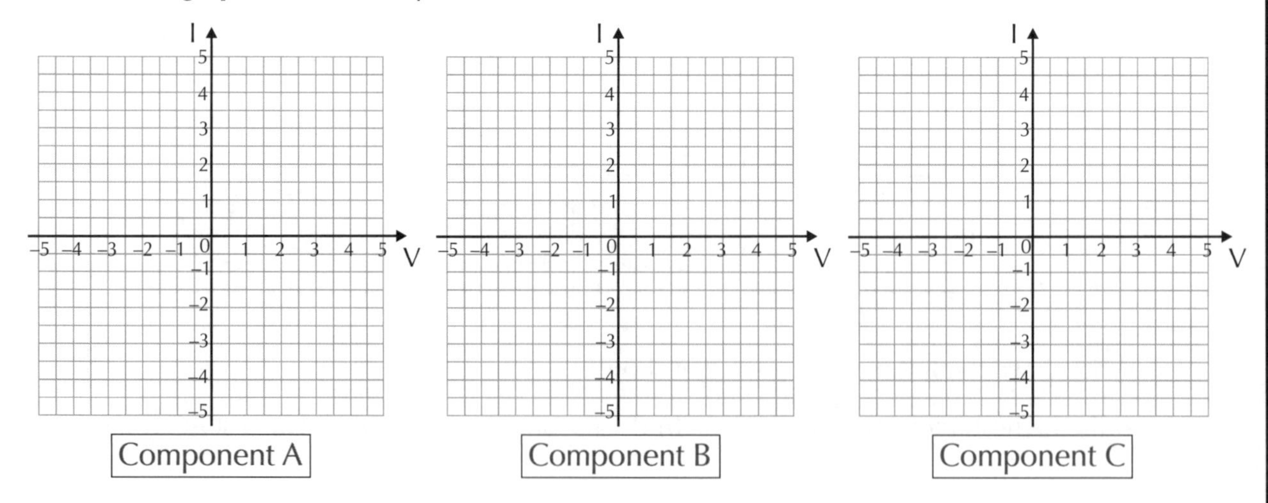

b) Complete Peter's **conclusions**:

Component **A** is a ....

Component **B** is a ....

Component **C** is a ....

Top Tips: There are two very important skills you need to master for resistance questions — **interpreting V-I graphs** and using the formula **V = I × R**. Make sure you can do both.

Circuit Symbols and Devices

Q1 Write out the names of the **numbered circuit devices** in the spaces below.

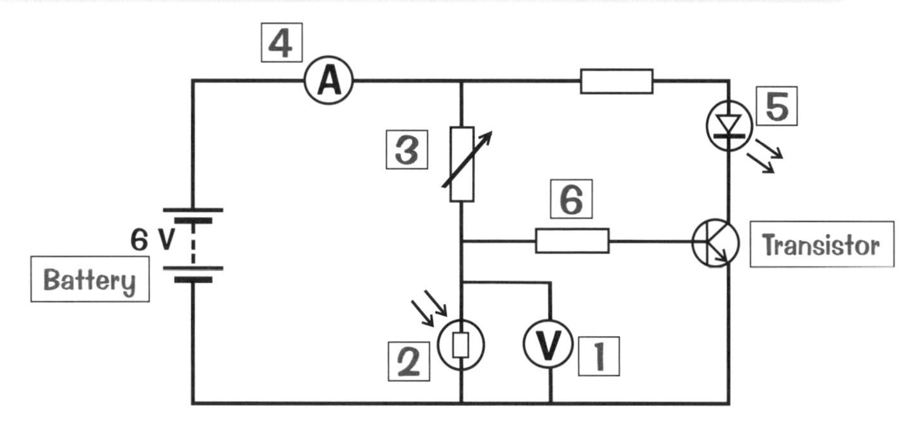

1. ....   4. ....

2. ....   5. ....

3. ....   6. ....

Q2 Use the words below to fill in the gaps.

light-dependent	diode	thermistor	fixed	variable	circuit

Some resistors always have the same resistance. These are called .... resistors. A .... resistor can be used for altering the current in a circuit. The resistance of a .... drops when the temperature increases. The resistance of a .... resistor drops when light shines on it.

Q3 Give one **similarity** and one **difference** between the following:

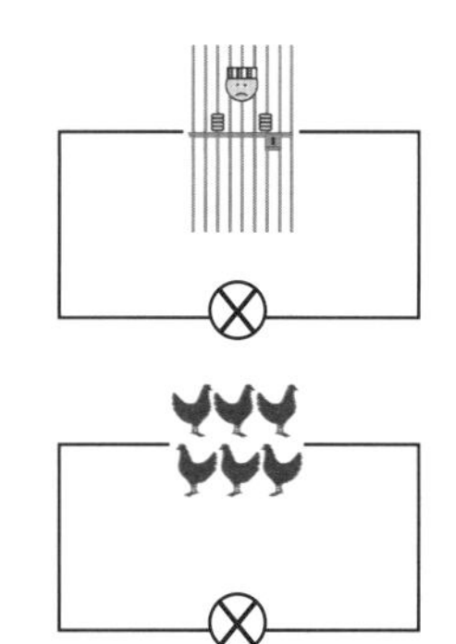

a) a cell and a battery

....

....

....

b) an ammeter and a voltmeter

....

....

c) a thermistor and a light-dependent resistor.

....

....

Series Circuits

Q1 Match up these descriptions with what they describe in a series circuit.

Same everywhere in the circuit

Shared by all the components

The sum of the resistances

Can be different for each component

Potential difference

Current

Total potential difference

Total resistance

Q2 The diagram shows a series circuit.

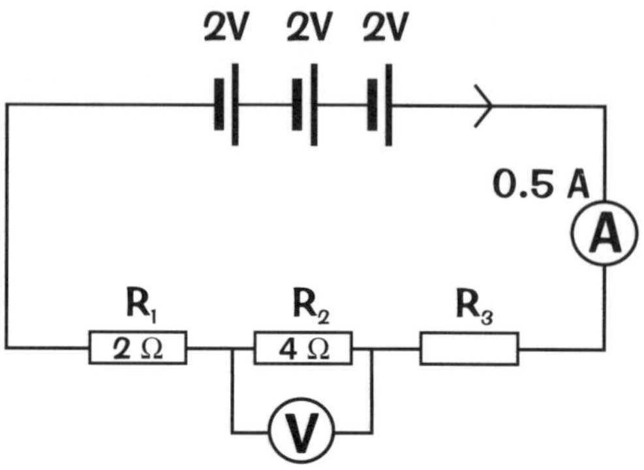

2V 2V 2V

0.5 A

A

R_1 2 Ω

R_2 4 Ω

R_3

V

a) Calculate the total potential difference across the battery.

....

b) Work out the total resistance.

....

c) Calculate the resistance of resistor R_3.

....

For parts b) and d), you'll need to use the formula connecting V, I and R.

d) What would you expect the reading on the voltmeter to be?

....

Q3 Vikram does an experiment with different numbers of lamps in a series circuit. The diagram below shows his three circuits.

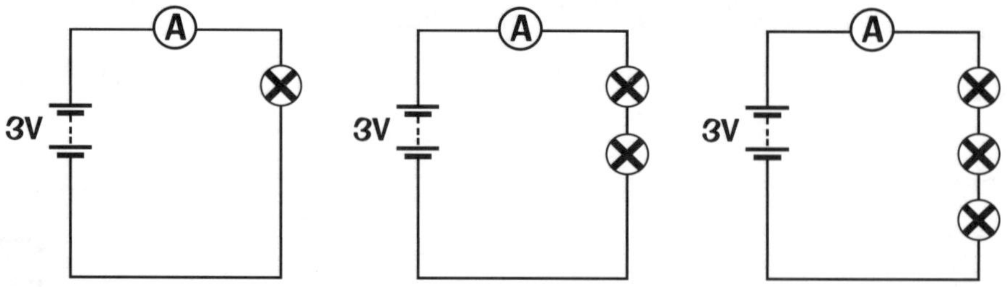

A 3V | A 3V | A 3V

a) What do you think happens to the **brightness** of the lamps as he adds more of them? **Explain** your answer.

....

....

b) How does the **current** change as more lamps are added? **Explain** your answer.

....

....

Parallel Circuits

Q1 Tick to show whether these statements about parallel circuits are **true** or **false**.

		True	False
a)	Components are connected side-by-side (instead of end-to-end).	☐	☐
b)	Each component has the same potential difference across it.	☐	☐
c)	The current is the same everywhere in the circuit.	☐	☐
d)	Components can be switched on and off independently.	☐	☐

Q2 Karen does an experiment with different numbers of lamps in a parallel circuit. The diagrams below show her three circuits.

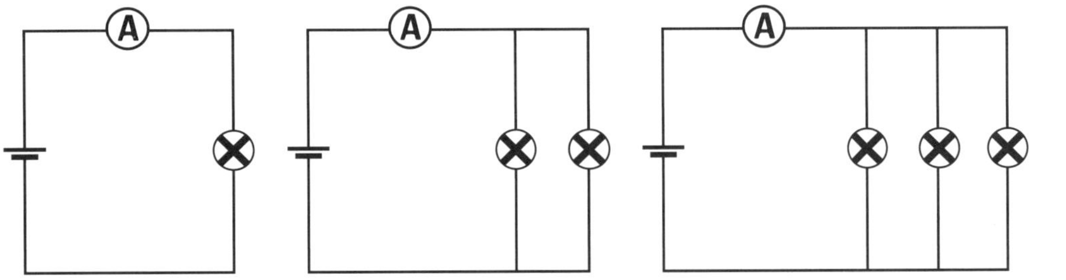

a) What happens to the **brightness** of the lamps as Karen adds more of them? **Explain** your answer.

....

....

b) One of the lamps in the third circuit is **unscrewed**.
What happens to the brightness of the other lamps?

....

Q3 The diagram opposite shows a **parallel** circuit.

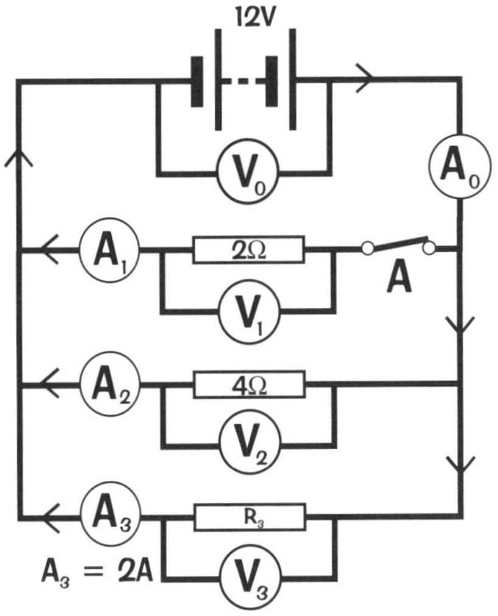

a) Calculate the readings on ammeters:

i) A_1 ....

ii) A_2 ....

b) Find the readings on voltmeters:

i) V_1 ....

ii) V_2 ....

c) What is the resistance of resistor R_3?

....

12V

A_0 V_0 A_1 2Ω V_1 A A_2 4Ω V_2 A_3 R_3 V_3

A_3 = 2A

d) What is the reading on ammeter A_0 when switch A is open?

....

Fuses and Safe Plugs

Q1 Answer the following questions about **plugs**:

a) Why is the body of a plug made of rubber or plastic?

....

b) Explain why some parts of a plug are made from copper or brass.

....

c) What material is the cable insulation made from, and why?

....

Q2 Use the words below to complete these rules for wiring a plug.

outer bare live earth neutral insulation firmly green and yellow

a) Strip the .... off the end of each wire.

b) Connect the brown wire to the .... terminal.

c) Connect the blue wire to the .... terminal.

d) Connect the .... wire to the .... terminal.

e) Check all the wires are .... screwed in with no .... bits showing.

f) The cable grip must be securely fastened over the .... covering of the cable.

Q3 Put **ticks** in the table to show which wires match each description.

Description	Live	Neutral	Earth
Must always be connected			
Just for safety			
Electricity normally flows in and out of it			
Alternates between +ve and –ve voltage			

Morris thought it best to be earthed at all times — just in case.

Q4 These sentences describe how a **fuse** and **earth wire** work together to help prevent you getting an electric shock from your toaster. Put numbers in the boxes to show the order they should go in.

☐ The surge in current causes the fuse wire to heat up.

☐ Everything is now safe.

☐ A fault develops and the earthed casing becomes connected to the live supply.

☐ The live supply is cut off.

☐ The fuse blows.

☐ A large current now flows in through the live wire and out through the earth wire.

Energy and Power in Circuits

Q1 Fill in the gaps using the words in the box. You might need to use some of the words more than once, or not at all.

power	current	lower	higher	how long	voltage

The total energy transferred by an appliance depends on .... it's used for and its .... The power of an appliance can be calculated using the formula: power = ... × .... The fuse rating for an appliance should be a little .... than its normal ....

Q2 Calculate the **amount** of electrical energy used by the following. For each component, say what **forms** of energy the electrical energy is converted to.

a) A 100 watt lamp in 10 seconds: .... J.

Electrical energy is converted to .... and .... energy.

b) A 500 watt motor in 2 minutes: .... J.

Electrical energy is converted to ...., ... and .... energy.

c) A 1 kW heater in 20 seconds: .... J.

Electrical energy is converted to .... energy.

d) A 2 kW heater in 10 minutes: .... J.

Electrical energy is converted to .... energy.

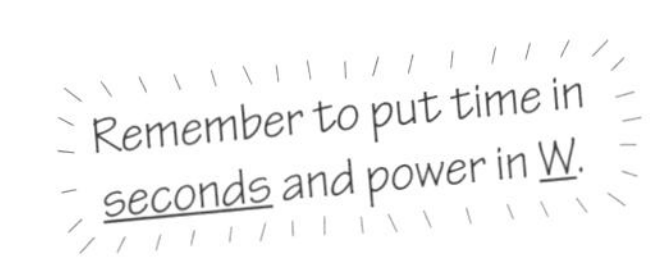

Q3 Lucy is comparing **three lamps**. She connects each lamp in a circuit and measures the **current**. Her results are shown in the table below.

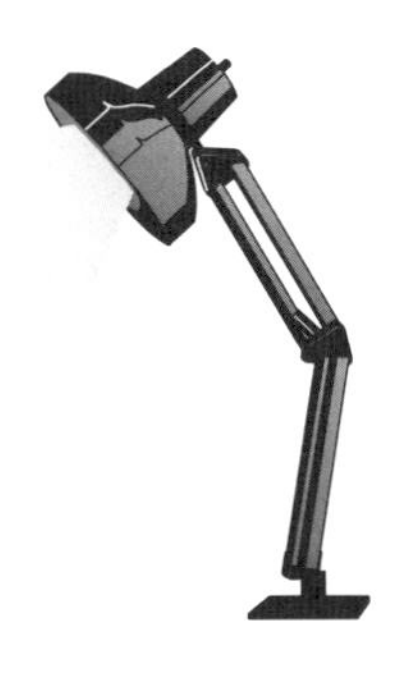

	Lamp A	Lamp B	Lamp C
Voltage (V)	12	3	230
Current (A)	2.5	4	0.1
Power (W)			
Energy used in one minute (J)			

a) Complete the table by filling in the missing values.

b) What rating of fuse would each lamp need? (Choose from 2 A, 3 A, 5 A, 7 A or 13 A.)

A = ..., B = ..., C = ...

Top Tips: Anything which supplies electricity is supplying **electrical energy**, which can be converted to other forms of energy — like heat or light. Remember that. And there are two **important formulas** for you to learn — one for energy and one for power.

Charge, Voltage and Energy Change

Q1 A 3 volt battery can supply a current of 5 amps for 20 minutes before it needs recharging.

a) Calculate:

i) the number of seconds in 20 minutes.

....

ii) how much charge the battery can provide before it needs recharging.

....

b) Each coulomb of charge from the battery can carry 3 J of energy.
How much energy can the battery transform before it needs recharging?

....

Q2 Sally is comparing two lamps, A and B. She takes the measurements shown in the table.

	Lamp A	Lamp B
Current through lamp (A)	2	4
Voltage drop across lamp (V)	3	2
Charge passing in 10 s (C)		
Energy transformed in 10 s (J)		

Calculate the **missing values** and write them in the table.

Q3 The motor in a fan is attached to a 9 V battery.
If a current of 4 A flows through the motor for 7 minutes:

a) Calculate the total charge passed.

....

b) Calculate the energy transformed by the motor.

....

Q4 The following statements are wrong.
Write out a correct version of each.

Look back at the formulas for charge and energy if you're puzzled.

a) Higher voltage means more coulombs of charge per second.

....

b) One ampere (amp) is the same as one coulomb per joule.

....

c) One volt is the same as one joule per ampere.

....

Mixed Questions — Section Nine

Q1 The diagram shows part of a type of ink-jet printer. Each droplet of ink is given a positive charge as it leaves the nozzle. Plates A and B are also charged.

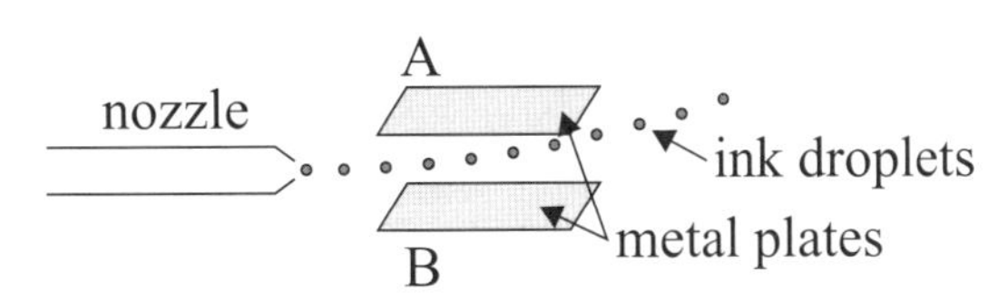

a) What charges would plates A and B have to make the droplets bend upwards as shown?

b) Explain how the droplets can be steered up or down to any desired position.

Q2 Maria walks across the nylon carpet in her living room and touches the radiator to see if the heating is on. When she touches the radiator, which is earthed, she feels an electric shock. Explain why.

Q3 Some railways use overhead electric cables at a voltage of 25 kV (25 000 V). Suggest why these cables must be kept a certain distance away from bridges and other structures.

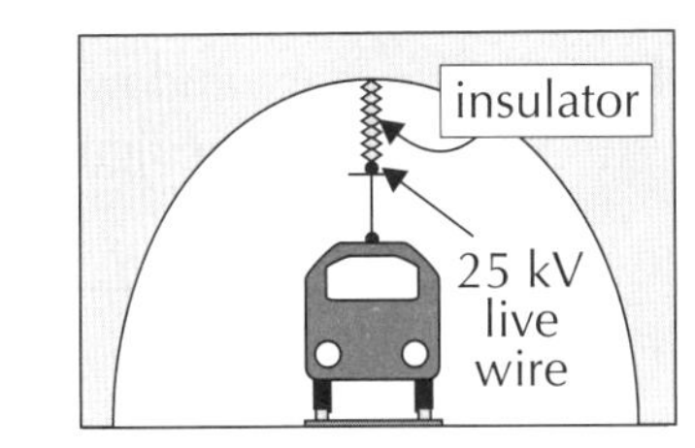

Q4 The diagram shows a circuit in which three resistors are connected in series.

a) Calculate the total resistance of the 3 resistors.

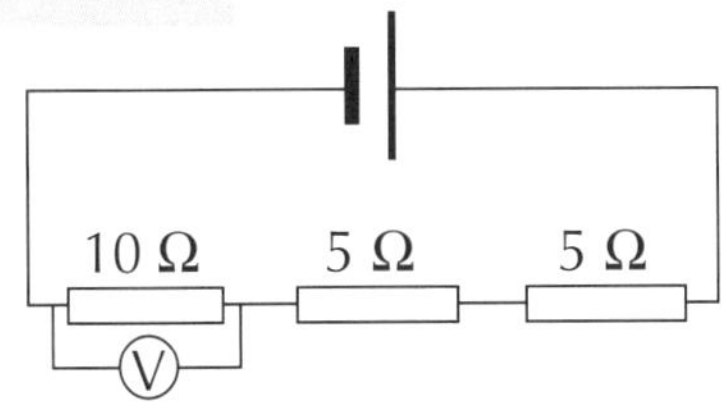

b) If the voltmeter shown reads 4 V, find:

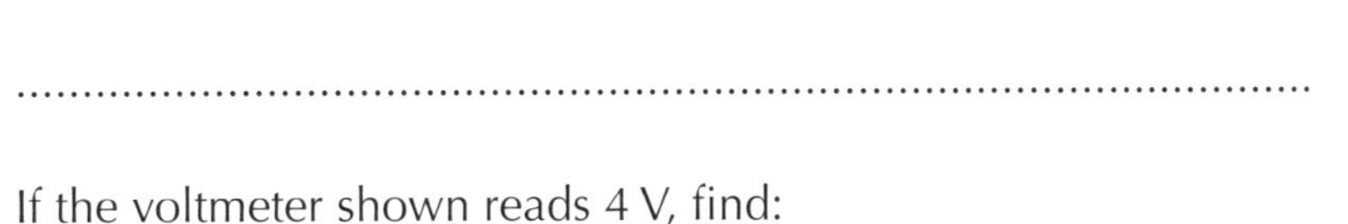

i) the current flowing in the circuit.

ii) the voltage of the power supply.

iii) the energy dissipated in each of the 5 Ω resistors in 2 minutes.

Mixed Questions — Section Nine

Q5 The diagram shows a circuit which could be used for the lights on a car.
Each headlight bulb is rated at 12 V, 6 A and each side light bulb is rated at 12 V, 0.5 A.

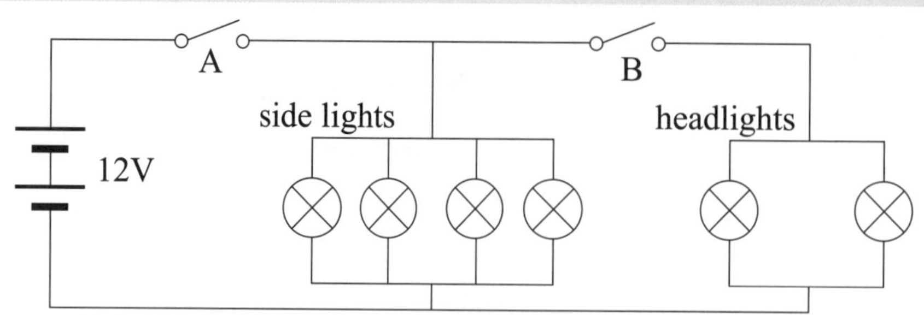

a) Calculate the total current flowing from the battery when:

i) Switch A is closed and switch B is open.

....

ii) Switch A is open and switch B is closed.

....

iii) Switches A and B are both closed.

....

b) A car's rear window de-mister is also connected to the battery in parallel.
Explain why the lights dim slightly when the de-mister is switched on.

....

....

c) A car battery supplies direct current (DC), but mains electricity is alternating current (AC).

i) The diagram shows a CRO trace from the mains electricity supply on the island of Bezique.
The **timebase** dial was set to 10 ms per large division.

Calculate the **frequency** of Bezique's electricity supply.

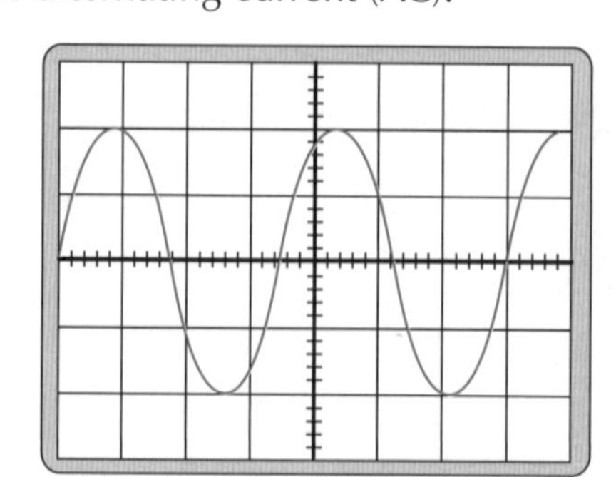

....

....

ii) On the diagram, illustrate the CRO trace you would expect to see from a 12 V car battery when the **gain** dial is set to 6 V per large division.

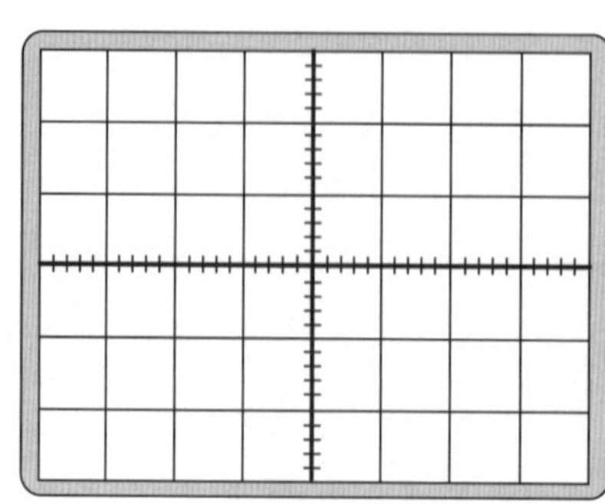

Atomic Structure

Q1 Put these different ideas about atoms in the order they were first thought of.

A An atom is like a plum pudding, with electrons stuck into a ball of positive charge.

B All materials are made of identical tiny particles called atoms.

C An atom has a small nucleus with electrons whizzing around it.

D Atoms contain electrons which can be removed from atoms.

E Each element has its own kind of atom.

Correct order: .... , ... , ... , ... , ...

Q2 Match up the key words with their meanings.

Keyword	Meaning
Isotopes	The part of an atom that has protons and neutrons.
Unstable atoms	Forms of an element which have different numbers of neutrons.
Nuclear decay	High-energy particles or waves that a decaying atom spits out.
Radiation	Atoms which are likely to break up (decay).
Nucleus	The random break-up of atomic nuclei.

Q3 Ernest Rutherford and his assistants, Geiger and Marsden, investigated the structure of atoms by firing alpha particles at a thin gold film.

a) What was the new idea about atoms put forward by **Ernest Rutherford**?

....

b) Describe the experimental evidence that led Rutherford to this new idea.

....

....

Q4 What are the important similarities and differences between:

a) protons and neutrons?

....

....

b) protons and electrons?

....

....

Radioactive Decay Processes

Q1 Complete the table showing the properties of the three types of radiation from radioactive decay.

	Alpha (α)	Beta (β)	Gamma (γ)
Ionising power			weak
Relative mass	4		
Penetrating power		moderate	
Speed			very fast
Charge	2+		

Q2 When a nucleus emits an alpha or beta particle, the nucleus changes.

a) What happens to a nucleus when it emits an **alpha particle**?

....

....

....

b) What happens to a nucleus when it emits a **beta particle**?

....

....

Q3 What is the connection between the ionising power of radiation and its penetrating power?

....

....

Q4 Explain clearly why:

Hint — think about the number of protons and neutrons.

a) an alpha particle is written as ${}^{4}_{2}\text{He}$ or ${}^{4}_{2}\alpha$.

....

b) a radium atom ${}^{226}_{88}\text{Ra}$ turns into a radon atom ${}^{222}_{86}\text{Rn}$ when it emits an alpha particle.

....

c) a beta particle is written as ${}^{0}_{-1}\text{e}$ or ${}^{0}_{-1}\beta$.

....

d) a carbon-14 atom ${}^{14}_{6}\text{C}$ turns into a nitrogen atom ${}^{14}_{7}\text{N}$ when it emits a beta particle.

....

Background Radiation

Q1 Tick any of the following statements that are **true**.

- [ ] Radon gas is given off by rocks such as granite.
- [ ] Exposure to radon gas increases the risk of getting lung cancer.
- [ ] Scientists are sure that radon gas is only dangerous at high levels of concentration.
- [ ] If you live where there is a lot of radon gas, there is nothing you can do about it.
- [ ] The risk from radon gas is the same whether you smoke or not.

Q2 List **five** sources of background radiation.

....

....

Q3 Peter did an experiment to compare equal quantities of two radioactive materials. Here are his results and conclusion.

Material tested	Radiation measured (counts per second)
None	50
Material A	200
Material B	400

CONCLUSION
"Both materials are radioactive. Material B is twice as radioactive as Material A."

Is Peter's conclusion correct? Give a reason for your answer.

....

....

Q4 Radon gas building up in people's houses is a problem.

a) Explain why it's a problem.

....

b) Why is the level of radon gas in homes different in different parts of the country?

....

....

c) What can be done to reduce the build up of radon gas in homes?

....

....

Radioactivity Safety

Q1 The three different types of radiation can all be dangerous.

a) Which **two** types of radiation can pass through the human body?
Circle the correct answers.

alpha beta gamma

b) Which type of radiation is usually most dangerous if it's inhaled or swallowed?

....

c) What effects can nuclear radiation have on the human body:

i) in the short-term? ....

ii) in the long-term? ....

Q2 It's important to take suitable precautions when handling radioactive materials in the lab.

a) List three safety precautions that should always be taken when handling radioactive sources.

1. ....
2. ....
3. ....

b) How should radioactive sources be stored when not in use? Explain your answer.

....

....

Q3 In 1986, a nuclear reactor at Chernobyl (in Ukraine) exploded, and a lot of radioactive material was released. Many people were exposed to high doses of radiation. Since then scientists have monitored the health of people living in the affected areas.

a) Why have scientists monitored people's health for so long after the explosion?

Think about half-life and dose.

....

....

....

....

b) The Chernobyl explosion provided scientists with a unique opportunity to study the **effects** of radiation exposure on **humans**. Why could scientists not study this by collecting data in a laboratory?

....

Half-Life

Q1 The graph shows how the count rate of a radioactive isotope decreases with time.

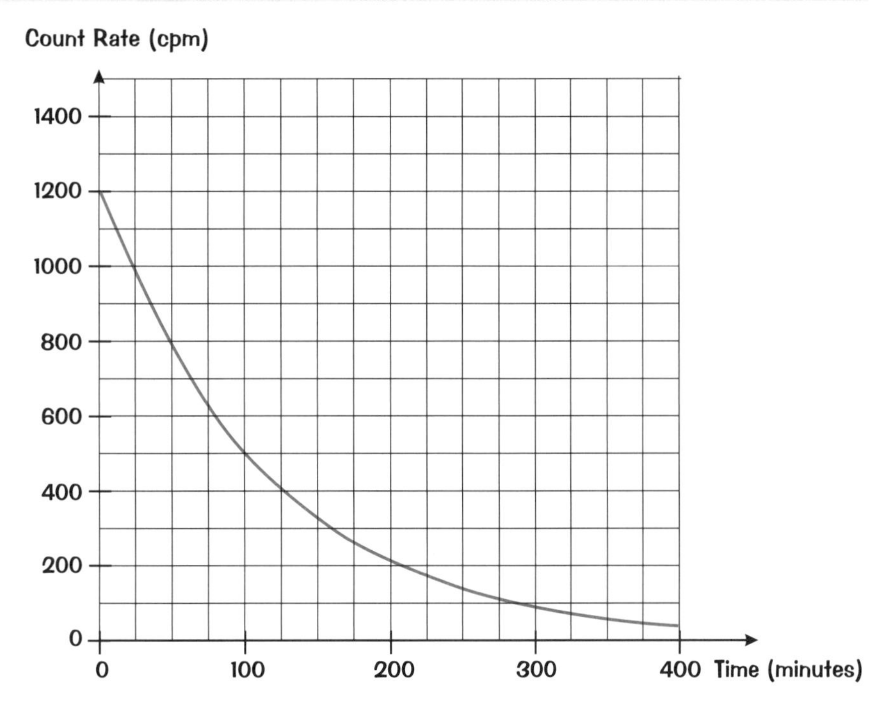

a) What is the half-life of this isotope? ....

b) What was the count rate after 3 half-lives? ....

c) What fraction of the original radioactive nuclei will still be unstable after 5 half-lives?

....

d) After how long was the count rate down to 100? ....

Q2 A radioactive isotope has a half-life of 40 seconds.

You'll need to change 6 minutes into seconds.

a) What fraction of the unstable nuclei will still be radioactive after 6 minutes?

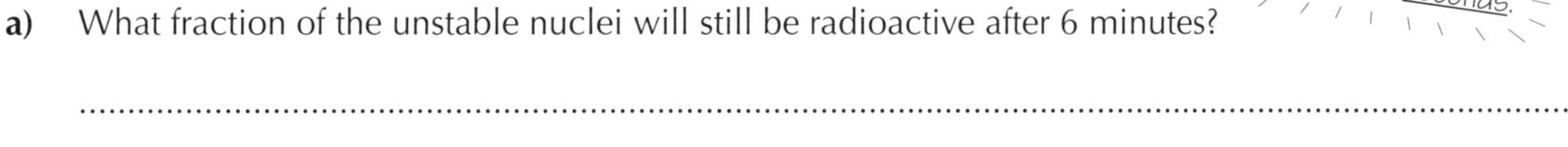

....

....

b) **i)** If the initial count rate of the sample was 8000 counts per minute, what would be the approximate count rate after 6 minutes?

....

....

ii) After how many whole **minutes** would the count rate have fallen below 10 counts per minute?

....

....

Uses of Ionising Radiation

Q1 The diagram shows how radiation can be used to sterilise surgical instruments.

radioactive source

thick lead

a) What kind of radioactive source is used, and why? In your answer, mention the **type** of radiation emitted (α, β or γ) and the **half-life** of the source.

....

....

b) What is the purpose of the thick lead?

....

Q2 Skin cancers are often surgically removed.
Tumours deeper within the body are often treated by radiotherapy, using **gamma rays**.

a) How does radiotherapy treat cancer?

....

b) What properties do gamma rays have which make them suitable for radiotherapy?

....

....

c) Why is a high dose used?

....

Q3 A patient has a radioactive source injected into her body to test her kidneys.

A healthy kidney will get rid of the radioactive material quickly (to the bladder). Damaged kidneys take longer to do this.

The results of the test, for both the patient's kidneys, are shown opposite.

Kidney A

Count Rate

Time

Kidney B

Count Rate

Time

a) Explain how the doctor knew which kidney was working well and which was not.

....

....

b) Explain why an alpha source would **not** be suitable for this investigation.

....

....

Radioactive Dating

Q1 Carbon-14 makes up 1/10 000 000 of the carbon in living things.

a) What happens to the proportion of carbon-14 in a plant or animal when it dies?

....

b) The half-life of carbon-14 is 5730 years. Explain what this means.

....

Q2 A leather strap from an archaeological dig was found to have 1 part in 80 000 000 carbon-14.

a) Use the data given in Q1 to help you estimate the age of the strap.

....

....

b) Suggest two reasons why your answer to part **a)** might be inaccurate.

1. ....

2. ....

Q3 Some Egyptian leather sandals are known to be from 3700 BCE.

Approximately what fraction of the carbon in the sandals would you expect to be carbon-14?

....

Q4 A website is advertising "woolly mammoth tusks" for sale. An investigator buys one and carries out a radiocarbon test. The tusk contains 1 part in 15 000 000 carbon-14.

Given that woolly mammoths are believed to have become extinct 10 000 years ago, is the tusk likely to be genuine? Explain your answer.

....

....

....

MAMMOTHS Я US

Q5 Uranium-238 decays with a half-life of 4.5 billion years into a stable form of lead.

A meteorite is found to contain some uranium-238 and some lead in the ratio of 1:1.
If there was no lead in the meteorite when it was created, how old is the meteorite?

....

....

Nuclear Fission and Fusion

Q1 Match up each keyword (or phrase) with its meaning.

Keyword	Meaning
Fission	Any process which changes atomic nuclei.
Nuclear reaction	Joining together.
Fusion	A device using an uncontrolled fission reaction.
Atomic bomb	Splitting apart.
Nuclear reactor	A device using nuclear fusion.
Hydrogen bomb	A device using a controlled nuclear reaction.

Q2 Explain how a nuclear fission **chain reaction** occurs, starting with a single **plutonium** nucleus absorbing a **slow-moving neutron**.

....

....

....

....

Q3 List four differences between nuclear **fission** and nuclear **fusion**.

1. ....
2. ....
3. ....
4. ....

Q4 Give two good points and two bad points about **fusion reactors**.

Good points ....

....

Bad points ....

....

Top Tips: Nuclear fuel can provide **millions** of times more energy than the same mass of fossil fuel. Given the current concerns about CO_2 emissions from burning fossil fuels, you can see why many people see nuclear fuel as an attractive alternative. Nuclear waste is really **dangerous** though.

Mixed Questions — Section Ten

Q1 An atom of the radioactive isotope uranium-238 is made up of electrons, protons and neutrons.

a) Write "electron", "proton" and "neutron" in the correct places in the table below.

		electric charge		
		-1	0	+1
mass	1/2000			
	1			

b) Explain the meanings of both words in the phrase "radioactive isotope".

....

....

c) State three practical uses of radioactive materials.

1. ....

2. ....

3. ....

Q2 Approximately one in ten million carbon molecules found in living plants and animals are the radioactive isotope carbon-14. After a plant or animal dies, this proportion starts to decrease. Carbon-14 has a half-life of 5730 years.

a) Calculate the fraction of atoms in a pure sample of carbon-14 that will still not have decayed after ten half-lives have gone by.

....

....

b) Approximately how old is a bone fragment in which the proportion of carbon-14 is one part in fifty million? Explain your answer.

....

....

....

c) Suggest why carbon dating is unreliable for samples more than 50 000 years old.

....

....

Mixed Questions — Section Ten

Q3 When radioactive decay occurs, α, β or γ radiation is emitted and new elements may be formed.

a) Write a nuclear equation to show thorium-234, $^{234}_{90}Th$, decaying to form protactinium, $^{234}_{91}Pa$.

....

b) **i)** Write a nuclear equation to show radon, $^{222}_{86}Rn$, decaying by **alpha** emission.

....

ii) Radon gas makes up about 51% of the UK's background radiation. About 14% is from rocks and building materials. How could **houses** be designed to minimise exposure to radiation?

....

....

Q4 Thallium is a radioactive element. One isotope, thallium-201, has a half-life of just over three days. Another isotope, thallium-204, has a half-life of 3.8 years.

a) Which isotope would be suitable for injecting into a patient to check the health of their heart? Explain your answer.

....

....

b) Why is a radioactive tracer that gives off gamma rays less of a health risk than a tracer that gives off beta particles?

....

....

c) Complete this sentence: "It is impossible to use substances that emit alpha particles as tracers within the human body because alpha radiation cannot...

...."

Q5 The diagram shows a nuclear reaction.

n → U → Kr, Ba, n, n, n

a) Underline the correct name for this type of reaction.

fission fusion

b) Describe how this process generates heat in nuclear reactors.

....

....

Answers

Higher Level

Section One — Life and Cells

Section One — Life and Cells

Page 1 — Cells

Q1a) True
b) False — they often have several different organ systems.
c) True
d) True
e) True
Q2a) Plant, animal
b) cell wall
c) Both plant and animal cells
d) photosynthesis, glucose
Q3 Lots of chloroplasts... for photosynthesis.
Tall shape... gives a large surface area for absorbing CO_2.
Thin shape... means you can pack more cells in at the top of the leaf.
Q4 stomata, turgid, photosynthesis, flaccid, night
Q5a) The **nucleus** contains genetic material / chromosomes / genes / DNA. Its function is controlling the cell's activities.
b) **Chloroplasts** contain chlorophyll. Their function is to make food by photosynthesis.
c) The **cell wall** is made of cellulose. Its function is to support the cell and strengthen it.

Page 2 — DNA

Q1 1. gene
2. chromosome
3. nucleus
4. cell
Q2 nucleus (not true with certain organisms like bacteria), helix, nucleotides, base, adenine/guanine, adenine/guanine
Q3 1. The DNA double helix 'unzips' to form two single strands.
2. Free-floating nucleotides join on where the bases fit.
3. Cross links form between the bases of the nucleotides and the old DNA strands.
4. The result is two molecules of DNA identical to the original molecule of DNA.
5. The new nucleotides are joined together.
Q4a)

A	C	T	G	C	A	A	T	G
T	G	A	C	G	T	T	A	C

b) It ensures an exact copy because only one base will correctly join onto another base.

Page 3 — DNA Fingerprinting

Q1 1. Collect the sample for DNA testing.
2. Cut the DNA into small sections.
3. Separate the sections of DNA.
4. Compare the unique patterns of DNA.
Q2 separated, chromatography, suspended, negatively, positive, small, big
Q3

	Foal	Mother	Father
DNA sample	Sample 1	**Sample 3**	**Sample 4**

Q4a) DNA from a crime scene could be checked against everyone in the country to see whose it was. Or any other sensible answer.

b) E.g. some people consider it an invasion of privacy. Or false positives could occur if there was a mistake in the analysis.

Page 4 — Making Proteins

Q1a) amino acids
b) liver
c) ribosomes
d) three
Q2 1. The DNA strand unzips.
2. A molecule of RNA is made using DNA as a template.
3. RNA moves out of the nucleus.
4. RNA joins with a ribosome.
5. Amino acids are joined together to make a polypeptide.
Q3a) DNA is too big to move out of the nucleus into the cytoplasm. RNA is small enough.
b) E.g. RNA is smaller and it's only one strand.
Q4a) a gene
b) The number and order of amino acids gives a protein a particular shape and therefore a particular function.
c) Our body can change some amino acids into others. This is called transamination and it happens in the liver. (Some amino acids are essential and can't be made.)
d) DNA controls which genes are switched on or off. This determines which proteins the cell produces, e.g. haemoglobin, which determines what type of cell it is.
e) A sequence of three bases in a strand of DNA codes for a particular amino acid. Amino acids are stuck together to make proteins, following the order of the code on the DNA.

Page 5 — Biological Catalysts — Enzymes

Q1a) Enzymes are biological catalysts. They increase the speed of a reaction without being changed or used up in the reaction.
b)

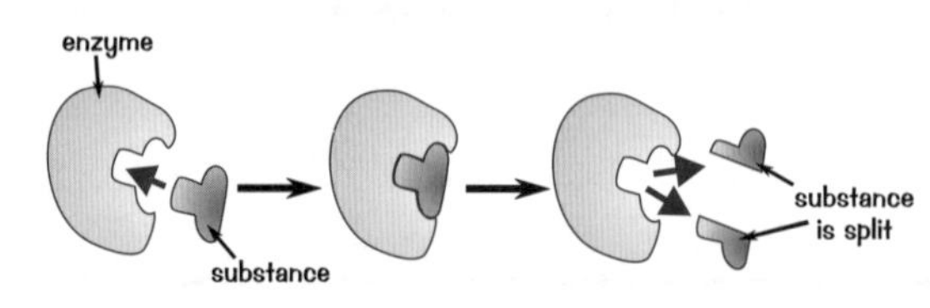

Q2a) i) False
ii) True
iii) True
iv) False

Section One — Life and Cells

b) i) All enzymes are made of protein.
iv) Most enzymes only catalyse one specific reaction.

Q3a)

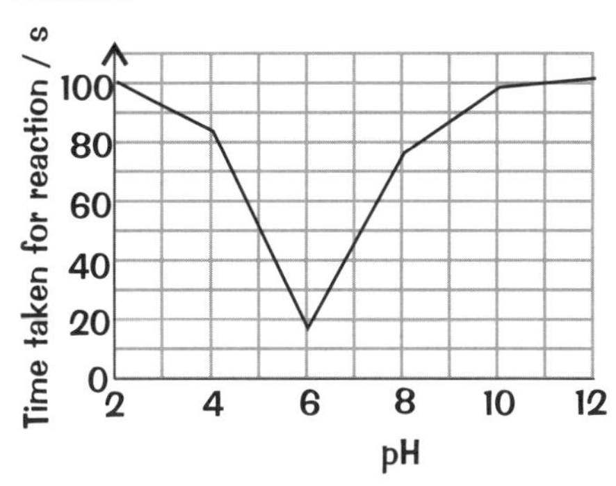

b) About pH 6.
c) At very high and very low pH levels the bonds in the enzymes are broken / the enzyme is denatured, meaning that it can't speed up the reaction.
d) No. This enzyme works very slowly at pH 2 / in strongly acidic conditions.

Page 6 — Diffusion

Q1 random, higher, lower, bigger, gases, large, less
Q2a) False
b) False
c) True
d) True
e) False
Q3a)

(The sugar particles will have spread out evenly.)
b) i) The rate of diffusion would **speed up**.
ii) The rate of diffusion would **speed up**.
iii) The rate of diffusion would **slow down**.
c) The sugar particles will move from an area of higher concentration (the sugar cube) to an area of lower concentration (the tea).

Page 7 — Diffusion in Cells

Q1 amino acids, small, diffusion, lower, out of
Q2 nerve, synapse, impulse, transmitter, diffuses, binds, receptor
Q3a) and **b)**

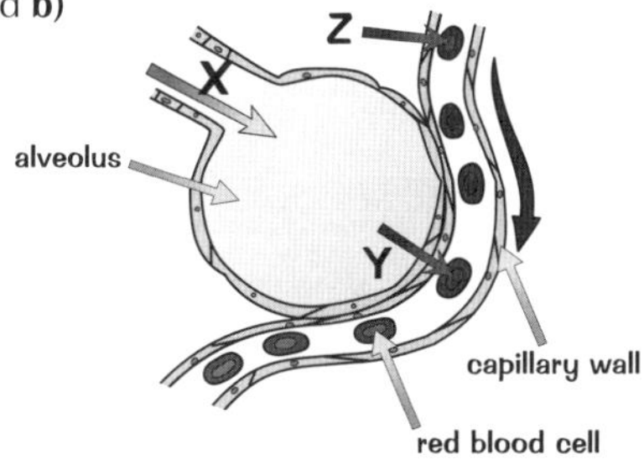

c) Into the blood. Although the person is breathing out, the concentration gradient still allows diffusion from the alveolus into the bloodstream.

Page 8 — Osmosis

Q1a) A membrane that only allows certain substances to diffuse through it.
b) side B
c) from B to A
d) The liquid level on side B will **fall**, because water will flow from side B to side A by osmosis.
Q2a) tissue fluid
b) More water will move by osmosis from the tissue fluid into the body cells as the tissue fluid has a higher water concentration and the body cells have a lower water concentration.
c) The net movement of water molecules stops when there is an equal concentration of water molecules on either side of the membrane — when they have reached equilibrium.

Pages 9-10 — Mixed Questions — Section One

Q1a)

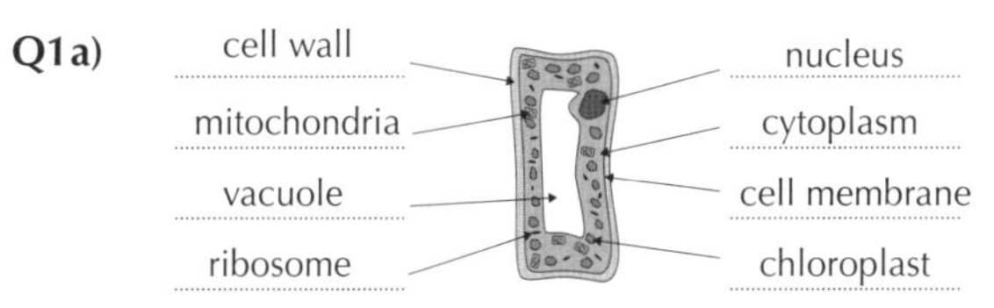

b) i) mitochondria
ii) chloroplasts
iii) nucleus
iv) cell wall (and vacuole)
Q2a) The DNA double helix unzips, and a molecule of RNA is made using DNA as a template. Base pairing ensures it's an exact match.
b) nucleus
c) ribosomes
Q3a) The victim and suspect A — they share a significant amount of their DNA.
b) Suspect B
c) Suspect B's DNA matches the DNA found at the crime scene.
d) No. Just because suspect B's DNA was found at the crime scene, it doesn't mean that he/she committed the murder. He/she could have simply been to the crime scene on a different occasion.
Q4a) The level will fall.
b) Water leaves the visking tubing by osmosis. This is because the concentration of water is higher inside the tubing than outside.
Q5a) 33 °C (a few degrees either way acceptable)
b) They are denatured / damaged.
Q6a)

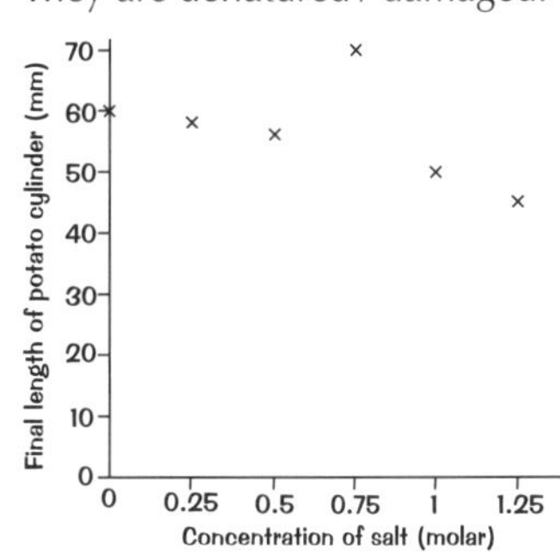

Section Two — Growth and Development

b)

Concentration of salt (molar)	Final length of potato cylinder (mm)	Change in length of potato cylinder (mm)
0	60	+10
0.25	58	+8
0.5	56	+6
0.75	70	+20
1	50	0
1.25	45	-5

c) i) 0.75 molar (it doesn't follow the pattern)
ii) Repeat the experiment at least twice more to find more reliable values.

Section Two — Growth and Development

Page 11 — Growth

Q1a) Any two of: height, length, width, circumference
b) i) The weight of an organism including all the water in its body.
ii) It varies a lot, depending on how much water it has gained or lost during the day.
Q2 E.g. Any two of: Some types of worm are able to grow a new 'tail' if cut in half. A young spider can regrow a leg. Some reptiles can regrow a lost leg or tail.
Q3 E.g. Animals tend to grow when they are young, plants grow continuously. Growth in animals happens by cell division, whereas in plants growth in height is mainly due to cell elongation.
Q4a)

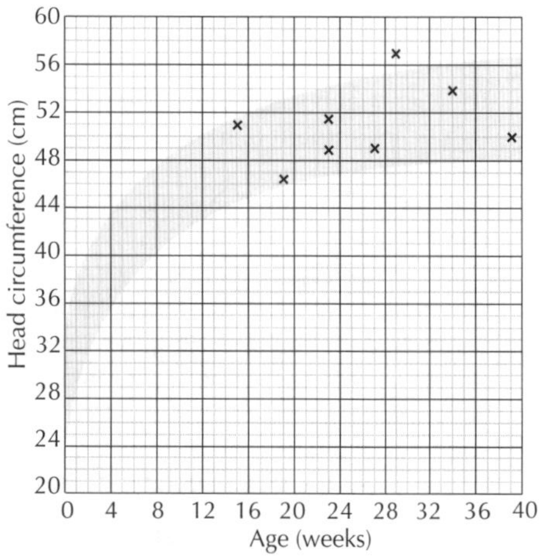

b) Oliver's
c) It gives a representation of the rate of growth of the baby. If the baby is growing too fast or too slow it could alert the doctor to developmental problems / if it's relatively very large or small.

Page 12 — Cell Division — Mitosis

Q1a) True
b) False (there are 23 pairs of chromosomes)
c) False (they're found in the nucleus)
d) True
e) True
f) True
g) True
Q2a) DNA is spread out in long strings.
b) DNA is duplicated and forms X-shaped chromosomes.
c) The chromosomes line up at the centre of the cell and cell fibres pull them apart. The left and right arms go to opposite ends of the cell.
d) Membranes form around each of the sets of chromosomes. They become the nuclei of the two new cells.
e) The cytoplasm divides to form two new cells.
Q3 reproduce, strawberry, runners, asexual, genes, variation

Page 13 — Cell Division — Meiosis

Q1a) Meiosis
b) Mitosis, Meiosis
c) Meiosis
d) Meiosis
Q2a) The DNA is spread out in long strands. Before the cell starts to divide it duplicates its DNA to produce an exact copy.
b) For the first meiotic division the chromosomes line up in their pairs across the centre of the cell.
c) The pairs are pulled apart, mixing up the mother and father's chromosomes into the new cells. This creates genetic variation.
d) The chromosomes line up across the centre of the nucleus ready for the second division, and the left and right arms are pulled apart.
e) There are now 4 gametes, each containing half the original number of chromosomes.
Q3a) Sex cells that only have one copy of each chromosome.
b) Gametes have half the usual number of chromosomes so that when two gametes join together during fertilisation the resulting fertilised egg will have the full number of chromosomes.

Page 14 — Sexual Reproduction

Q1 acrosome containing enzymes —to digest the membrane of the egg cell
produced in large numbers — to increase the chance of fertilisation
small with long tails — so they can swim to the egg
lots of mitochondria — to provide the energy needed to move.
Q2a) i) The offspring get half their chromosomes from each parent, so they get features from both parents.
ii) When the chromosomes are first pulled apart in meiosis, it creates a random mixture (assortment) of the father's and the mother's chromosomes, so each new cell is unique.

Section Two — Growth and Development

b) It increases the gene pool. This increases the chance of an individual being resistant to a new disease.

Q3a) 24 weeks

b) It was based on the point that a foetus became able to survive outside the womb.

c) When the pregnancy is putting the mother's health at serious risk, or if there is a major foetal abnormality.

d) Human life begins at fertilisation so ending a pregnancy at any time is the same as killing a human being.

e) E.g. Some people believe that a foetus can feel pain at 7 weeks old, so termination should not be allowed after this time. / Some people believe the foetus can't feel pain until the pain receptors are connected to the brain at about 26 weeks, so termination should be allowed up to this time. / With medical advances foetuses are becoming viable earlier in the pregnancy so some people feel this limit should be dropped.

Page 15 — Stem Cells and Differentiation

Q1a) cells that are well-suited to perform a particular job

b) the process by which a cell changes to become specialised for a job

c) cells that can develop into different types of cell depending on what instructions they get

Q2 Embryonic stem cells can differentiate into any type of body cell. Adult stem cells are less versatile — they can only turn into certain types of cell.

Q3 Possible answer:
People with some blood diseases (e.g. sickle cell anaemia) can be treated by bone marrow transplants. Bone marrow contains stem cells that can turn into new blood cells to replace the faulty old ones.

Q4 diabetes — insulin-producing cells
paralysis — nerve cells
heart disease — heart muscle cells
Alzheimer's — brain cells

Q5a) Possible answer:
Stem cell research may lead to cures for a wide variety of diseases.

b) Possible answer:
Embryos shouldn't be used for experiments as each one is a potential human life.

Page 16 — Growth in Plants: Plant Hormones

Q1a) False

b) True

c) False

d) True

Q2a) auxins

b) At the tips of the shoots and roots.

c) i) In the shoot, auxin moves away from the light, where it stimulates growth on the shaded side, so the shoot bends towards the light.

ii) In the root, auxin moves to the lower side of the root, where it inhibits growth, making the root grow downwards.

Q3a) The flowers aren't pollinated. Instead a growth hormone is applied.

b) Unripe fruit is firmer, so it's less easily damaged and bruised during picking and transport. (Or any sensible answer.)

c) They are sprayed with a ripening hormone during transport.

Page 17 — Selective Breeding

Q1 Fruit plant: e.g. any two of: larger fruit, sweeter/better tasting fruit, fruit with better colour, fruit that ripens more quickly, more resistant to disease, faster growth rate.
Ornamental house plant: e.g. any two of: more colourful leaves/flowers, more scented flowers, more resistant to disease, faster growth rate.

Q2 E.g. There's less variety in the gene pool of the organism — this means that they will have similar level of disease resistance and some diseases may be able to wipe out the whole lot. The characteristics selective for by humans may not be beneficial for the organism e.g. increasing the milk yield of cows causes inflammation of the udders.

Q3a) Female sheep who produce large numbers of offspring can be bred with rams whose mothers produced large numbers of offspring.

b) Tall wheat plants with a good grain yield can be bred with dwarf wheat plants that are more able to resist the wind and rain.

Q4a) Yes, the average milk yield has increased over the generations.

b) 5375 – 5000 = 375 litres

Page 18 — Genetic Engineering

Q1a) 1. The human insulin gene is cut from human DNA.
2. The human insulin gene is inserted into the host DNA of a bacterium.
3. The bacteria are cultivated in a fermenter.
4. Insulin is extracted from the medium.

b) E.g. Bacteria can be easily cultivated in large numbers without taking up too much room / they divide quickly.

Q2a) Genes could be added that make plants resistant to herbicides, frost damage and disease.

b) Genes involved in the production of a vitamin e.g. beta-carotene, could be added to a plant that's commonly eaten.

Q3a) E.g. some people think that it's unnatural, and could cause unforeseen problems that could then be passed to future generations.

Section Two — Growth and Development

b) E.g. yes — because it can help people (e.g. it can help people with diseases like diabetes, it can help to grow more food, etc.)
OR: No — there could be consequences that nobody has thought of yet / it might not be safe / it's not fully understood what the long-term effects might be.

Q4 The GM salmon might breed with wild salmon and the gene would spread through the wild population. Faster-growing salmon could disrupt natural food chains.

Page 19 — Cloning

Q1 a) Clones are genetically identical organisms.
b) A female in which an embryo is implanted. The embryo is not the natural offspring of this female.
c) An animal in it's early stages of development, which has arisen from a ball of genetically identical cells.

Q2 a) Embryo transplants.
b) Sperm from the prize bull is used to artificially fertilise an egg from the prize cow. The resulting embryo is split at an early stage in its development to give lots of clones. These can then be implanted into the other cows in the herd to grow into calves.
c) The new calves will all be genetically identical to one another.
d) A reduced gene pool, meaning all the new calves will be vulnerable to the same diseases, etc.

Q3 a) All the plants have cells with the same DNA, since they have all arisen by replication and cell division.
b) tissue culture

Q4 a) False
b) False
c) True
d) False

Page 20 — Adult Cloning

Q1 a) removing and discarding a nucleus = **A**
implantation in a surrogate mother = **D**
useful nucleus extracted = **B**
formation of a diploid cell = **C**
b) mitosis
c) The embryo may not develop normally.

Q2 a) More animals that can produce the blood clotting agent would increase the yield of the agent; also the process of genetic engineering would only have to happen once.
b) Some people might think it is unethical to either genetically engineer or clone an animal. / Cloning is a new science and we might be unaware of the problems associated with it.

Q3 a) Transplanting organs from animals into humans.
b) Animals could be genetically engineered to make organs that can be safely transplanted into humans, and then these animals could be cloned to increase the number of organs available for transplantation.

Q4 Lots of women will have to be willing to donate eggs. There would have to be a lot of surrogate pregnancies. There could be high rates of miscarriage and stillbirth. At the moment, evidence suggests that animal clones are unhealthy and die prematurely — it could be the same for humans. We are playing about with genetics that we don't completely understand. The clone may be psychologically damaged knowing that it's a clone of another human being.

Page 21 — Genetic Diagrams

Q1 a) Cross 1

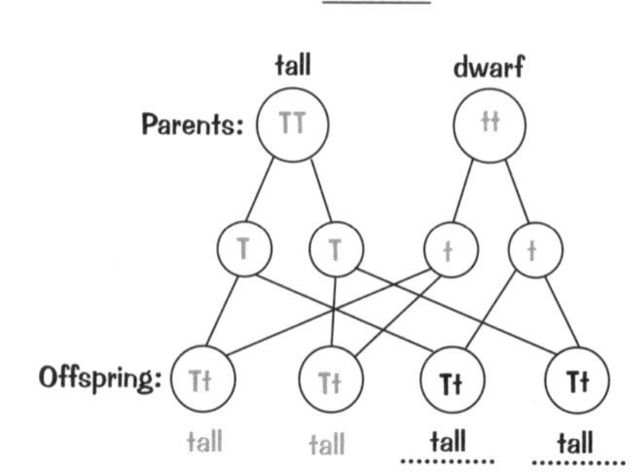

Cross 2

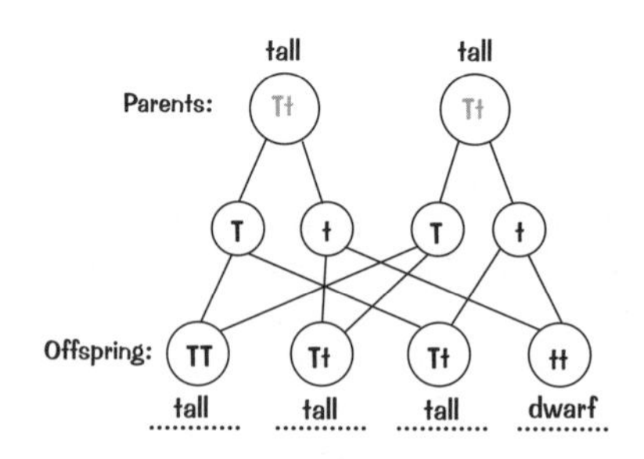

b) 75% (0.75, 3 in 4, ¾)

Q2 a) i) red eyes
ii) white eyes
iii) red eyes
iv) white eyes

b) i)

parent's alleles		**R**	**r**
	R	RR	Rr
	r	Rr	rr

ii) 25% (0.25, 1 in 4, ¼)
iii) There are likely to be 72 with red eyes (three quarters).

Section Three — Human Biology

Page 22 — Genetic Disorders

Q1a)

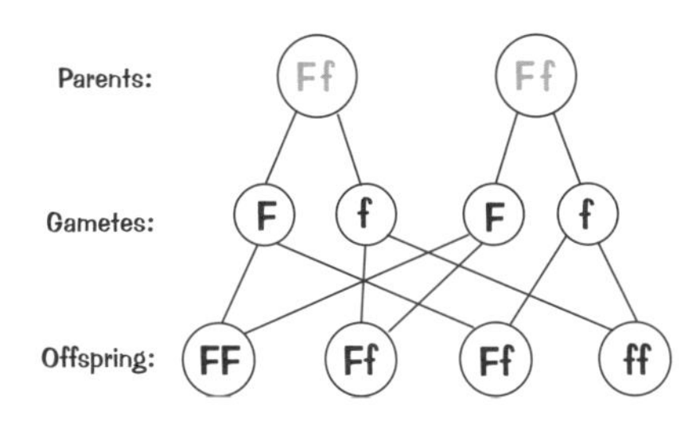

b) i) 25% (quarter, 0.25, 1 in 4, ¼)
ii) 50% (half, 0.5, 1 in 2, ½)

Q2a) 50% (half, 0.5, 1 in 2, ½)
b) People may have children before they realise they have the disease.

Q3a) Possible answers include:
- Embryonic screening implies that people with genetic disorders are 'undesirable' and may increase prejudice against such people.
- The rejected embryos are destroyed. Each one is a potential human life.
- There's a risk that embryonic screening could be taken too far, e.g. parents might want to choose embryos who fulfil their vision of the ideal child.

b) Possible answers include:
- If embryonic screening means healthy children are born, then this stops the suffering associated with many genetic disorders.
- During IVF, most of the embryos are destroyed anyway — screening just allows the selected one to be healthy.

Pages 23-24 — Mixed Questions — Section Two

Q1a) Stem cells have the ability to differentiate into different types of cell.
b) i) mitosis
ii) Stem cells from embryos can differentiate into any different type of cell in the human body.
c) Possible answer: Some people feel that using embryos for stem cell research is unethical; they feel that every embryo has a right to life.

Q2a) Yes
b) No. Neither of the parents carry the allele, so they can't pass it on to their children.

Q3a) A: mitosis; B: meiosis; C: mitosis; D: mitosis; E: fertilisation.
b) Meiosis halves the number of chromosomes. This compensates for the doubling of chromosomes at fertilisation, and allows the number of chromosomes to remain constant down the generations. Meiosis also helps to create variety.

Q4a) E.g. Any two of: Increase meat/egg yield; better temperament for living in confinement; resistance to disease; better tasting meat/eggs, etc.
b) E.g. Bigger meat yield/egg production could harm the health of the birds. / It would reduce their gene pool.

Q5a) To check that the gene for growth hormone had been inserted successfully. The piece of DNA that was inserted contained both these genes, so if the bacteria were resistant to the penicillin they would also be able to produce growth hormone.
b) E.g. any 2 from: Bacteria reproduce quickly. They take up little space. They can be grown relatively cheaply.
Less chance of passing on disease than if hormone from corpses is used.

Section Three — Human Biology

Page 25 — Respiration and Exercise

Q1a) True
b) False
c) True
d) False
e) True
f) True
g) False

Q2a) glucose + oxygen → carbon dioxide + water + energy
b) glucose → lactic acid + energy

Q3a) 45 – 15 = **30** breaths per minute
b) During exercise, aerobic respiration in the muscles increases to provide more energy. The breathing rate increases to provide more oxygen for respiration in the muscles.
c) Because Jim has an oxygen debt after the race. Extra oxygen is needed to break down the lactic acid produced by anaerobic respiration in his muscles during the race.

Q4a) Any two from: large surface area, moist surface, thin / permeable walls, good blood supply
b) Reduced rate of diffusion, because the oxygen concentration in the alveoli will fall (so a smaller concentration gradient).

Page 26 — Enzymes and Digestion

Q1

a) protein $\xrightarrow{\text{protease}}$ amino acids

b) fat $\xrightarrow{\text{lipase}}$ glycerol + fatty acids

c) carbohydrate $\xrightarrow{\text{amylase}}$ simple sugars

Q2

Amylase	Protease	Lipase	Bile
salivary glands pancreas small intestine	stomach pancreas small intestine	pancreas small intestine	liver

Section Three — Human Biology

Q3a) gall bladder, small intestine, neutralises, enzymes, fat
b) Emulsification breaks fat into smaller droplets which gives a larger surface area for lipase to work on, speeding up digestion.

Page 27 — The Digestive System

Q1

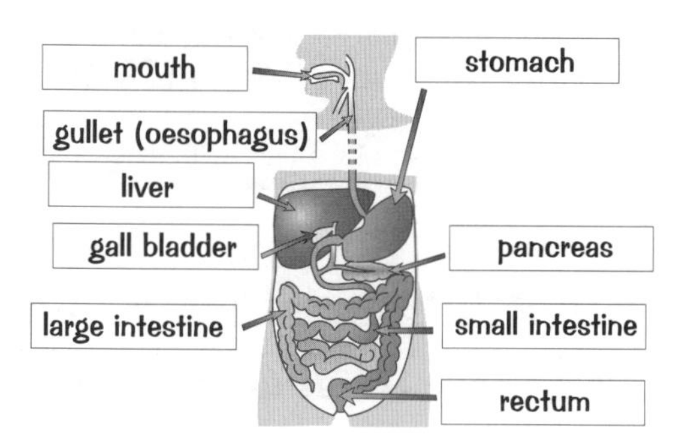

Q2a) Produces amylase.
b) Stores bile / releases bile into the small intestine.
c) Produces enzymes (protease, amylase and lipase) / releases enzymes into the small intestine.
d) Produces bile which emulsifies fats and neutralises stomach acid.
e) Absorbs excess water from food.

Q3a) i) capillary network
ii) longitudinal muscle
iii) villus
iv) circular muscle
b) i) Provides a very large surface area for diffusion to happen across.
ii) To allow time for all the food to be digested and absorbed before it reaches the end. It also increases the surface area.

Page 28 — Functions of the Blood

Q1a) False
b) False
c) True
d) False
e) True

Q2a)

Substance	Travelling from	Travelling to
Urea	liver	kidneys
Carbon dioxide	body cells	lungs
Glucose	gut	body cells

b) E.g. any six from: red blood cells, white blood cells, platelets, water, amino acids, hormones, antibodies, antitoxins

Q3 large, nucleus, haemoglobin, oxygen, oxyhaemoglobin, flexible

Q4a) antibodies
b) antitoxins
c) White blood cells have a flexible shape which enables them to wrap around the microorganism, before digesting it using enzymes.

Page 29 — Circulatory System: Blood Vessels

Q1 artery — vessel that takes blood away from the heart capillary — microscopic blood vessel
cholesterol — fatty substance
lumen — hole in the middle of a tube
vein — vessel that takes blood towards the heart

Q2a) veins
b) capillaries
c) arteries
d) arteries, veins

Q3a) E.g. for making cell membranes.
b) saturated fat
c) Cholesterol can build up in your arteries as plaques. These restrict and may block the lumen preventing blood getting through. This can lead to a heart attack or stroke.

Q4a) Any two from: The vein has a wider lumen, thinner wall, and valves.
b) The length of the blood vessel, because this is the dependent variable.
c) The vein, because it has a thinner wall.
d) To make his experiment a fair test (the vessels are the same age, etc.)

Page 30 — Circulatory System: The Heart

Q1a) pulmonary artery
b) vena cava
c) right atrium
d) tricuspid valve
e) right ventricle
f) aorta
g) pulmonary vein
h) semi-lunar valve
i) bicuspid valve
j) left ventricle

Q2a) False
b) True
c) True
d) True

Q3a) The heart is made up of two separate pumps. The right side pumps blood to the lungs. The left side pumps blood to the body.
b) The atria only have to pump blood into the ventricles, whereas the ventricles have to pump blood out of the heart at a very high pressure, so they need to have thick muscular walls to do this.
c) The right ventricle only has to pump blood to the lungs, so it doesn't need as much muscle. The left ventricle has to pump blood to the rest of the body, so it needs to be more muscular.

Q4 pacemaker, irregular, artificial, valves

Page 31 — Homeostasis

Q1 Homeostasis is the maintenance of a constant internal environment.

Q2a) E.g. temperature, water content, ion content, blood sugar level.

Section Three — Human Biology

b) E.g. carbon dioxide and urea.

Q3a) If the temperature deviates too much from 37 °C the enzymes in the body are denatured / don't work as efficiently.

b) The thermoregulatory centre in the brain detects the temperature of the blood.

Q4

	Too hot	Too cold
hair	hairs lie down flat	hairs stand up
sweat glands	more sweat produced	less sweat produced
blood vessels	dilate near skin	constrict near skin
muscles	no shivering occurs	shivering occurs

Page 32 — The Kidneys and Homeostasis

Q1a) False

b) True

c) True

d) False

e) True

Q2a) They're taken into the body in food and drink, and then absorbed into the blood.

b) E.g. too much or too little water would be drawn into the cells, which would damage the cells / nerves and muscles wouldn't work properly.

c) In the sweat.

Q3a) E.g. any three from: in sweat, in our urine, in the air we breathe out, in faeces.

b)

	Do you sweat **a lot** or **a little**?	Is the amount of urine you produce **high** or **low**?	Is the urine you produce **more** or **less** concentrated?
Hot Day	A lot	low	more
Cold Day	A little	high	less

c) Sheona would have lost a lot of water as sweat when she got hot during the run. To try to avoid dehydration her kidneys will have excreted as little water as possible, meaning that there was little urine and it was concentrated.

Pages 33 — Controlling Blood Sugar

Q1a) From food and drink

b) Liver and pancreas

c) Insulin

Q2 Missing words are: insulin, pancreas, insulin, liver, glucose, blood, reduced / lower.

Q3a) A disorder where the pancreas doesn't produce enough insulin so a person's blood sugar level can get too high.

b) Diabetics can monitor their blood sugar levels by testing a small sample of their blood using a special device.

c) Any two from: by injecting insulin at meal times / by avoiding foods that are rich in simple carbohydrate, i.e. sugars / by exercising after eating meals.

Page 34 — Insulin and Diabetes

Q1a) False

b) True

c) False

d) False

e) False

Q2a) Dogs' pancreases.

b) i) The blood sugar levels dropped quickly.

ii) Insulin

Q3a) Diabetics used to use insulin from animals such as pigs. Now they can use human insulin produced by genetically modified bacteria.

b) Diabetics used to use glass syringes that had to be boiled. Now they can use disposable syringes that are already sterile. There are also needle free devices.

Q4a) A pancreas transplant.

b) Risk of infection, risk of rejecting the organ, having to take immunosuppressive drugs.

c) Two of the following: transplanting just the cells which produce insulin, artificial pancreases, using stem cells.

Pages 35-36 — Mixed Questions — Section Three

Q1a) C — this arrow shows movement from the blood vessel to the body cells. Sugar is carried in the blood plasma, not in the red blood cells (like arrow A).

b) **glucose** + **oxygen** → **carbon dioxide** + **water** + energy

c) Any two of: to make larger molecules from smaller ones, to make muscles contract, to maintain a constant body temperature

Q2a) Dilation of the blood vessels causes more blood to flow to the surface of the skin so more heat is lost.
Constriction of the blood vessels causes less blood to flow to the surface of the skin so less heat is lost.

b) Hairs standing on end trap more air next to the body for insulation.

c) Heat is lost from the body as the sweat evaporates.

Q3a) Glucose is needed for respiration / to provide energy.

b) pancreas

c) insulin

Q4a) i) A, G, H

ii) F

iii) G

iv) H

v) D

b) To kill bacteria and to provide the optimum pH for stomach proteases to work.

c) They will find it difficult to digest fats, as bile emulsifies fats to give a greater surface area. Conditions in the small intestine will be too acidic, as bile neutralises the acid from the stomach. This may stop enzymes in the small intestine from working properly.

Section Four — Plants and the Environment

Q5a) W — pulmonary artery
X — vena cava
Y — pulmonary vein
Z — aorta

b) E.g. Blood in the vena cava is deoxygenated, blood in the aorta is oxygenated.

c) Narrow lumen and thick muscle / elastic layer to cope with high blood pressure.

d) i) veins

ii) valves prevent the backflow of blood.

Section Four — Plants and the Environment

Page 37 — Photosynthesis

Q1a) carbon dioxide + water → glucose + oxygen

b) chloroplast — the structure in a cell where photosynthesis occurs
chlorophyll — a green pigment needed for photosynthesis
sunlight — supplies the energy for photosynthesis
glucose — the food that is produced in photosynthesis

Q2 leaves, energy, convert, cells, fructose, sucrose, fruits, cellulose, walls, lipids

Q3a) 00.00 (midnight)

b) There's no light at night so photosynthesis won't occur.

c) Plants use the food they have stored as starch.

d)

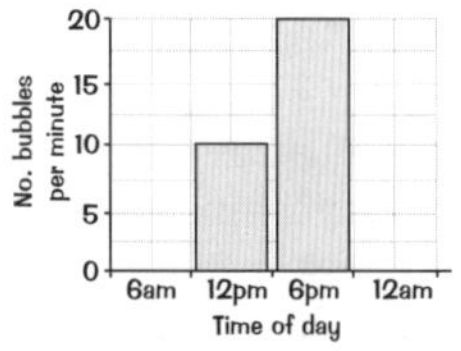

Page 38 — Rate of Photosynthesis

Q1a) blue light (approx. 440 nm), red light (approx. 660 nm)

b) You could use blue or red light to increase the rate of photosynthesis, and therefore the growth rate.

Q2a)

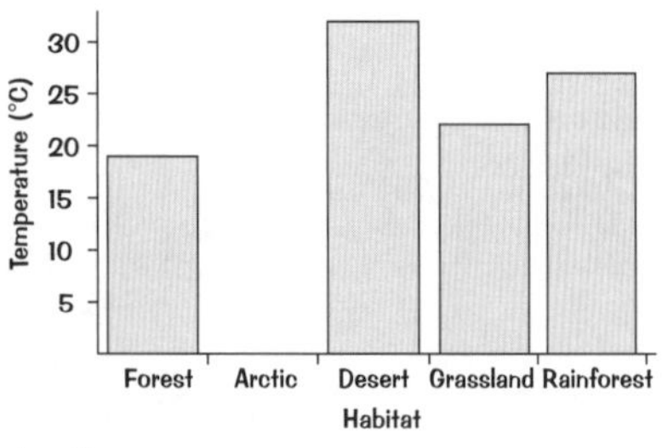

b) Arctic

c) The temperatures are extremely low there, so the rate of photosynthesis will be slower because the enzymes needed for photosynthesis will be working very slowly.

Q3a) Increasing the concentration of carbon dioxide increases the rate of photosynthesis up to a certain point.

b) The rate of photosynthesis does not continue to increase because the amount of light stops acting as the limiting factor.

Page 39 — Leaf Structure

Q1 A — palisade mesophyll layer
B — upper epidermis
C — waxy cuticle
D — stoma
E — guard cell

Q2a) photosynthesis

b) respiration

Q3a) A — oxygen / water vapour
B — oxygen / water vapour
C — carbon dioxide

b) The leaf will not be photosynthesising as there is no light. This means that mainly carbon dioxide will be diffusing out of the leaf and oxygen will be diffusing in. Less water will diffuse out.

Q4a) Provide a large surface area for gas exchange. / Lets gases easily move between cells.

b) Means a large surface area is exposed to light.

c) Deliver water and nutrients to leaf cells.

d) Contain chlorophyll to absorb lots of light energy.

Page 40 — Transpiration

Q1a) b) c)

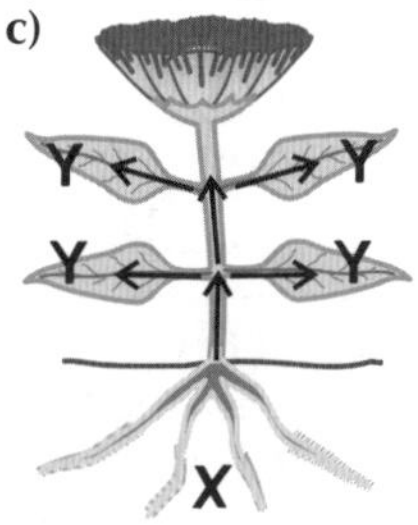

Q2a) False

b) True

c) True

d) False

Q3 leaves, diffusion/evaporation, diffusion/evaporation, leaves, xylem, roots, transpiration

Q4 Any three of: It helps to keep the plant cool, the plant has a constant supply of water for photosynthesis, it creates a turgor pressure which provides support, essential minerals from the soil are constantly brought into the plant with the water.

Q5a) Open, because the plant will be using the sunlight to photosynthesise and so it needs to take in CO_2.

b) Most of the stomata close at night, which avoids losing water by transpiration.

c) The plant won't lose even more water by transpiration, but it won't be able to photosynthesise either.

Section Four — Plants and the Environment

Page 41 — Water Flow in Plants

Q1

XYLEM VESSELS	PHLOEM VESSELS
transport water have no end-plates made of dead cells	made of living cells have end-plates transport food

Q2a) minerals, water
b) support
c) It has very thick side walls that are strong and stiff.
Q3a) A — normal
B — turgid
C — flaccid
D — plasmolysed
b) The cells lose water and their contents are no longer able to push up against the cell wall supporting the cell (turgor pressure).
c) The inelastic cell wall doesn't collapse completely.
Q4a) Any two of: Stomata are mostly found on the lower surface of the leaf where it's cool and dark. There is a waterproof waxy cuticle covering the leaf surface.
b) They have no stomata on the upper epidermis and fewer and smaller ones on the underside of the leaf.

Page 42 — Minerals Needed for Healthy Growth

Q1 **magnesium** — for making chlorophyll
potassium — for helping enzymes to function
phosphates — for making DNA and cell membranes
nitrates — for making proteins
Q2a) root hair cell
b) Absorbing water and minerals from the soil.
c) It has a very large surface area for absorbing the minerals and water.
d) The soil generally has a lower concentration of minerals than the root hair cells. Diffusion only takes place from areas of higher concentration to areas of lower concentration.
e) The cells use active transport to absorb the minerals. This requires energy, which is released by respiration.
Q3a) nitrates
b) Poultry manure — its contains the highest percentage of nitrogen.

Page 43 — Pyramids of Number and Biomass

Q1

Feature	Pyramid of numbers	Pyramid of biomass
Values for mass are shown at each level.		✓
Nearly always a pyramid shape.		✓
Each bar represents a step in a food chain.	✓	✓
Always starts with a producer.	✓	✓
Can only have 3 steps.		
Numbers are shown at each step.	✓	

Q2a) A
b) C
c) The total mass of the organisms decreases at each trophic level as shown by this pyramid.
Q3a)

ladybirds
aphids
oak tree

b) There is a single, large organism at the bottom of the chain.
Q4a) The population of lions might increase as there would be more food for them.
b) The number of zebras might decrease as they would be competing with the increased gazelle for food. / The number of zebras might decrease as there are more lions to eat them.

Page 44 — Energy Transfer and Energy Flow

Q1a) energy
b) Plants, photosynthesis
c) eat
d) respiration
e) lost, movement
f) inedible, hair
Q2a) i) 100 000 – 90 000 = **10 000 kJ**
ii) (10 000 ÷ 100 000) × 100 = **10%**
b) i) 5 ÷ 100 × 1000 = **50 kJ**
ii) 1000 – 50 = **950 kJ**
Q3a) (2070 ÷ 103 500) × 100 = **2%**
b) 2070 ÷ 10 = **207**
207 – (90 + 100) = **17 kJ**
c) heat loss / movement / excretion
d) So much energy is lost at each stage of a food chain that there's not enough left to support more organisms after about five stages.

Page 45 — Biomass and Fermentation

Q1 E.g. eat the biomass, feed it to livestock, grow the seeds of plants, use the biomass as fuel.
Q2a) False (the culture medium is a liquid)
b) False (the food is contained in the liquid culture medium)
c) True
d) False (the microorganisms need to be kept at the right temperature)
e) False (air is piped in to supply oxygen to the microorganisms)
Q3a) More trees can be planted to replace those that are burnt. The new trees are photosynthesising so remove CO_2 from the atmosphere.
b) A digester or fermenter.
c) It is burnt and used for heating or to generate electricity.
Q4a) A protein from a fungus used to make meat substitutes.

Section Four — Plants and the Environment

b) E.g. any two of: they grow very quickly, they're easy to look after, they can use waste products from agriculture and industry as food, food is produced whether the climate is hot or cold.

c) i) To keep the fermenter at the correct temperature.

ii) To supply oxygen for aerobic respiration of the fungi.

iii) To mix the contents.

Page 46 — Managing Food Production

Q1a) True

b) True

c) False

Q2a) Wheat → Human

b) There are fewer steps in this food chain so less energy is lost.

Q3a) It creates a favourable environment for the spread of disease e.g. avian flu. / The animals may be uncomfortable.

b) When the animals are eaten, the antibiotics will enter humans. This may help microbes that infect humans to develop resistance to the antibiotic.

c) This often means using power from fossil fuels (which we wouldn't be using if the animals were grazing naturally.) / Some people may think it's cruel to keep animals inside all the time.

Q4a) Breeding season — lots of small fish born, so average size decreases when they are included in calculations.

b) E.g. a high number of fish lice, an increased water pH, predators may eat the fish, competition for food by other species.

c) In this experiment the fish farm (Ecosystem A) produces larger fish and more fish survive.

Page 47 — Pesticides and Biological Control

Q1a) Pesticides are chemicals that are used to kill creatures to prevent them damaging crops, gardens, buildings etc.

b) Any one of: they may kill organisms that are not pests, they can disrupt food chains, they could be harmful to humans eating food that has been sprayed.

Q2 The frog population would decrease as there is less for them to eat, so the foxes would have to eat more rabbits. The populations of both rabbits and foxes could therefore decrease too.

Q3a) Biological control is when living organisms rather than chemicals are used to control a pest species.

b) E.g. any two of: using a predator — ladybirds are introduced into garden to keep the numbers of aphid down; a parasite — certain types of wasps and flies produce larvae inside a host insect, this eventually kills the insect pest; a disease to control numbers of the pest organism — myxomatosis is a virus that was introduced to control the rabbit population.

c) Advantage: e.g. no chemicals are used / only the pest species is usually affected, so there is less disruption of food chains / there is less risk to people eating the food.
Disadvantage: e.g. it's slower to take effect / more difficult to manage / may not kill all the pests / there is a risk that control organisms could become pests themselves or drive out native species.

Q4a) The birds of prey ate animals that had eaten the crops that were covered in pesticide.

b) Each small animal ate a lot of crops, and each bird ate a lot of the small animals. If the chemical was not excreted it would build up through the food chain and reach toxic levels.

Page 48 — Alternatives to Intensive Farming

Q1a) A mixture of fertilisers dissolved in water / a nutrient solution.

b) e.g. tomatoes / cucumbers

c) i) Advantage

ii) Disadvantage

iii) Advantage

iv) Advantage

v) Disadvantage

vi) Disadvantage

Q2a) **Insecticides**: Alternatives include biological control / crop rotation / varying seed planting times. **Advantage**: No chemicals used so safer for humans eating the crops / less likely to disrupt food chains / doesn't kill harmless or beneficial organisms.

b) **Herbicides**: Alternatives include weeding. **Advantage**: No chemicals used so safer for humans eating the crops / less likely to disrupt food chains / doesn't kill harmless or beneficial organisms.

c) **Chemical fertilisers**: Alternatives include manure, compost or crop rotation. **Advantage**: No chemicals used so safer for humans eating the crops / less likely to disrupt food chains / doesn't kill harmless or beneficial organisms. Less chance of polluting rivers with chemical fertiliser and causing eutrophication.

Q3a) Cost — the farmer won't have to pay for expensive chemical fertilisers and herbicides. However, he or she might have to pay extra staff. The yields will be lower so there won't be as much profit. This may mean that more land is required to get the same amount of crop, which is expensive.

b) Labour — weeding is much more labour intensive than simply spraying a field with a chemical. Spreading manure and compost could also take more work than spraying a liquid over the crop.

c) Environment — Without the use of chemicals there will be less disruption to food chains and less pollution to waterways. A greater variety of wildlife will be able to survive on the farm.

Section Four — Plants and the Environment

Pages 49-50 — Recycling Nutrients

Q1a) b) c)

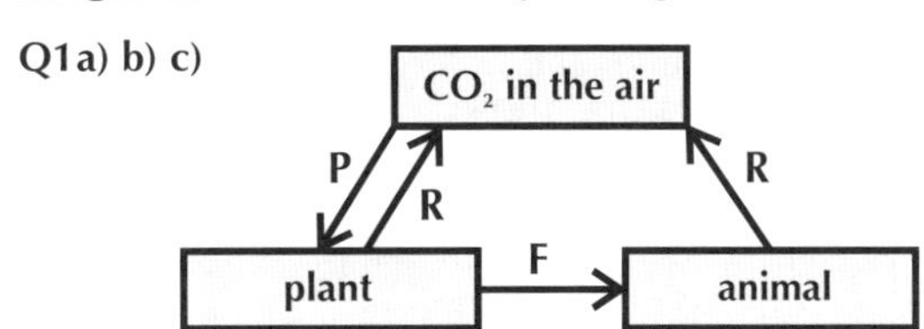

Q2 1. Plants take up minerals from the soil.
2. Plants use minerals and the products of photosynthesis to make complex nutrients.
3. Nutrients in plants are passed to animals through feeding and used in respiration to provide energy.
4. Waste and dead tissues are decayed by microorganisms.
5. Materials are recycled and returned to the soil by decay.

Q3a) Photosynthesis
b) It's present in all organic molecules like carbohydrates, proteins and lipids.
c) By animals feeding on other organisms.
d) Respiration

Q4

Type of organism involved in decay	Example	How they help in decay
Detritivores	**E.g. Earthworms / maggots / woodlice**	**They break up decaying material into smaller bits, which provides a larger surface area for smaller decomposers to work on.**
Saprophytes	Bacteria / fungi	**They secrete digestive enzymes onto decaying material which breaks down the material into bits that can be absorbed.**

Q5a) protein
b) 78 %
c) an unreactive gas

Q6 Plants — From nitrates in the soil
Animals — By eating other organisms
Bacteria — By breaking down dead organisms and animal waste

Q7a) Decomposers — Decompose proteins and urea into ammonia.
b) Nitrifying bacteria — Turn ammonia in decaying matter into nitrates which plants can use.
c) Denitrifying bacteria — Turn nitrates back into nitrogen gas.
d) Nitrogen-fixing bacteria — Turn nitrogen gas into nitrogen compounds that plants can use.

Q8a) Nitrogen-fixing bacteria converting nitrogen from the air into nitrogen compounds in the soil.
b) Nitrifying bacteria converting ammonia into nitrates.
c) Denitrifying bacteria converting nitrates in the soil into nitrogen gas.

Q9 Legume plants have root nodules that contain nitrogen-fixing bacteria. These bacteria convert nitrogen gas into nitrogen compounds, increasing the fertility of the soil.

Page 51 — Air Pollution

Q1 The main cause of acid rain is... sulfur dioxide.
Acid rain kills trees and... acidifies lakes.
Limestone buildings and statues are affected by... acid rain.
In clouds sulfur dioxide reacts with water to make... sulfuric acid.

Q2 the greenhouse effect, sulfur dioxide, sulfuric, nitrogen oxides, nitric

Q3a) Carbon monoxide is formed when there is not enough oxygen for a hydrocarbon fuel to burn completely.
b) Carbon monoxide is dangerous because it is poisonous. (It combines with haemoglobin preventing your blood from carrying as much oxygen.)

Q4a) The percentage of carbon dioxide in the atmosphere is increasing at an increasing (exponential) rate.
b) The burning of fossil fuels for energy.
c) The average temperature is increasing.

Page 52 — Water Pollution

Q1 E.g. any four of: Fertilisers / sewage / industrial chemicals / pesticides / acid rain / oil spills / metals.

Q2 1. Excess fertiliser washes off fields into rivers and streams.
2. The amounts of nitrates and phosphates in the water increases.
3. There's a rapid growth of plants and algae.
4. Plants die because they don't receive enough light.
5. Decomposers feed off the dead plants using up all the oxygen in the water.
6. Fish and other living organisms start to die.

Q3 DDT can't be broken down, so it remains in the bodies of organisms and is passed on to animals higher in the food chain when they feed.

Q4a) An indirect measure.
b) Collect samples of the same size, in the same way, at the same time of day, etc.
c) Mayfly larvae prefer clean water and sludge worms prefer water that contains sewage.
d) E.g. Sewage is full of bacteria, which use up a lot of oxygen. Animals like mayfly larvae might not have enough oxygen to survive.

Page 53 — Pollution Indicators

Q1a) E.g. chemical test, satellite picture
b) E.g. any two of: weathering on rocks/buildings, visibility, melting ice

Q2a) air pollution
b) There are more lichen species further away from the town centre.
c) Lichen are sensitive to the levels of pollutants in the air. So it is likely that the air outside the town centre contains less pollutants.

Q3a) increased, decrease, less, more, air, destroy them
b) As the amount of ozone in the atmosphere decreases the number of skin cancer cases increases.
c) No, it doesn't. Something else could be causing the increase in the number of cases of skin cancer.

Section Five — Classifying Materials

Page 54 — Conservation and Recycling

Q1a) True
b) True
c) False
d) False
e) False

Q2 coppicing — cutting trees down to just above ground level
reforestation — replanting trees that have been cut down in the past
replacement planting — new trees are replanted at the same rate that others are cut down

Q3a) Recycling is when things are reprocessed to make new goods instead of being thrown away.
b) E.g. any three of: glass, paper, plastics, metal
c) less energy

Q4a) Decreasing the number of different species in an area.
b) E.g. we could miss out on things like new medicines, foods or fibres.

Q5 E.g. conservation measures may help protect our food supply for the future, e.g. fishing quotas. Recycling metals and paper means using less raw materials, cuts energy use and reduces pollution.

Page 55-56 — Mixed Questions — Section Four

Q1a) The lower side. Water is lost from the stomata, which are mainly found on the lower side of the leaf.
b) transpiration
c) from the soil
d) A lower light intensity / a lower temperature / less air movement / higher humidity.

Q2a) Gas A = carbon dioxide
Gas B = oxygen
b) As it gets lighter, the level of oxygen should increase as the plant will photosynthesise more and produce more oxygen. Carbon dioxide levels should decrease as light intensity increases, because the plant uses up carbon dioxide in photosynthesis.

Q3a) Farmers use pesticides to kill pest animals that damage their crops. They use fertilisers to put more nutrients into the soil. Both these things help them to have bigger crop yields.
b) Any three of: Fertilisers can pollute rivers and streams, causing eutrophication. Pesticides can kill harmless / beneficial species as well as pests. Food chains can be disrupted. Animals and birds at the top of food chains can be harmed — these might be rare or endangered species.
c) Any two sensible answers, for example: Organic farming does not use chemicals, so there is little risk to animals at the top of food chains. Organic farming does not disrupt food chains as much, so endangered species don't have their food sources taken away. Organic farming techniques allow a greater variety of plants and insects to live on the farm, including endangered species. There is less risk of eutrophication with organic farming, so rare aquatic creatures and water birds are less at risk.

Q4a) 500 – 250 – 150 = 100 kJ.
b) 150 – 75 – 20 = 55 kJ.
c) The pigs could be kept in small cages and crowded close together so that they're warm and can't move much. This means they will respire less, as they won't need to release as much energy for movement and for keeping warm.
d) The pigs could be missed out of the food chain and the barley eaten directly by the humans.

Q5a) Nitrogen-fixing bacteria turn atmospheric nitrogen gas into nitrogen compounds in the soil that plants can use. The legumes therefore put nitrogen back into the soil for the cereal crop to use.
b) Plants need nitrogen to make proteins for cell growth. If they don't have enough the plants will be stunted and will have yellow older leaves.

Q6a) More sewage means more nutrients for bacteria, so they reproduce rapidly near to the outflow pipe.
b) i) Sludgeworm
ii) Mayfly nymph

Section Five — Classifying Materials

Page 57 — Atoms

Q1a) neutral
b) ion
c) protons, electrons (in either order)
d) negatively

Q2

Particle	Mass	Charge
Proton	1	**+1**
Neutron	**1**	0
Electron	$\frac{1}{2000}$	–1

Q3a) nucleus
b) electron
c) electron
d) proton
e) neutron
f) proton

Q4a) The total number of protons and neutrons in an atom.
b) The number of protons in an atom.
c)

Element	Symbol	Mass Number	Number of Protons	Number of Electrons	Number of Neutrons
Sodium	Na	**23**	11	**11**	**12**
Oxygen	**O**	16	8	8	8
Neon	**Ne**	**20**	10	10	10
Calcium	Ca	**40**	**20**	20	20

Section Five — Classifying Materials

Page 58 — Elements, Compounds and Isotopes

Q1a) A = element; B = compound; C = element; D = compound
b) i) C
ii) A
iii) D
iv) B
Q2a) Compounds
b) completely different to
c) difficult
d) a compound, an element
e) electrons
Q3 Isotopes, element, protons, neutrons.
Q4 W and Y, because these two atoms have the same number of protons but a different mass number.
Q5 Yes. It's the number of electrons that determines the chemistry of an atom. Isotopes of an element have the same numbers of electrons.

Page 59 — The Periodic Table

Q1a) radon and krypton
b) sodium
c) nickel
d) iodine
e) silicon or iodine
Q2a) true
b) false
c) true
d) false
e) true
Q3a) The following should be ticked: **A** and **D**
b) Fluorine and chlorine are both in Group 7, so they both contain the same number of electrons in their outer shell. The properties of elements are decided by the number of electrons they have in their outer shell.
Q4

	Alternative Name for Group	Number of Electrons in Outer Shell
Group 1	Alkali metals	**1**
Group 7	**Halogens**	7
Group 0	**Noble gases / Inert gases**	**8**

Page 60 — Electron Shells

Q1a) true
b) false
c) false
d) true
e) false
Q2a) 2,2
b) 2,6
c) 2,8,4
d) 2,8,8,2
e) 2,8,3
f) 2,8,8
Q3a) Noble gases are unreactive elements because they have full outer shells of electrons.
b) Alkali metals are reactive elements, because they have an incomplete outer shell of electrons.

Q4a) 2,8,7
b)
c) It's outer shell isn't full (it's keen to get an extra electron).
Q5

Page 61 — Ionic Bonding

Q1a) Group 1
b) 1
c) +1
d) NaCl
Q2a) 2
b) 2
c)

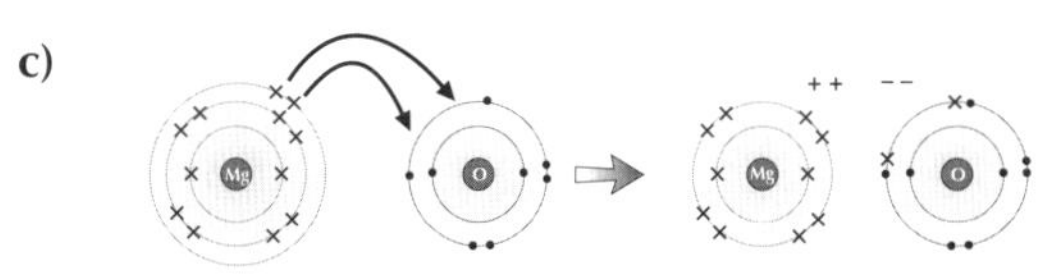

d) MgO
e) giant ionic
Q3a) strong, positive, negative, large
b) i)

	Conducts electricity?
When solid	No
When dissolved in water	Yes
When molten	Yes

ii) When solid, the ions are held tightly in a giant ionic structure (so they're unable to move and conduct electricity). When dissolved or molten, the ions are free to move and so can conduct electricity.

Page 62 — Electron Shells and Ions

Q1a) ions
b) readily
c) rarely
d) cations
Q2a) i) 1
ii) 2
iii) 1
b) i) 2
ii) 1
iii) 1
Q3a)

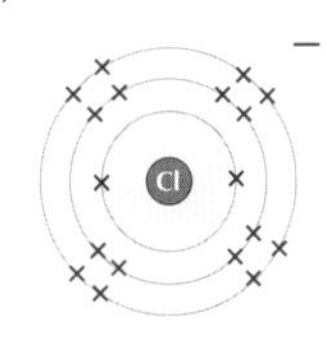

Cl [2,8,8]$^-$

Section Five — Classifying Materials

b)

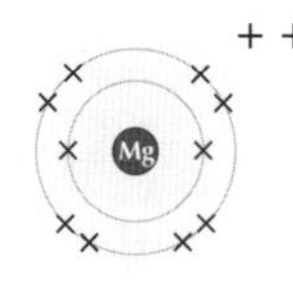

Mg $[2,8]^{++}$

c)

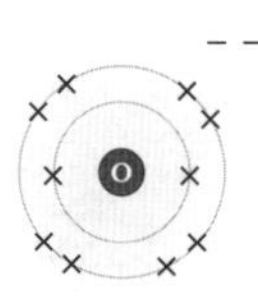

O $[2,8]^{--}$

Q4a) $[2,8,8]^{+}$
b) $[2,8,8]^{++}$
c) $[2,8]^{-}$
d) $[2]^{++}$

Page 63 — Reactivity Trends

Q1a)

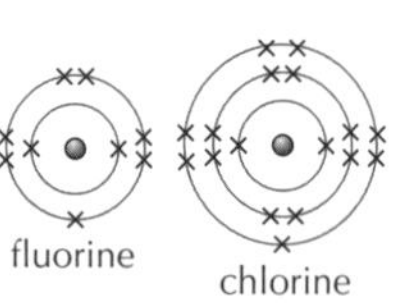

b) Similarity: E.g. they both have 7 electrons in their outer shell.
Difference: chlorine has one more full shell that fluorine does.
c) They gain one more outer electron so that they have a full outer shell.
d) Fluorine, because it gains an electron more easily — chlorine's outer shell is further from the nucleus and more shielded, so it's harder for the positive nucleus to pull an electron in.
Q2a) They lose their single outer electron, leaving them with only full shells.
b) (Least) lithium, sodium, potassium (most).
c) Reactivity increases because the outer electron is more easily lost because it is further from the nucleus and is more shielded from the positive nuclear charge.
Q3a)

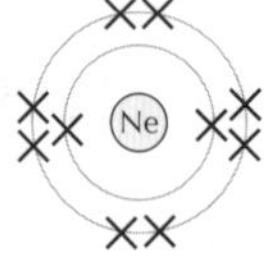

b) It has a full outer shell of electrons.

Page 64 — Covalent Bonding

Q1a) true
b) true
c) true
d) false
e) true
Q2

Atom	Carbon	Chlorine	Hydrogen	Nitrogen	Oxygen
Number of electrons needed to fill outer shell	4	1	1	3	2

Q3a)

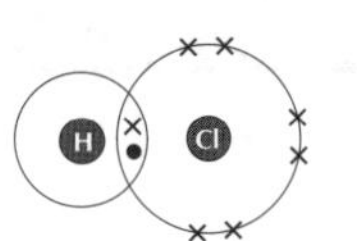

b)

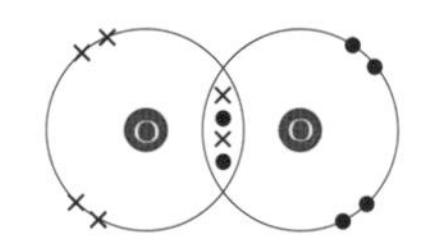

c)

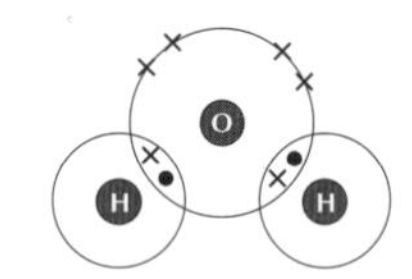

d)

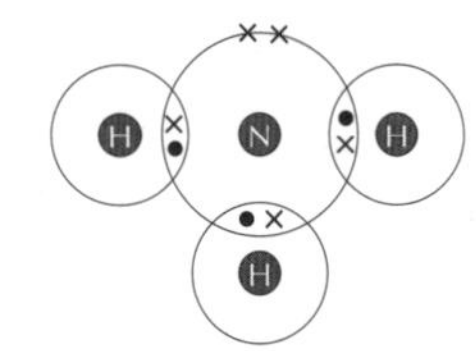

e)

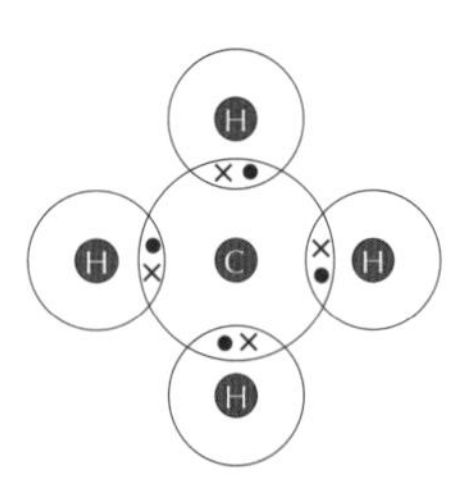

Q4 Sharing electrons allows both atoms to achieve the stable 'full outer shell' of electrons.

Page 65 — Covalent Substances: Two Kinds

Q1 Diamond — I am used in jewellery; I am the hardest natural substance; My carbon atoms form four covalent bonds.
Graphite — I have layers which move over one another; I am used in pencils; I am the only non-metal which is a good conductor of electricity; My carbon atoms form three covalent bonds.
Silicon dioxide — I am used to make glass; Sand is made from me; I am not made from carbon.
Q2 uncharged atoms, strong, high, don't, insoluble
Q3 Any two of: low melting point; low boiling point; usually a gas/liquid at room temperature; doesn't conduct electricity.
Q4a) Each carbon atom in graphite only forms three covalent bonds. This leaves free electrons to carry electricity.
b) Each carbon atom forms four covalent bonds in a very rigid giant covalent structure.

Page 66 — Molecular Substances: The Halogens

Q1 Chlorine — dense green gas.
Iodine — dark grey solid.
Bromine — orange liquid.

Section Five — Classifying Materials

Q2a) False
b) True
c) False
d) True
Q3 The halogen atoms (and molecules) get bigger down the group. Larger molecules have stronger intermolecular forces of attraction. More energy is needed to overcome stronger forces, so the melting and boiling points increase.
Q4a) Bromine is more reactive than iodine so displaces it from the potassium iodide solution. Bromine is less reactive than chlorine so doesn't displace it from the potassium chloride solution.
b) $Br_2(aq) + 2KI(aq) \rightarrow I_2(aq) + 2KBr(aq)$
Q5a) sodium bromide
b) $2Na(s) + Br_2(g) \rightarrow 2NaBr(s)$

Page 67 — Metallic Structures

Q1

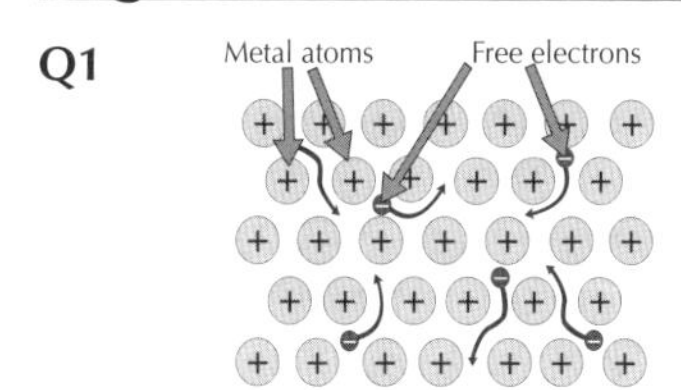

Q2 Metals contain free electrons which transfer heat and move under the influence of a voltage.
Q3a) iron, nickel, vanadium, copper, manganese
b) E.g. Iron — ammonia production.
Nickel — hydrogenation of oils (converting natural oils into fats).
Q4a) They heat up, which means some of the electrical energy is wasted as heat.
b) A superconductor is a material that has no electrical resistance. You can make some metals superconduct by cooling them to very low temperatures.
Q5a) Any 2 of, e.g.
Power cables that transmit electricity without losing power; electromagnets that don't need a power source; very fast-working electronic circuits.
b) The temperatures that the superconductors have to reach before they superconduct are extremely low, and therefore very expensive to produce.

Page 68 — New Materials

Q1a) C_{60}
b) 3
c) Yes, each carbon atom only forms three covalent bonds, leaving free electrons that can conduct electricity.
Q2a) Materials that behave differently depending on the conditions.
b) dyes, temperature, liquids, solid, contract
c) It remembers its original shape — so if you bend it too far, you can heat it and it goes back to its 'remembered' shape.
Q3a) 1 ÷ 0.000 001 = **1 000 000**
b) They have a huge surface area, so individual catalyst molecules could be attached to carbon nanoparticles (or nanotubes). This gives the catalyst an increased surface area, making it more effective.
c) Building a product molecule-by-molecule either by positioning each molecule exactly where you want it or by starting with a bigger structure and taking bits off it.
d) Any 2 of, e.g.
reinforcing tennis rackets; making stronger, lighter building materials; as conductors in electric circuits.

Pages 69-70 — Mixed Questions — Section Five

Q1 a) R = graphite; S = diamond; T = buckminsterfullerene
b) i) R: D; S: B
ii) giant ionic
iii) C — it has a low boiling point and is a non-conductor.
Q2a) Ca atom: [2,8,8,2]
Ca^{2+} ion: $[2,8,8]^{++}$
b) 20
c) Any of: beryllium, magnesium, strontium, barium, radium.
Q3a)

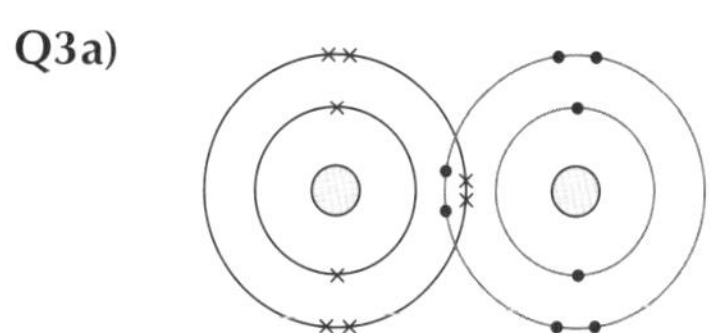

b) A single covalent bond is where each of the atoms involved in the bond donates one electron to a shared pair.
Q4a)

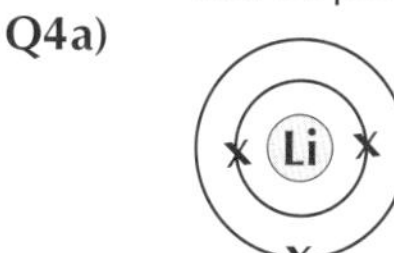

b) Lithium forms ions by losing its outer electron to give an ion with a full outer shell and a charge of +1.
c) i) Two or more elements chemically joined together.
ii) LiF
iii) Nothing would happen. Chlorine is less reactive than fluorine so would not displace it.
d) i) Faster. Bromine is less reactive than fluorine. This is because its extra shells of electrons provide more shielding and its outer shell is further from the nucleus. This makes it harder for it to gain an electron.
ii) Slower. Sodium is more reactive than lithium. This is because its extra shell of electrons provides more shielding and its outer shell is further from the nucleus. This makes it easier for it to lose an electron.
Q5a) They have no resistance, so when electricity flows through them none is wasted as heat.
b) E.g. two from: very strong, very tiny, conduct electricity.

Section Six — Equations and Calculations

c) i) titanium and nickel
ii) transition metals

Section Six — Equations and Calculations

Page 71 — Balancing Equations

Q1a) Li^+
b) O^{2-}
c) Fe^{3+}
d) Cl^-
Q2a) CH_4
b) $AgNO_3$
c) Li_2O
d) Na_2CO_3
e) KOH
f) $AlCl_3$
Q3a) The reactants are methane and oxygen and the products, are carbon dioxide and water.
b) Methane + oxygen → carbon dioxide + water
c) $CH_4 + 2O_2 \rightarrow CO_2 + 2H_2O$
Q4a) $CuO + \mathbf{2}\ HBr \rightarrow CuBr_2 + H_2O$
b) $H_2 + Br_2 \rightarrow \mathbf{2}\ HBr$
c) $\mathbf{2}\ Mg + O_2 \rightarrow 2MgO$
d) $2NaOH + H_2SO_4 \rightarrow Na_2SO_4 + \mathbf{2}\ H_2O$
Q5a) $\mathbf{3}\ NaOH + AlBr_3 \rightarrow \mathbf{3}\ NaBr + Al(OH)_3$
b) $\mathbf{2}\ FeCl_2 + Cl_2 \rightarrow \mathbf{2}\ FeCl_3$
c) $N_2 + \mathbf{3}\ H_2 \rightarrow \mathbf{2}\ NH_3$
d) $\mathbf{4}\ Fe + \mathbf{3}\ O_2 \rightarrow \mathbf{2}\ Fe_2O_3$
e) $\mathbf{4}\ NH_3 + \mathbf{5}\ O_2 \rightarrow \mathbf{4}\ NO + \mathbf{6}\ H_2O$

Page 72 — Relative Formula Mass

Q1a) How heavy (or how massive) an atom of an element is compared to an atom of carbon-12.
b) i) 24
ii) 20
iii) 16
iv) 1
v) 12
vi) 64
vii) 39
viii) 40
ix) 35.5
Q2 Element A is helium
Element B is (3 × 4) = 12 = carbon
Element C is (4 × 4) = 16 = oxygen
Q3a) You add the relative atomic masses of all the atoms in (the formula of) the compound together.
b) i) (2 × 1) + 16 = 18
ii) 39 + 16 + 1 = 56
iii) 1 + 14 + (3 × 16) = 63
iv) (2 × 1) + 32 + (4 × 16) = 98
v) 14 + (4 × 1) + 14 + (3 × 16) = 80
Q4 $2XOH + H_2 = 114$
2 × (X + 16 + 1) + (2 × 1) = 114
2 × (X + 17) + 2 = 114
2 × (X + 17) = 112
X + 17 = 56
X = 39
so X = potassium

Page 73 — Two Formula Mass Calculations

Q1a) Percentage mass of an element in a compound = $\frac{A_r \times \text{No. of atoms (of that element)}}{M_r \text{ (of whole compound)}} \times 100$
b) i) (14 × 2) ÷ [14 + (4 × 1) + 14 + (3 × 16)] × 100 = 35%
ii) (4 × 1) ÷ [14 + (4 × 1) + 14 + (3 × 16)] × 100 = 5%
iii) (3 × 16) ÷ [14 + (4 × 1) + 14 + (3 × 16)] × 100 = 60%
Q2a) 14 ÷ (14 + 16) × 100 = 47% or 46.7%
b)

	Nitrogen	Oxygen
Percentage mass (%)	30.4	69.6
$\div A_r$	(30.4 ÷ 14) = 2.17	(69.6 ÷ 16) = 4.35
Ratio	1	2

empirical formula = NO_2

Q3

	Calcium	Oxygen	Hydrogen
Mass (g)	0.8	0.64	0.04
$\div A_r$	(0.8 ÷ 40) = 0.02	(0.64 ÷ 16) = 0.04	(0.04 ÷ 1) = 0.04
Ratio	1	2	2

empirical formula = $Ca(OH)_2$ (or CaO_2H_2)

Q4a) A = (3 × 16) ÷ [(2 × 56) + (3 × 16)] × 100 = 30%
B = 16 ÷ [(2 × 1) + 16)] × 100 = 89% or 88.9%
C = (3 × 16) ÷ [40 + 12 + (3 × 16)] × 100 = 48%
b) B

Page 74 — Calculating Masses in Reactions

Q1a) $2Mg + O_2 \rightarrow 2MgO$
b) 2Mg | 2MgO
2 × 24 = 48 | 2 × (24 + 16) = 80
48 ÷ 48 = 1 g | 80 ÷ 48 = 1.67 g
1 × 10 = 10 g | 1.67 × 10 = **16.7 g**
Q2 4Na | $2Na_2O$
4 × 23 = 92 | 2 × [(2 × 23) + 16] = 124
92 ÷ 124 = 0.74 g | 124 ÷ 124 = 1 g
0.74 × 2 = **1.5 g** | 1 × 2 = 2 g
Q3a) $2Al + Fe_2O_3 \rightarrow Al_2O_3 + 2Fe$
b) Fe_2O_3 | 2Fe
[(2 × 56) + (3 × 16)] = 160 | 2 × 56 = 112
160 ÷ 160 = 1 g | 112 ÷ 160 = 0.7
1 × 20 = 20 g | 0.7 × 20 = **14 g**
Q4 $CaCO_3 \rightarrow CaO + CO_2$
$CaCO_3$ | CaO
40 + 12 + (3 × 16) = 100 | 40 + 16 = 56
100 ÷ 56 = 1.786 kg | 56 ÷ 56 = 1 kg
1.786 × 100 = **178.6 kg** | 1 × 100 = 100 kg

Page 75 — The Mole

Q1a) mass, relative formula mass
b) i) 20 ÷ 40 = 0.5 moles
ii) 112 ÷ 32 = 3.5 moles
iii) 200 ÷ (64 + 16) = 2.5 moles
c) i) 2 × 23 = 46 g
ii) 0.75 × (24 + 16) = 30 g
Q2a) 4.5 × 24 = 108 litres

Section Seven — Industrial Chemistry

b) $0.48 \times 24 = 11.52$ litres

Q3a) i) $2 \times 0.05 = 0.1$ moles

ii) $0.5 \times 0.25 = 0.125$ moles

b) moles per litre = no. of moles ÷ volume
$= 0.25 \div 0.2$
$= 1.25$ M

c) volume = no. of moles ÷ moles per litre
$= 2 \div 1.5$
$= 1.33$ litres

Q4a) $Mg + H_2SO_4 \rightarrow MgSO_4 + H_2$

b) number of moles of magnesium $= 0.6 \div 24 = 0.025$
number of moles of hydrogen produced = 0.025
volume of hydrogen produced $= 0.025 \times 24 = 0.6$ litres

c) number of moles of $MgSO_4$ formed = 0.025
$0.025 \times [24 + 32 + (16 \times 4)] = 3$ g

Page 76 — Atom Economy

Q1a) copper

b) M_r CuO $= 64 + 16 = 80$
$(2 \times 64) \div [(2 \times 80) + 12] \times 100 = 74\%$ or 74.4%

c) $100 - 74 = 26\%$ or 25.6%

Q2a) Reactions with a high atom economy use up resources less rapidly and produce less waste. This lowers the cost of disposing of the waste safely, and is cheaper as the resources can often be very expensive. This all means a higher profit.

b) Reactions that only have one product, e.g. the Haber process.

Q3a) M_r $TiCl_4 = (48 + (4 \times 35.5) = 190$
With magnesium: $48 \div [190 + (2 \times 24)] \times 100 = 20.2\%$
With sodium: $48 \div [190 + (4 \times 23)] \times 100 = 17.0\%$

b) The reaction with magnesium has the better atom economy.

Q4 $Cr_2O_3 + 2Al \rightarrow Al_2O_3 + 2Cr$
M_r $Cr_2O_3 = (2 \times 52) + (3 \times 16) = 152$
$(2 \times 52) \div [152 + (2 \times 27)] \times 100 = 50.5\%$

Page 77 — Percentage Yield

Q1a) percentage yield $= \dfrac{\text{actual yield}}{\text{predicted yield}} \times 100$

b) $1.2 \div 2.7 \times 100 = 44.4\%$

Q2a) Not all the reactants are turned into products.

b) Some of the liquid remains with the solid and filter paper, and in the original container.

c) Some of the liquid remains on the inside surface of the old container.

d) The reactants form an unexpected product.

Q3a) $6 \div 15 \times 100 = 40\%$

b) E.g. When they transferred the solid to a clean piece of filter paper, some of the solid would have remained on the filter paper; some of the solid may have remained in the liquid during filtration.

Pages 78-79 — Mixed Questions — Section Six

Q1 The third equation should be circled.

Q2a) no. of moles = mass ÷ A_r
$= 13 \div 65$
$= 0.2$ moles

b) $2 \times 0.2 = 0.4$ moles

Q3a)

C	2CO
12	$2 \times (12 + 16) = 56$
$12 \div 12 = 1$ g	$56 \div 12 = 4.67$ g
$1 \times 10 = 10$ g	$4.67 \times 10 = 46.7$ g

46.7 g of CO is produced in stage B — all this is used in stage C.

3CO	$3CO_2$
$3 \times (12 + 16) = 84$	$3 \times [12 + (2 \times 16)] = 132$
$84 \div 84 = 1$ g	$132 \div 84 = 1.57$ g
$1 \times 46.7 = 46.7$ g	$1.57 \times 46.7 =$ **73.3 g**

b) It could be recycled and used in stage B.

Q4a) $2NaOH + H_2SO_4 \rightarrow Na_2SO_4 + 2H_2O$

b)

2NaOH	Na_2SO_4
$2 \times (23 + 16 + 1) = 80$	$(2 \times 23) + 32 + (4 \times 16) = 142$
$80 \div 142 = 0.563$ g	$142 \div 142 = 1$ g
$0.563 \times 75 =$ **42.3 g**	$1 \times 75 = 75$ g

c) M_r $Na_2SO_4 = (23 \times 2) + 32 + (16 \times 4) = 142$
M_r $2NaOH + H_2SO_4 = 2(23 + 16 + 1) + (1 \times 2) + 32 + (16 \times 4) = 178$
atom economy $= (142 \div 178) \times 100 =$ **80%** or **79.8%**

Q5a)

	Silicon	Chlorine
Mass (g)	1.4	7.1
$\div A_r$	$(1.4 \div 28) = 0.05$	$(7.1 \div 35.5) = 0.2$
Ratio	1	4

Empirical formula = $\mathbf{SiCl_4}$

b) $(35.5 \times 4) \div [(35.5 \times 4) + 28] \times 100 =$ **83.5%**

c) number of moles of $Cl_2 = 7.1 \div (35.5 \times 2) = 0.1$
volume $= 0.1 \times 24 = 2.4$ litres

d) $Si + 2Cl_2 \rightarrow SiCl_4$

e) i) $6.5 \div 8.5 \times 100 = 76\%$ or 76.5%

ii) E.g. some product was lost when liquid was transferred between containers. Unexpected reactions took place.

f) Yes, there's only one product, so the atom economy is 100%.

Q6a) $24 + [2 \times (14 + 16 \times 3)] = 148$

b) i) Mg: $0.12 \div 24 = 0.005$ mol
$Mg(NO_3)_2$: $0.74 \div 148 = 0.005$ mol

ii) $0.005 \div 0.2 = 0.025$ mol/dm^3

c) $0.025 \times [1 + 14 + (16 \times 3)] = 1.575$ g

Section Seven — Industrial Chemistry

Page 80 — Rates of Reaction

Q1a) higher

b) lower

c) gases, faster

Section Seven — Industrial Chemistry

d) increases
e) isn't
Q2a) i) Z
ii) It has the steepest initial gradient.
b) So that all the marble reacts/is used up.
c) Equal masses of marble chips were used each time.
d) The curve should be steeper and show that a larger volume of gas is produced, e.g. like this:

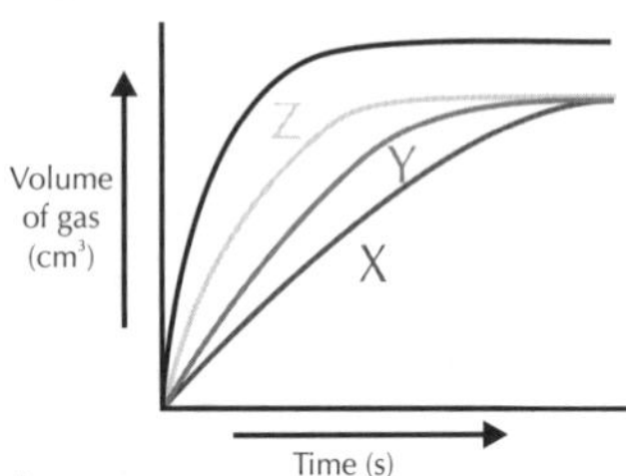

Q3a) decrease
b) More reactant(s) was used.
c) The reactants in Q might be in smaller pieces/ have a larger surface area/be more concentrated/ be at a higher temperature. OR A catalyst/more catalyst could have been used in Q.

Page 81 — Measuring Rates of Reaction

Q1a) 94
64
45.5
35
9
b) 50 in the third column of the table should be circled.
c) 2 mol/dm^3
d) i) Gas syringe
ii) Stopwatch/stopclock/timer/balance/measuring cylinder
e) Sketch should look something like this:

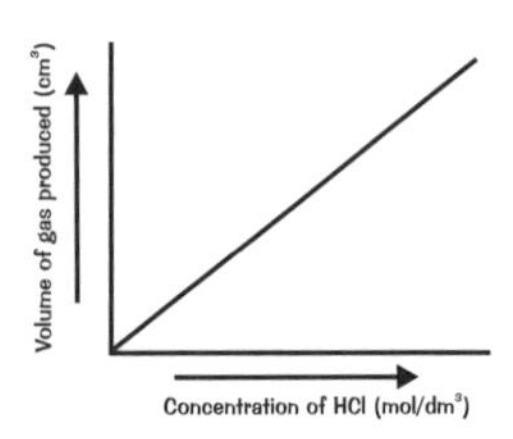

f) To improve the reliability of the results
g) For example, bad experimental technique, e.g. misreading the value from the gas syringe, not emptying the gas syringe before starting.
h) Any 2 reasonable suggestions, e.g. take more readings for each concentration, use more concentrations, improve dilution technique.

Page 82 — Collision Theory

Q1 increasing the temperature — makes the particles move faster, so they collide more often
decreasing the concentration — means fewer particles of reactant are present, so fewer collisions occur
adding a catalyst — provides a surface for particles to stick to and lowers the activation energy
increasing the surface area — gives particles a bigger area of solid reactant to react with
Q2a) energy
b) faster, more
c) rate of reaction.
Q3a) i) increase
ii) The particles are closer together so there's more chance of successful collisions.
b)

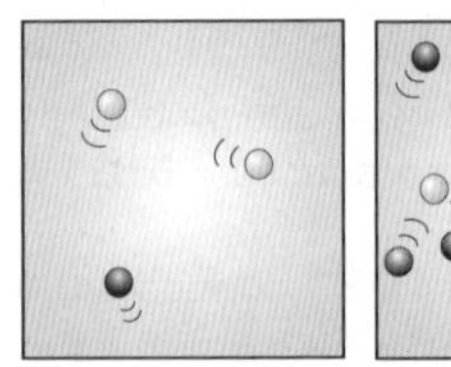
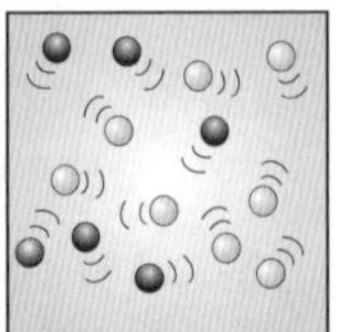

Q4a) False
b) True
c) False
d) True
Q5 Increase

Page 83 — Catalysts

Q1a) activation energy
b) A
c)

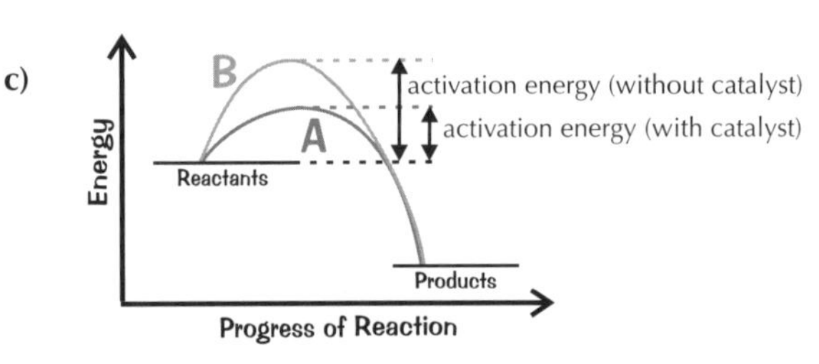

Q2a) E.g. powder
b) To give them a large surface area.
c) They increase the number of successful collisions by lowering the activation energy, e.g. by giving the reacting particles a surface to stick to.
d) E.g. They can be expensive to buy, they need to be removed and cleaned, they can be poisoned by impurities and stop working.
Q3a) Transition metals.
b) e.g. nickel is used for cracking hydrocarbons, iron is used in the Haber process.
Q4 CO reacts very slowly with air to form CO_2. Before this happens it can be inhaled by people. The catalyst speeds up the reaction so most of the CO is converted to CO_2 before the gases even pass out of the exhaust.

Page 84 — Energy Transfer in Reactions

Q1 give out, heat, rise, temperature
Q2a) N, B, N, B.
b) combustion
c) methane + oxygen → carbon dioxide + water
or ethanol + oxygen → carbon dioxide + water

Section Seven — Industrial Chemistry

Q3 E.g. take in, heat, fall/decrease/drop, temperature.

Q4a) $CaCO_3 \rightarrow CaO + CO_2$

b) i) endothermic

ii) Because the reaction takes in heat.

c) i) 1 800 000 ÷ 1000 = 1800 kJ

ii) 90 000 ÷ 1 800 000 = 0.05 tonnes or 50 kg

Page 85 — Reversible Reactions

Q1a) products, react, reactants

b) balance

c) closed, escape

Q2a) i) A, B

ii) AB

b) i) Y

ii) X

c) $A + B \rightleftharpoons AB$

d) At the same rate.

Q3a) i) Forward, because there are three molecules on the left-hand side of the equation and only two molecules on the right-hand side of the equation.

ii) It will move it to the right / increase the amount of SO_3 produced.

b) B

Page 86 — The Haber Process

Q1a) i) Nitrogen and hydrogen.

ii) The left-hand side.

b) E.g. fertiliser / explosives / dyestuffs

Q2a) 200 atmospheres, 450 °C.

b) 1. High enough to give a good % yield.
2. Not so high that the plant becomes too expensive to build.

Q3a) This will move the position of equilibrium to the left.

b) To increase the rate of reaction.

c) They are recycled.

Q4a) It has no effect on % yield.

b) It would make it cheaper to produce. Ammonia can be made more quickly, meaning lower running costs for the same amount of ammonia produced.

Page 87 — Acids and Alkalis

Q1a) acid + base → **salt** + **water**

b) neutralisation

Q2a) Test the acid solution with universal indicator or a pH meter.

b) Baking soda or soap powder, because they are weak bases and so would neutralise the acid but would be unlikely to irritate or harm the skin. (Stronger bases like caustic soda might damage the skin.)

Q3a) i)

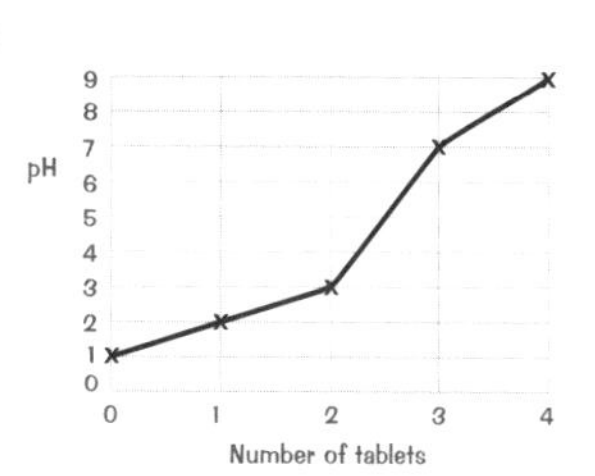

ii) The pH increases from pH 1 to pH 9. It increases most sharply between pH 3 and pH 7.

iii) 3

b) E.g. the new line should be above the previous one and reach pH 7 at 2 tablets.

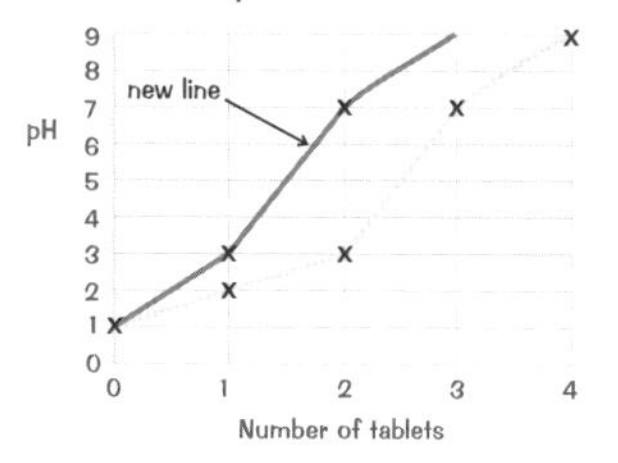

Page 88 — Acids Reacting with Metals

Q1a)

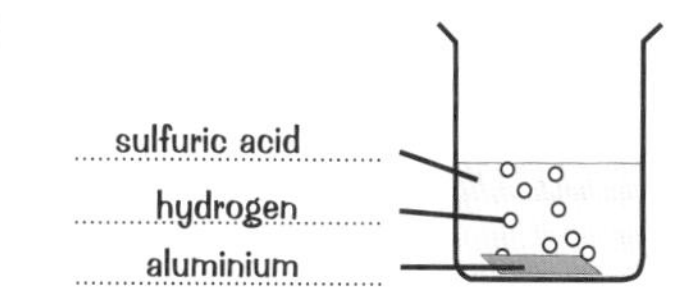

b) aluminium + **sulfuric acid** → aluminium sulfate + **hydrogen**

c) $\mathbf{2Al + 3H_2SO_4 \rightarrow Al_2(SO_4)_3 + 3H_2}$

Q2 metals, hydrogen, silver, reactive, more, chlorides, sulfuric, nitric.

Q3a) i) $Ca + \mathbf{2}HCl \rightarrow CaCl_2 + H_2$

ii) $\mathbf{2}Na + \mathbf{2}HCl \rightarrow \mathbf{2}NaCl + H_2$

iii) $\mathbf{2}Li + H_2SO_4 \rightarrow Li_2SO_4 + H_2$

b) i) magnesium bromide

ii) $2Al + 6HBr \rightarrow 2AlBr_3 + 3H_2$

Page 89 — Neutralisation Reactions

Q1a) hydrochloric acid + lead oxide → **lead** chloride + water

b) nitric acid + copper hydroxide → copper **nitrate** + water

c) sulfuric acid + zinc oxide → zinc sulfate + **water**

d) hydrochloric acid + **nickel** oxide → nickel **chloride** + **water**

e) **nitric** acid + copper oxide → **copper** nitrate + **water**

Q2a) i) $\mathbf{2}HCl + CaCO_3 \rightarrow CaCl_2 + \mathbf{H_2O} + CO_2$

ii) $H_2SO_4 + \mathbf{Na_2CO_3} \rightarrow Na_2SO_4 + \mathbf{H_2O} + \mathbf{CO_2}$

iii) $\mathbf{2HNO_3} + \mathbf{CaCO_3} \rightarrow Ca(NO_3)_2 + H_2O + CO_2$

iv) $\mathbf{2HCl} + Na_2CO_3 \rightarrow \mathbf{2}NaCl + \mathbf{H_2O} + \mathbf{CO_2}$

b) Bubble the gas through **limewater**. If the gas is carbon dioxide then the limewater will become **milky**.

Q3a) gas, alkaline, nitrogen, proteins, salts, fertilisers

b) ammonia + nitric acid → ammonium nitrate

c) Because it has nitrogen from two sources, the ammonia and the nitric acid.

Section Seven — Industrial Chemistry

Page 90 — Making Salts

Q1a) soluble
b) insoluble
c) insoluble, neutralised
d) precipitation
e) more, less
Q2a) B
b) A
c) D
d) C
Q3a) 1. The nickel carbonate no longer dissolves / solid remains in the flask.
2. Bubbles no longer form.
b)

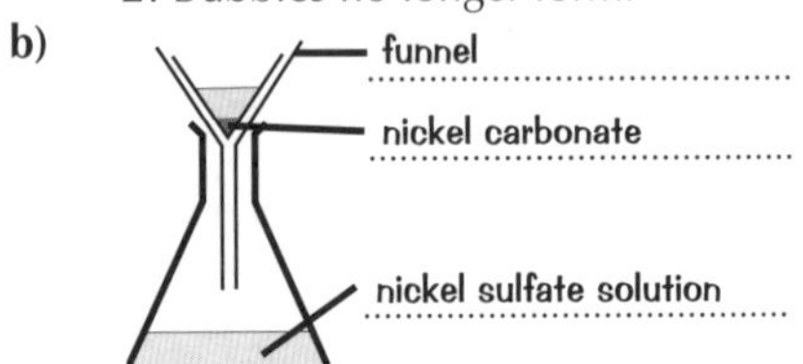

c) filtration
d) Heat the nickel sulfate solution to evaporate off the water.

Page 91 — Electrolysis and the Half-Equations

Q1 For electricity to flow, charged ions need to be free to move, and so you need a liquid.
Q2a) A: H^+
B: Cl^-
C: H_2
D: Cl_2
b) Cathode: $2H^+ + 2e^- \rightarrow H_2$
Anode: $2Cl^- \rightarrow Cl_2 + 2e^-$
Q3a) It could be melted.
b) Cathode: $Pb^{2+} + 2e^- \rightarrow Pb$
Anode: $2Br^- \rightarrow Br_2 + 2e^-$
Q4a) Chlorine gas was produced in the experiment, and it is also used in solution to kill bacteria in swimming pools.
b) Chlorine gas is toxic.
c) E.g. The experiment should be carried out in a fume cupboard / The lab should be checked to make sure it is well ventilated.

Page 92 — Crude Oil

Q1 E.g. Most technology around today is set up to use crude oil fractions as fuel and converting to alternatives would be time-consuming and costly. We need more energy than can currently be created using alternatives alone. We're simply not ready to stop using crude oil as our main source of fuel.
Q2a) E.g. any 3 of: plastics, paints, medicines, solvents, detergents, etc.
b) They form four covalent bonds.
Q3a) Cracking takes excess long-chain hydrocarbons (which aren't very useful) and turns them into shorter molecules, useful for fuels and making plastics.
b) Breaking down molecules by heating them.
c) i) $C_{12}H_{26} \rightarrow C_8H_{18} + 2C_2H_4$
ii) The alkenes.

Page 93 — Alkanes and Alkenes

Q1a) i) A saturated hydrocarbon contains only single covalent bonds.
ii) An unsaturated hydrocarbon contains at least one double (or triple) covalent bond.
b)

```
   H H
   | |
 H-C-C-H
   | |
   H H
```

c)

```
 H     H
  \   /
   C=C
  /   \
 H     H
```

d) Shake a sample of each with a few drops of bromine water. Result for ethane — bromine water remains unchanged. Result for ethene — bromine water is decolourised.
Q2a) C_5H_{10}
b) C_7H_{16}
c) C_8H_{16}
d) C_5H_{12}
e) C_6H_{12}
f) $C_{10}H_{22}$
g) C_9H_{20}
h) $C_{12}H_{24}$
Q3a) hydration
b) $C_2H_4 + H_2O \rightarrow C_2H_5OH$
c) The following should be circled: high pressure, 300 °C, phosphoric acid catalyst.

Page 94 — Vegetable Oils

Q1 Saturated animal fat — bottom diagram
Polyunsaturated grape seed oil — top diagram
Monounsaturated olive oil — middle diagram
Q2a) Reaction with hydrogen with a nickel catalyst at about
60 °C. The double bonds open up and bond to the hydrogen atoms.
b) It increases the melting points of vegetable oils.
c) A double bond makes a kink in the carbon chain. Straight chains fit together better than kinked ones, so the bonds between them are stronger, giving a higher melting point. (Partial hydrogenation also leaves
trans-fats.)
Q3 Spread A. It contains mainly polyunsaturated fats, which tend to lower blood cholesterol. It also has less saturated (and trans) fat which tend to increase blood cholesterol.

Section Seven — Industrial Chemistry

Page 95 — Plastics

Q1

$$n\begin{pmatrix} H & & H \\ & C{=}C & \\ H & & Cl \end{pmatrix} \longrightarrow \left(\begin{matrix} H & H \\ -C- & C- \\ H & Cl \end{matrix}\right)_n$$

Q2a) E.g. plastics do not biodegrade, so they will just fill up the landfill sites rather than decay away.
b) When you burn plastic, toxic fumes are given off.
c) Plastics need to be sorted by type before they can be recycled.
Q3a) Ruler 2
b) The forces between the polymer chains are weaker in Ruler 1 — there are fewer cross-links which allows the long chains of atoms to slide over one another and to separate more easily.

Page 96 — Chemical Production

Q1a) batch production
b) continuous production
c) continuous production
d) batch production
Q2a) large-scale, highly automated, low, high, low
b) E.g. Any two of: It can be expensive to build the plant. It needs to be run at full capacity to be cost-effective. It only makes one product.
c) They are specialist chemicals, so they are complicated to make and there's relatively low demand for them.
Q3a) Step A: Crush the plant.
Step B: Dissolve it in a suitable solvent.
Step C: Extract the substance using chromatography.
b) i) For: e.g. It helps to make sure the drug isn't dangerous before being given to humans.
Against: e.g. Animals may suffer in the trials. / Animal tests may not be accurate.
ii) To prove that the drug works on humans, and to find how effective it is and if there are any side effects. / Drugs may have different effects on humans than they do in animals.

Page 97 — Detergents and Dry-Cleaning

Q1 solvent — A liquid that can dissolve a substance.
solution — A liquid mixture made from dissolving one substance in another.
solute — A substance that's dissolved in a liquid.
Q2a) hydrophilic → ○〰〰 ← hydrophobic
b) i) the hydrophilic head
ii) the hydrophobic tail
Q3 dissolve, grease, intermolecular, water, pull
Q4a) Washing powder A
b) Washing powders A and E — they don't work as well at higher temperatures.

Pages 98-99 — Water Purity

Q1a) aquifers
b) E.g. as a coolant, raw material, solvent.
Q2a) E.g. repair pipes to prevent leaks / install water meters where possible
b) E.g. do not waste water at home (various methods) / install a water butt to collect rainwater for garden use
Q3a) 1. Filtration through a wire mesh
2. Filtration through sand beds
3. Sedimentation
4. Chlorination
b) Mesh filtration removes large solids, whilst sand filtration removes smaller solids.
c) E.g. iron sulfate, aluminium sulfate
d) Ammonium nitrate dissolves in water.
e) Chlorine gas is bubbled through to kill bacteria.
Q4a) Lead compounds from old lead pipes.
b) Nitrate residues from fertiliser run-off. Pesticide residues from spraying too near rivers/the reservoir.
Q5a) A reaction between two chemicals in solution that produces an insoluble solid.
b) sodium sulfate + barium chloride → barium **sulfate + sodium chloride**
c) $K_2SO_4 + \mathbf{BaCl_2} \rightarrow \mathbf{BaSO_4} + 2KCl$
Q6a)

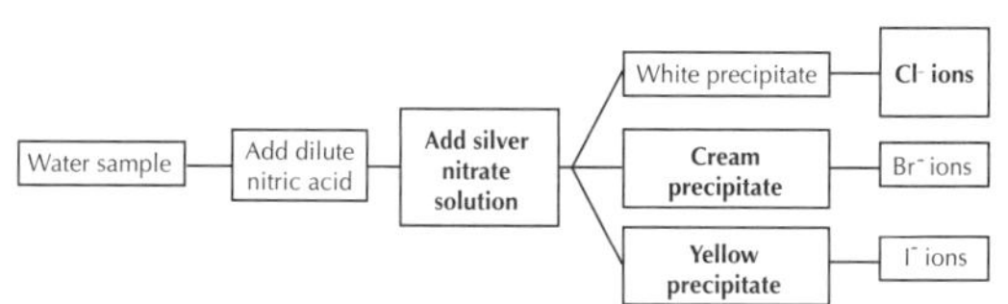

b) i) $AgNO_3 + KCl \rightarrow \mathbf{AgCl} + KNO_3$
ii) $\mathbf{AgNO_3} + \mathbf{NaI} \rightarrow AgI + NaNO_3$
iii) $Ag^+ + Br^- \rightarrow \mathbf{AgBr}$
Q7a) Dirty water can carry dangerous microbes that cause diseases like cholera and dysentery.
b) E.g. their governments can give communities a clean water supply and teach people the skills to maintain it.
Q8a) E.g. Seawater is in plentiful supply. The water produced is pure and clean.
b) E.g. It is an energy-intensive and expensive process. Generating the required energy can cause pollution. For example, burning oil releases carbon dioxide, a greenhouse gas.

Pages 100-101 — Mixed Questions — Section Seven

Q1a) Increasing the temperature.
Increasing the concentration/pressure.
Adding a catalyst.
Increasing the surface area of solid reactants.
b) One factor should be explained in terms of collision theory: Increasing concentration or surface area increases the number of collisions. Adding a catalyst increases the number of successful collisions by lowering the activation energy. Increasing the temperature increases both the number and speed of collisions.

Section Eight — Forces and Motion

c) E.g. any 2 of: Measuring the change in mass of the reactants using a mass balance. Measuring the volume of gas given off with a gas syringe. Measuring the time it takes for a mark to disappear (precipitation reaction).

Q2a) $N_2 + 3H_2 \rightleftharpoons 2NH_3$

b) i) increase, lowering, lower

ii) This increases their surface area and so increases the rate of reaction.

c) decrease

Q3a) $Mg + \mathbf{2}HCl \rightarrow MgCl_2 + H_2$

b) The pH would increase / it would become less acidic, until it finally reached neutral pH / pH 7 (if there was enough magnesium).

c) Magnesium sulfate.

Q4a) i) They gain electrons to become aluminium atoms.

ii) $Al^{3+} + \mathbf{3e^-} \rightarrow \mathbf{Al}$

b) $2O^{2-} \rightarrow \mathbf{O_2} + \mathbf{2e^-}$

Q5a) E.g.

```
    H   H           H     H
    |   |            \   /
  H-C-C=C-H   or      C=C
    |  |             /   \
    H  H            H     CH3
```

b) An unsaturated hydrocarbon is one that contains at least one carbon-carbon double (or triple) bond.

c) i)

```
   / H    H \        / H  H \
   |  \  /  |        |  |  |  |
  n|  C=C   |  ---> -|--C--C--|-
   |  /  \  |        |  |  |  |
   \ H   CH3/        \ H  CH3 / n
```

ii) E.g. Plastics aren't biodegradable, so they don't break down in landfill. They shouldn't be burnt either, because that gives off toxic fumes.

Q6a) Solvent A — it dissolves more paint than the other solvents so is likely to form stronger intermolecular bonds.

b) Solvent C — it dissolves paint nearly as well as solvent A, but it's a lot cheaper.

Section Eight — Forces and Motion

Page 102 — Velocity and Acceleration

Q1 $\text{Speed} = \frac{\text{distance}}{\text{time}}$, so distance = speed × time = $3 \times 10^8 \times 1.3$ = 390 000 000 m. Dividing by 1000 gives **390 000 km** (3.9×10^5 km).

Q2a) Since the egg was dropped from rest, its change in speed is 80 m/s. Putting the numbers into the formula you get

$$\text{acceleration} = \frac{\text{change in velocity}}{\text{time}} = \frac{80}{8} = \mathbf{10\ m/s^2}.$$

b) Now rearrange the formula to get

$$\text{time} = \frac{\text{change in velocity}}{\text{acceleration}} = \frac{40}{10} = \mathbf{4\ s}.$$

Q3 First work out how fast the train is going in m/s — 12 km × 1000 = 12 000 m, 20 mins × 60 = 1200 s.

$$\text{Speed} = \frac{\text{distance}}{\text{time}} = \frac{12\ 000}{1200} = 10\ \text{m/s}.$$

The speed rules out **A** and **C**.

The train is travelling east so **E** is wrong. Velocity should have a direction so you can discount **B**. So the answer is **D**. The train's average speed is 10 m/s.

Q4 You need to find the total time it would take for each of the takeaways to reach the house.

Ludo's Pizza:

$$\text{Time for delivery} = \frac{\text{distance}}{\text{speed}} = \frac{6.5}{30} = 0.217\ \text{hours}.$$

Time taken to cook the food is 0.25 hours, so the total time is 0.47 hours.

Moonlight Indian Takeaway:

$$\text{Time for delivery} = \frac{\text{distance}}{\text{speed}} = \frac{4}{40} = 0.1\ \text{hours}.$$

Time taken to cook the food is 0.5 hours, so the total time is 0.6 hours.

So they should order from **Ludo's Pizza**.

Q5 Rearranging the formula for acceleration you get: change in velocity = acceleration × time = 2 × 4 = 8 m/s. Change in velocity = final velocity – initial velocity, so initial velocity = final velocity – change in velocity = 24 – 8 = **16 m/s**.

Page 103 — D-T and V-T Graphs

Q1a) 180 s (or 3 mins)

b) $\text{Speed} = \frac{\text{distance}}{\text{time}} = \frac{450}{180} = \mathbf{2.5\ m/s}.$

c) He runs there in half the time it took him to walk there — 90 s. See graph:

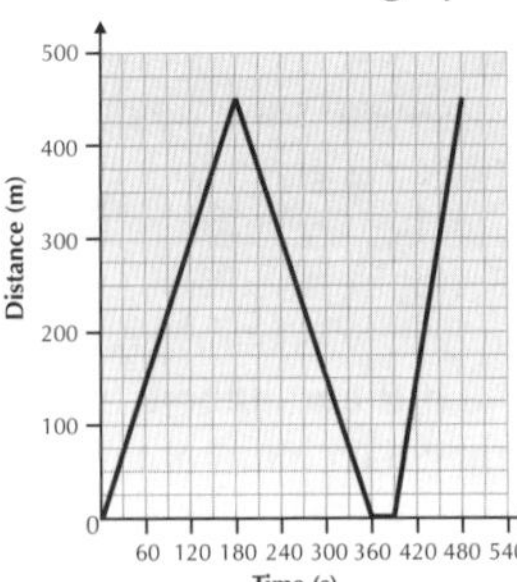

Q2 The graph shows that the motorist accelerates for about 1.5 seconds, then travels at a constant speed. So the gradient of the graph between 1.5 s and 3.0 s will give you the speed. Gradient = vertical change ÷ horizontal change = (72 – 18) ÷ (3.0 – 1.5) = 54 ÷ 1.5 = 36 m/s — i.e. she was exceeding the speed limit.
So the motorist wasn't telling the truth.

Q3 The distance the motorist travels before stopping is equal to the area under the graph. To find it, split the graph into a rectangle and a triangle. Area of the rectangle = base × height = 0.75 × 12 = 9 m. Area of the triangle = half × base × height. 0.5 × 2.5 × 12 = 15 m. Total distance = 9 m + 15 m = 24 m. He didn't hit the kitten.

Section Eight — Forces and Motion

Page 104 — Mass, Weight and Gravity

Q1 The fourth statement should be ticked.

Q2a) Professor White's reasoning is incorrect. The mass of the rocket will be the same on any planet — it's the weight that will change.

b) $\text{Mass} = \frac{\text{weight}}{\text{gravity}}$, and gravity on Earth is 10 m/s^2, so the extinguisher must have a mass of 5 kg.

$\frac{1.9 \text{ kg}}{5 \text{ kg}} = 0.38.$

The balance reads 38% of the true mass, so the gravitational field strength on Mars is 38% of that on Earth. 10 m/s^2 × 38% = **3.8 m/s^2**.

Q3a) i) Plot the points and draw a line of best fit. It will go through the origin, since a mass of 0 kg will have no weight.

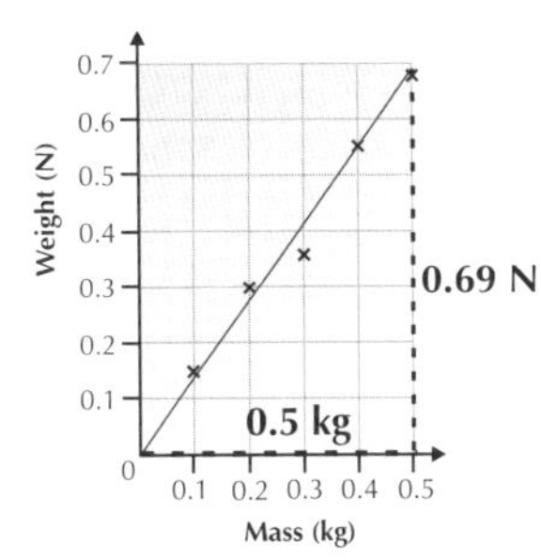

ii) Gravitational field strength = $\frac{\text{weight}}{\text{mass}}$, so find the gradient of the line to find the gravity on Europa.

$\text{Gradient} = \frac{\text{rise}}{\text{tread}} = \frac{0.69 \text{ N}}{0.5 \text{ kg}} = \mathbf{1.38 \text{ N/kg}}.$

b) This is more likely to give an accurate result than a single measurement.

Page 105 — Friction Forces and Terminal Speed

Q1 greater, accelerates, increase, balances, constant, greater, decelerates, decrease, balances, constant.

Q2 All the boxes except 'carrying less cargo' should be ticked.

Q3a) Paola is **wrong** because although gravity (the accelerating force per unit mass) is the same for both objects, air resistance will affect them differently because they have different shapes.

b) Guiseppe is **right** because drag will be greater for the feather compared to its weight, so drag will balance its weight sooner. The hammer will continue to accelerate for longer than the feather.

c) Raphael is **right** because the hammer is more streamlined.

Q4 No, Mavis can't draw any conclusions.
The terminal velocity depends not only on drag (which is determined by the size, shape and smoothness of the object) but on the weight of the object, and the weights of the balls will be different.

Pages 106-107 — The Three Laws of Motion

Q1 balanced, stationary, constant /
resultant, accelerates, force, proportional, inversely proportional /
opposite reaction.

Q2 The second statement should be ticked.

Q3 If there is acceleration in any direction, the forces can't be balanced:

a) Unbalanced — the ball is slowing down, which is negative acceleration.

b) Unbalanced — motion in a circle means constantly changing direction, which requires acceleration.

c) Unbalanced — the vase will be accelerating due to gravity.

d) Unbalanced — as **b)**.

e) Balanced — without air resistance or gravity there will be no acceleration — the bag will continue travelling in the direction it was ejected at the speed it was given when ejected.

Q4 Force = Mass × Acceleration.
Disraeli 9000: 800 kg × 5 m/s^2 = 4000 N
Palmerston 6i: 1560 kg × 0.7 m/s^2 = 1092 N
Heath TT: 950 kg × 3 m/s^2 = 2850 N
Asquith 380: 790 kg × 2 m/s^2 = 1580 N
So the correct order is: **Palmerston 6i**, **Asquith 380**, **Heath TT**, **Disraeli 9000**.

Q5a) The force of the engine is 110 kg × 2.80 m/s^2 = 308 N.

b) $\text{Mass} = \frac{\text{Force}}{\text{Acceleration}} = \frac{308 \text{ N}}{1.71 \text{ m/s}^2} = \mathbf{180.1 \text{ kg}}.$

Q6 Since the probe came back, it must have changed direction, which requires acceleration.
Acceleration requires a force, so some fuel must have been burnt.
(Although it's possible that the change in direction could be made by using the gravity of a planet or other body in space.)

Q7 Using F = ma, the resultant force on the mass must be
1 kg × 0.25 m/s^2 = 0.25 N.
Resultant force = force on the newton-meter – force of friction (they act in opposite directions).
0.25 N = 0.4 N – force of friction, so force of friction =
0.4 N – 0.25 N = **0.15 N**.

Q8 A

Page 108 — Stopping Distances

Q1a) How far a car travels once the brakes are applied.

b) i) Thinking distance = **speed** × **reaction time**. (Or the other way round.)

ii) Stopping distance = **thinking** distance + **braking** distance. (Or the other way round.)

Section Eight — Forces and Motion

Q2

Thinking Distance	Braking Distance
Tiredness	Road surface
Alcohol	Tyres
Speed	Weather
	Brakes
	Speed
	Load

Q3 The third box should be ticked — thinking distance will double and braking distance will more than double.

Q4 The friction between the brake discs and pads will be reduced if they are covered in water. This means the braking force will be reduced and the car will take longer to stop (i.e. the braking distance increases).

Page 109 — Momentum and Collisions

Q1 Truck A's momentum = 30 m/s × 3000 kg = 90 000 kg m/s.
Truck B's momentum = 10 m/s × 4500 kg = 45 000 kg m/s.
Truck C's momentum = 20 m/s × 4000 kg = 80 000 kg m/s.
Truck D's momentum = 15 m/s × 3500 kg = 52 500 kg m/s.
So the order of increasing momentum is: **B, D, C, A**.

Q2 Momentum_{before} = 60 kg × 5 m/s = 300 kg m/s
$\text{Momentum}_{before} = \text{momentum}_{after}$
so, 300 kg m/s = $m_{(skater + bag)}$ × 4.8 m/s
so, $m_{(skater + bag)}$ = 300 ÷ 4.8 = 62.5 kg
so, the mass of the bag = 62.5 – 60 = **2.5 kg**.

Q3 The **second** and **third** statements should be ticked.

Q4a) Momentum of car = 750 kg × 30 m/s = 22 500 kg m/s.
When the car has stopped its momentum = 0 kg m/s.
So the change in momentum is 22 500 kg m/s.
Average force = Change in momentum ÷ time = 22 500 kg m/s ÷ 1.2 s = **18 750 N**

b) Wearing slightly stretchy seatbelts means that the occupants will take slightly longer (than 1.2 seconds) to stop moving and the force exerted on their bodies will be lower (than 18 750 N).

Page 110 — Car Safety

Q1a) Kinetic energy
b) The kinetic energy is mainly converted to heat in the brakes (and a little bit of sound).

Q2a) A smaller deceleration means a smaller force acting on the passengers, reducing the risk of injury.
b) i) Parts of the car crumple up to slow the car down more gradually.
ii) The airbag is soft, so it slows down the passengers over a longer time.
c) The seat belt stretches slightly to absorb some of the energy of the impact.

Q3 safety, interact, crashes, power, control, skidding, lock, steering

Q4 The crash barrier crumples to slow the car down gradually and absorb some of the energy of the impact.

Page 111 — Work and Potential Energy

Q1a) Work involves the transfer of **energy**.
b) To do work a **force** acts over a **distance**.
c) Work is measured in **joules**.

Q2a) True
b) True
c) False
d) True

Q3a) Work done = force × distance = 1200 N × 8 m = **9600 J**
b) From the chemical energy in its food.
c) Heat energy (because of friction between the donkey's feet and the surface of the track) and some sound energy.

Q4a) Gravity / his weight.
b) It is transferred into kinetic energy — in his moving legs and arms — which is then transferred into potential energy — as he gains height. (Some of the energy supplied is also wasted as heat and sound.)
c) Work done = force × distance moved = 600 N × 2 m = **1200 J**
d) 15 kJ = 15 000 J = 600 N × distance
so, distance = 15 000 ÷ 600 = 25 m
Each step is 0.2 m high, so the number of rungs Ben must climb is 25 ÷ 0.2 = **125 rungs**.

Page 112 — Kinetic Energy

Q1 K.E. = $\frac{1}{2}mv^2 = \frac{1}{2} \times 200 \times (9)^2 = 0.5 \times 200 \times 81$ = **8100 J**

Q2 9 J = $\frac{1}{2} \times m \times (20)^2 = \frac{1}{2} \times m \times 400$
so, m = (9 × 2) ÷ 400 = **0.045 kg**

Q3 K.E. = 2000 J = $\frac{1}{2} \times 0.004 \text{ kg} \times v^2 = 0.002 \times v^2$, so rearranging gives:
$v = \sqrt{2000 \div 0.002} = \sqrt{1\,000\,000} =$ **1000 m/s**.

Q4 Kinetic energy is proportional to velocity^2 so if the speed increases to 5/3 (50/30) of its original value, the distance needed to stop will be approximately 25/9 its original value — just under 3 times. 14 × 25 ÷ 9 ≈ 39 m).

Q5a) Work done against gravity is mass × g × height = 70 × 10 × 20 = **14 000 J**.
b) The gravitational potential energy the skier gained is converted into kinetic energy when she skis down the slope.
So, K.E. = 14 000 J = $\frac{1}{2}mv^2 = \frac{1}{2} \times 70 \times v^2$
so rearranging gives $v = \sqrt{14\,000 \div 35} = \sqrt{400}$
= **20 m/s**.

Section Nine — Electricity

Page 113 — Roller Coasters

Q1a) A — maximum P.E.
B — P.E. is being converted to K.E.
C — minimum P.E., maximum K.E.
D — K.E. is being converted to P.E.

b) i) Decrease in K.E. = increase in K.E.
so you would expect K.E. = 300 ÷ 2 = **150 kJ**

ii) There is friction between the carriage and the track, so some of the P.E. is converted into heat.

c) No. (Assuming there's no friction) all things move with the same acceleration under gravity, so the mass of the carriage makes no difference.

Q2a) W = m × g = 1500 × 15 = **22 500 N** (or 22.5 kN)

b) i) P.E. = m × g × h = 1500 × 15 × 25 = **562 500 J** (or 562.5 kJ)

ii) 562 500 J (or 562.5 kJ)

c) i) change in P.E. = m × g × change in h
= 1500 × 15 × (25 – 7) = **405 000 J** (or 405 kJ)

ii) K.E. = 405 000 J = ½mv² = ½ × 1500 × v^2
so, v^2 = (405 000 × 2) ÷ 1500 = 540
v = 23.2 m/s

Page 114 — Power

Q1a) 10 minutes = 10 × 60 = 600 seconds
energy = power × time = 150 × 600 = **90 000 J** (or 90 kJ)

b) Fuel used = 90 kJ ÷ 30 kJ/ml = **3 ml**

c) Power = energy ÷ time = 120 000 ÷ 600 = **200 W**

Q2a) Final K.E. = ½mv² = ½ × (60 + 5) × 8² = 2080 J
power = energy ÷ time = 2080 ÷ 6 = **346.7 W**

b) P.E. = m × g × h = 60 × 10 × 5 = 3000 J
power = energy ÷ time = 3000 ÷ 4 = **750 W**

Q3a) sprint 4 (because he slipped)

b) **Fastest** K.E. = ½mv² = ½ × 70 × 8.2² = 2353.4 J
Power = energy ÷ time = 2353.4 ÷ 3.1 = **759 W**
Slowest K.E. = ½mv² = ½ × 70 × 7.9² = 2184.35 J
Power = energy ÷ time = 2184.35 ÷ 3.3 = **662 W**

c) His power output would be **higher**.

Pages 115-116 — Mixed Questions — Section Eight

Q1a) Energy transferred = Work done = force × distance
= 475 N × 100 m = **47 500 J** (or 47.5 kJ).

b) Power = work done ÷ time = 47 500 ÷ 27 = **1759 W**

c) i) Scott has a constant acceleration (of 0.8 m/s²).

ii) Scott has no acceleration / his acceleration is zero (or 0 m/s²).

iii) Scott has a decreasing deceleration — the graph's negative gradient is flattening out.

d) After 20 s Scott's speed is 4 m/s.
Kinetic energy = ½mv² = ½ × 75 × (4)² = **600 J**.

e) Distance travelled = area under graph
= (0.5 × 5 s × 4 m/s) + (15 s × 4 m/s) = **70 m**.

Q2a) F = ma. So, 270 N = 180 kg × a

$$a = \frac{270}{180} = \mathbf{1.5\ m/s^2}.$$

b) F = ma = 180 kg × 5 m/s² = **900 N**.

c) E.g. Any two of the following: his speed / the total mass of the scooter and load / how effective his brakes are / road surface / weather / tyres / gradient of the road.

d) Paul's reaction time would be increased if he was tired. Since distance = speed × time, the longer it takes to think about stopping, the further you'll travel until you start to brake — so the total stopping distance will be longer.

Q3a) In the first 5 seconds the motorbike changes speed from 0 m/s to 25 m/s (because 90 km per hour = 25 m/s).
So acceleration = 25 m/s ÷ 5 s = 5 m/s².
F = ma = 200 kg × 5 m/s² = **1000 N**.

b) Drag increases very rapidly as speed increases, meaning that the engine has to exert a much greater driving force in order to maintain a steady speed. So you can expect the fuel consumption to be greater for the faster bike.

c) Sudden braking requires a lot of heat to be dissipated very quickly, so the tyres may get hot enough to melt — the black marks are melted rubber.

Q4a) When Karl jumps the boat will exert a force on him (that moves him to the east) and Karl will exert an equal force on the boat in the opposite direction (that moves it to the west).

b) $\text{momentum}_{\text{before jump}}$
= (100 + 80) kg × 0 m/s = 0 kg m/s
$\text{momentum}_{\text{before jump}} = \text{momentum}_{\text{after jump}}$ = 0 kg m/s
= $\text{momentum}_{\text{boat}} + \text{momentum}_{\text{Karl}}$
So: 0 kg m/s = (100 kg × v) + (80 kg × 3 m/s)
Rearranging gives: v = –(80 × 3) ÷ 100 = –2.4 m/s
The minus sign indicates that the boat goes in the opposite direction to Karl so its velocity is **2.4 m/s west**.

c) $\text{momentum}_{\text{before Karl lands}}$
= $\text{momentum}_{\text{boat}} + \text{momentum}_{\text{Karl}}$
= (112 kg × 0) + (80 kg × 3 m/s)
= 240 kg m/s.
$\text{momentum}_{\text{before Karl lands}} = \text{momentum}_{\text{after he lands}}$
So: 240 kg m/s = (112 + 80) × v
Rearranging gives: v = 240 ÷ 192 = +1.25 m/s.
The plus sign indicates that the boat goes in the same direction to Karl so its velocity is **1.25 m/s east**.

Section Nine — Electricity

Pages 117-118 — Static Electricity

Q1 static, insulating, friction, electrons, positive / negative, negative / positive

Q2 circled: positive and negative, negative and positive
underlined: positive and positive, negative and negative

Q3a) Because rubber is an insulating material (and flexible).

b) So that electrons can move and charge can be transferred to the dome.

c) As Nadia becomes charged, so does her hair. Because each strand of hair has the same charge, the strands repel each other.

Section Nine — Electricity

Q4 Lisa: Because they rub against each other, which scrapes off electrons, causing static charge. The charge can't move (the clothes are insulators), so charge builds up throughout the day.
Sara: No. Charging mainly happens with synthetic
(man-made) materials. Cotton is a natural material.
Tim: The sound is caused by small sparks as the charges on the shirt are discharged.

Q5 sparks, fuel, explosion, metal, grain chutes / paper rollers, paper rollers / grain chutes

Q6 Raindrops and ice bump together and electrons move between them.
The bottoms of the clouds become negatively charged because they gain extra electrons.
As the charge increases, the voltage gets higher and higher.
If the voltage gets big enough there is a huge spark (a flash of lightning).

Page 119 — Uses of Static Electricity

Q1 shock, defibrillator, paddles, shock, insulated
Q2a) This gives the smoke particles a negative charge.
b) To attract the smoke particles.
c) The smoke is negatively charged and the plates are positively charged, so they are attracted to each other.
Q3a) Light shining on the image plate causes the charge to leak away.
b) The powder is negatively charged, so is attracted by the positively charged image plate.
c) The paper wouldn't attract the black powder, so the page would be blank.

Page 120 — Circuits — The Basics

Q1a) current
b) voltage, force
c) more
d) resistance, less
Q2

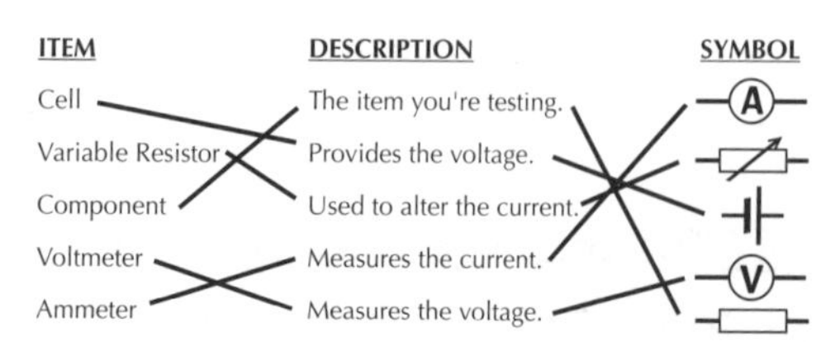

Q3a) i) ampere / amp
ii) volt
iii) ohm
b) E.g., any two from: increase the resistance of the variable resistor / insert a component of higher resistance / reduce the voltage from the battery.
Q4a) True
b) False. An ammeter should be connected in series with a component.
c) True
d) False. A voltmeter should be connected in parallel with a component.

Page 121 — Measuring AC

Q1 volts, alternating, AC, direction, changing, frequency, hertz
Q2a) Cathode ray oscilloscope
b) Voltage plotted against time (or another voltage).
c) Gain and timebase
Q3a) C
b) B
c) A
Q4a) 2 volts
b) 4 × 10 ms = **40 ms** or **0.04 s**
c) Frequency = 1 ÷ 0.04 = **25 Hz**

Page 122 — Resistance and V = I × R

Q1

Voltage (V)	Current (A)	Resistance (Ω)
6	2	**3**
8	**4**	2
9	3	3
4	8	**0.5**
2	**0.5**	4
1	0.5	2

Q2a)

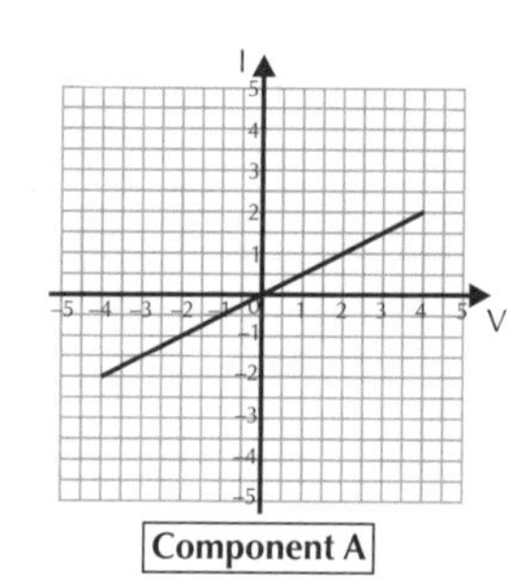

Component A

Component B

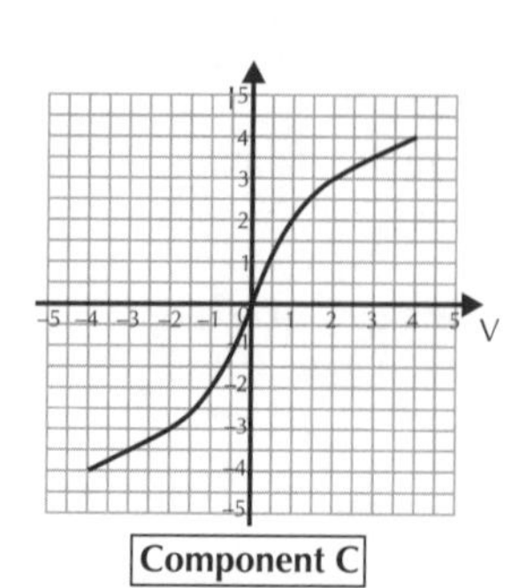

Component C

b) Component A is a resistor.
Component B is a diode.
Component C is a filament lamp.

Section Nine — Electricity

Page 123 — Circuit Symbols and Devices

Q1 1. Voltmeter
2. LDR / light-dependent resistor
3. Variable resistor
4. Ammeter
5. LED / light-emitting diode
6. (Fixed) resistor

Q2 fixed, variable, thermistor, light-dependent

Q3a) They both provide the voltage in a circuit, but a battery contains more than one cell.

b) They both measure variables in a circuit, but a voltmeter measures voltage / must always be connected in parallel, and an ammeter measures current / must always be connected in series.

c) They both change their resistance because of changes in their environment, but a thermistor responds to temperature changes and an LDR responds to changes in light.

Page 124 — Series Circuits

Q1 Same everywhere in the circuit — Current.
Shared by all the components — Total potential difference.
The sum of the resistances — Total resistance.
Can be different for each component — Potential difference.

Q2a) $2\text{ V} + 2\text{ V} + 2\text{ V} = \mathbf{6\text{ V}}$

b) $V = I \times R$, so total R = total $V \div$ total $I = 6 \div 0.5 = \mathbf{12\ \Omega}$

c) R_3 = total resistance $- R_1 - R_2 = 12 - 2 - 4 = \mathbf{6\ \Omega}$

d) $V = I \times R = 0.5 \times 4 = \mathbf{2\text{ V}}$

Q3a) The lamps get dimmer as more are added because the voltage is shared out between the lamps.

b) The current gets smaller as more lamps are added. Each lamp adds more resistance which means less current.

Page 125 — Parallel Circuits

Q1a) True

b) True

c) False

d) True

Q2a) Nothing, because each lamp gets its voltage from the battery separately.

b) Nothing happens to the brightness of the other lamps.
(The answers above assume that the internal resistance of the cell is ignored — in practice the current would decrease a little as lamps were added.)

Q3a) i) $I = V \div R = 12 \div 2 = \mathbf{6\text{ A}}$

ii) $I = V \div R = 12 \div 4 = \mathbf{3\text{ A}}$

b) i) **12 V**

ii) **12 V**

c) $R = V \div I = 12 \div 2 = \mathbf{6\ \Omega}$

d) $A_0 = A_2 + A_3 = 3\text{ A} + 2\text{ A} = \mathbf{5\text{ A}}$

Page 126 — Fuses and Safe Plugs

Q1a) Because these materials are electrical insulators.

b) These materials are electrical conductors, and are used for those parts that the electricity goes through.

c) Rubber or plastic because they are electrical insulators and are flexible.

Q2a) insulation

b) live

c) neutral

d) green and yellow, earth

e) firmly, bare

f) outer

Q3

Description	Live	Neutral	Earth
Must always be connected	✓	✓	
Just for safety			✓
Electricity normally flows in and out of it	✓	✓	
Alternates between +ve and –ve voltage	✓		

Q4 1. A fault develops and the earthed casing becomes connected to the live supply.
2. A large current now flows in through the live wire and out through the earth wire.
3. The surge in current causes the fuse wire to heat up.
4. The fuse blows.
5. The live supply is cut off.
6. Everything is now safe.

Page 127 — Energy and Power in Circuits

Q1 how long, power, voltage / current, current / voltage, higher, current.

Q2a) 1000 J, light, heat

b) 60 000 J, kinetic, heat, sound

c) 20 000 J, heat

d) 1 200 000 J, heat

Q3a)

	Lamp A	Lamp B	Lamp C
Voltage (V)	12	3	230
Current (A)	2.5	4	0.1
Power (W)	30	12	23
Energy used in one minute (J)	1800	720	1380

b) A = 3 A, B = 5 A, C = 2 A.

Page 128 — Charge, Voltage and Energy Change

Q1a) i) $20 \times 60 = \mathbf{1200\text{ seconds}}$

ii) $5 \times 1200 = \mathbf{6000\text{ C}}$

b) $3 \times 6000 = \mathbf{18\,000\text{ J}}$ (or **18 kJ**)

Q2

	Lamp A	Lamp B
Current through lamp (A)	2	4
Voltage drop across lamp (V)	3	2
Charge passing in 10 s (C)	20	40
Energy transformed in 10 s (J)	60	80

Q3a) $4 \times (7 \times 60) = \mathbf{1680\text{ C}}$

b) $1680 \times 9 = \mathbf{15\,120\text{ J}}$ (or **15.12 kJ**)

Section Ten — Nuclear Physics

Q4a) Higher **current** means more coulombs of charge per second.
b) One ampere (amp) is the same as one **coulomb** per second.
c) One volt is the same as one joule per **coulomb**.

Pages 129-130 — Mixed Questions — Section Nine

Q1 a) Plate A would be negative and Plate B would be positive.
b) By adjusting the size and the polarity (direction) of the voltage applied to the plates, the amount the ink droplets move up or down can be precisely controlled.
Q2 E.g. As she walks across the nylon carpet, electrons are transferred between the carpet and her feet, leaving her charged. When she touches the earthed radiator, she is discharged — and feels the charge flowing between her body and earth.
Q3 The distance must be large enough to prevent a spark jumping across the gap from the cables to 'earth' (the bridge or other structure).
Q4a) $10 + 5 + 5 =$ **20 Ω**.
b) i) I = V ÷ R = 4 ÷ 10 = **0.4 A** (current through 10 Ω resistor is the same as current in all parts of the circuit).
ii) V = IR = 0.4 × 20 = **8 V**.
iii) Voltage across 5 Ω resistor = I × R = 0.4 × 5 = 2 V
P = V × I = 2 × 0.4 = 0.8 W
Energy = P × t = 0.8 × (2 × 60) = **96 J**.
Q5a) i) 4 × 0.5 = **2.0 A**.
ii) 0 A
iii) (4 × 0.5) + (2 × 6.0) = **14.0 A**.
b) The battery (or alternator) can't provide the full voltage when there is a high current / heavy load.
c) i) Time period = 10 ms × 3.5 = 0.01 × 3.5 = 0.035 s
Frequency = 1 ÷ 0.035 = **29 Hz**.
ii)

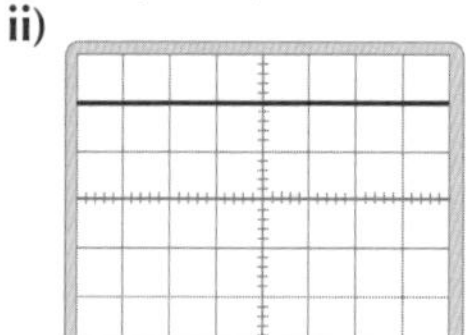

Section Ten — Nuclear Physics

Page 131 — Atomic Structure

Q1 Correct order: **B, E, D, A, C.**
Q2 **Isotopes** — Forms of an element which have different numbers of neutrons.
Unstable atoms — Atoms which are likely to break up (decay).
Nuclear decay — The random break-up of atomic nuclei.
Radiation — High-energy particles or waves that a decaying atom spits out.
Nucleus — The part of an atom that has protons and neutrons.
Q3a) Most of the mass of the atom is concentrated in a tiny positive nucleus in the centre of the atom.
b) Most alpha particles passed straight through gold foil. Only a few hit atomic nuclei and bounced back.
Q4a) Similarities: (Nearly) the same mass, both found in nucleus.
Differences: Protons have a positive charge, neutrons have no charge.
b) Similarities: Both have a single electrical charge; there's the same number of each in a neutral atom.
Differences: Protons have a positive charge, electrons have a negative charge; protons have a relative mass of 1, electrons have a relative mass of about $\frac{1}{2000}$; protons are found in nucleus, electrons are found whizzing round the outside of the nucleus.

Page 132 — Radioactive Decay Processes

Q1

	Alpha (α)	Beta (β)	Gamma (γ)
Ionising power	very strong	moderate	weak
Relative mass	4	1/2000	0
Penetrating power	low	moderate	very high
Speed	slow	moderate	very fast
Charge	2+	–1	0

Q2a) The nucleus loses two protons and two neutrons. / It changes into the nucleus of a different element.
b) One of its neutrons is converted into a proton. / It changes into the nucleus of a different element.

Q3 A particle with high penetrating power will have low ionising power and a particle with low penetrating power will have high ionising power.
Q4a) An alpha particle has 2 protons and 2 neutrons, exactly the same as the nucleus of a helium atom.
b) It loses 2 protons and 2 neutrons, so the mass number goes down by 4: 226 – 4 = 222; and the atomic number goes down by 2: 88 – 2 = 86. An atom with 86 protons is radon.
c) It is an electron and has no mass worth mentioning, and it has the opposite charge to a proton.
d) It gains a proton and loses a neutron. (A neutron changes into a proton). Carbon's atomic number is 6; nitrogen's atomic number is 7.

Page 133 — Background Radiation

Q1 The first two statements are true, the remaining three statements are false.

Section Ten — Nuclear Physics

Q2 Any five from: the air, rocks, food, building materials, space/the Sun/cosmic rays, fallout (from nuclear explosions/accidents), nuclear waste, medical activity/X-rays/radiotherapy/isotope tracing, other industrial uses of radioactive materials and X-rays.

Q3 Peter is correct to say that both materials are radioactive, but he is not correct to say that Material B is twice as radioactive as Material A. He has not taken account of background radiation, which should be subtracted from all experimental readings.

Q4a) Because radon gas is radioactive and can cause cancer.

b) Radon gas comes from certain rocks (such as granite) which contain unstable isotopes and are radioactive. Some locations have more of these rocks than others.

c) E.g. All new houses in problem areas should have good ventilation systems. This removes radon gas from houses so they are much safer.

Page 134 — Radioactivity Safety

Q1a) Beta and gamma.

b) Alpha radiation.

c) i) Radiation can kill cells outright. High doses can cause burns and radiation sickness.

ii) Damaged cells can survive and mutate, leading to cancer in the long term.

Q2a) E.g. any three of: Always use tongs to hold the sample. Hold the sample at arm's length. Keep the sample facing away from you and other people in the room. Never look directly at the sample.

b) In a thick-walled lead-lined container, to stop radiation escaping. (Could also mention in a locked cupboard, to stop any untrained people getting access to the source.)

Q3a) Many of the radioactive contaminants released in the explosion have long half-lives, so their effects will be felt for a long time e.g. if people eat contaminated food, their dose will increase for many years after the event. Some of the effects of radiation exposure take a long time to be seen e.g. some cancers develop many years after the exposure. Scientists also want to monitor the children of people who were exposed to radiation — radiation can damage the parents' sex cells and cause birth defects etc.

b) Exposing people to very high doses of radiation would cause them a lot of harm, so this would be unethical.

Page 135 — Half-Life

Q1a) Half-life is the time taken for the count rate to halve (e.g. from 1200 cpm to 600 cpm). This is about **80 minutes**.

b) After 240 minutes, the count rate was **150 cpm** (by reading from the graph or by calculating 1200 ÷ 8).

c) After 1 half-life, one half are still unstable.
After 2 half-lives, one quarter are still unstable.
After 3 half-lives, one eighth are still unstable.
After 4 half-lives, one sixteenth will be unstable.

So after 5 half-lives, $\frac{1}{32}$ of the atoms will be unstable.

d) Reading from the graph, approximately **285 mins**.

Q2a) $6 \times 60 = 360$ seconds. $360 \div 40 = 9$ half-lives.

After 9 half-lives, $\frac{1}{2^9} = \frac{1}{512}$ will still be radioactive.

b) i) $8000 \times \frac{1}{512} \approx$ **16** cpm.

ii) After 9 half-lives (6 minutes), the count rate is 16, so only one more half-life would be needed for the count to fall below 10 (to 8). So it would take **7 whole minutes**.

Page 136 — Uses of Ionising Radiation

Q1a) A gamma-emitter with a long half-life is used. Gamma radiation is needed because it is not stopped by air or metal parts of the instruments and it can kill the cells of living organisms (e.g. bacteria) on the instruments. A long half-life is needed because the sterilising machine will be in use over many years and replacing the source frequently would be inconvenient.

b) Lead is used to prevent the operator and anyone near the machine from getting a dose of radiation.

Q2a) The gamma rays kill the cells in the tumour.

b) They are highly penetrating and pass easily through the body. They can also be carefully directed towards the cancer cells.

c) A high dose is used to kill the cancer cells rather than just damage them.

Q3a) The level of radioactivity from kidney A decreases faster than that from kidney B. This shows that kidney A is working much better and has passed the radioactive material on to the bladder.

b) An alpha source would do a lot of damage to the cells of the patient's kidneys, because alpha radiation is highly ionising. Also, the radiation could not be detected outside the body.

Page 137 — Radioactive Dating

Q1a) The proportion of carbon-14 starts to decrease (it decays and isn't replaced by more carbon-14).

b) After 5730 years, you would expect the number of atoms of carbon-14 in a sample to have halved.

Q2a) After 1 half-life, there would be 1/20 000 000 C-14. After 2 half-lives, there would be 1/40 000 000. After 3 half-lives, there would be 1/80 000 000. So the strap is 3 half-lives old. The strap is 3 × 5730 = **17 190 years old**.

b) E.g. any two of: the sample may have got contaminated; there could have been a measuring error; the level of C-14 in the atmosphere hasn't stayed constant, so the result should be calibrated.

Section Ten — Nuclear Physics

Q3 3700 BC is about 1 C-14 half-life ago, so you would expect there to be about 1 part in 20 000 000 C-14.

Q4 If the tusk contains 1 part in 15 000 000 C-14, it is less than one half-life old. That makes the tusk less than 5730 years old, so it is unlikely to be genuine.

Q5 The ratio 1:1 means that 50% of the original uranium is still uranium, and the other 50% is lead. This would happen after 1 half-life.
So the meteorite is 4.5 billion years old.

Page 138 — Nuclear Fission and Fusion

Q1 **Fission** — Splitting apart.
Nuclear reaction — A process which changes atomic nuclei.
Fusion — Joining together.
Atomic bomb — A device using an uncontrolled nuclear reaction.
Nuclear reactor — A device using a controlled nuclear reaction.
Hydrogen bomb — A device using nuclear fusion.

Q2 E.g. The slow-moving neutron is absorbed by a plutonium nucleus. This plutonium nucleus splits up, forming new lighter elements and spitting out two or three neutrons. One or more of these 'extra' neutrons may then be absorbed by another plutonium nucleus, causing it to split and spit out more neutrons, which may cause other nuclei to split etc.

Q3 E.g. any four from:
Fission splits nuclei up, fusion combines nuclei.
Fission happens to big nuclei like uranium or plutonium, fusion happens between light nuclei like hydrogen.
Fission produces radioactive waste, fusion produces very little radioactive waste.
Fusion requires extremely high temperatures, fission does not.

Q4 **Good points**
E.g. Fuel is cheap and plentiful. / They produce very little radioactive waste.
Bad points
E.g. No known materials can withstand the high temperatures needed. / It requires a lot of energy to achieve such high temperatures.

Pages 139-140 — Mixed Questions — Section Ten

Q1a)

		electric charge		
		-1	0	+1
mass	1/2000	**electron**		
	1		**neutron**	**proton**

b) In a **radioactive** material, the atomic nuclei spontaneously decay, giving off charged particles or gamma rays. **Isotopes** are atoms which have the same number of protons but different numbers of neutrons.

c) E.g. any three from: tracers in medicine, finding leaks in pipes, sterilisation of surgical instruments, food irradiation, radiotherapy, thickness control, radioactive dating, smoke detectors, nuclear power.

Q2a) After 10 half-lives, $1/2^{10} = 1/1024$ atoms have not decayed.

b) After 11 460 years, the proportion is 1/40 000 000.
After 17 190 years, the proportion is 1/80 000 000.
So the bone fragment is between 11 460 and 17 190 years old.
It must be nearer 11 460 since 1/50 000 000 is nearer to 1/40 000 000 than 1/80 000 000.
So the bone fragment is about 12 000 to 13 000 years old.

c) E.g. After ten half-lives less than a thousandth of the original radioactive atoms are still there. Very old samples may have so few radioactive atoms that the randomness of when individual atoms decay starts to matter. It no longer evens out statistically.

Q3a) $^{234}_{90}\text{Th} \rightarrow {}^{234}_{91}\text{Pa} + {}^{0}_{-1}\text{e}$

b) i) $^{222}_{86}\text{Rn} \rightarrow {}^{218}_{84}\text{Po} + {}^{4}_{2}\alpha$

ii) New houses in high-radon areas should be designed with good ventilation systems to reduce the concentration of radon.

Q4a) Thallium-201, the type with a half-life of three days. With a short half-life the radiation quickly disappears from the body and does little harm.

b) Gamma rays pass straight out of the body. Unlike beta radiation, gamma rays scarcely cause any ionisation, so they do little cell damage.

c) Many possible answers — answer should make the point that the alpha particles cannot leave the body and so cannot be detected from outside.

Q5a) fission

b) When a slow-moving neutron gets absorbed by a uranium nucleus, the nucleus splits. This gives out lots of energy — heat — and two or three more neutrons which can hit other nuclei, creating a chain reaction (and releasing more heat energy).